MY FLAG GREW STARS

My Flag Grew Stars

WORLD WAR II REFUGEES' JOURNEY TO AMERICA

KITTY GOGINS

ISBN 1-4392-5819-8

Library of Congress Control Number 2009909684

Printed in the United States of America.

To order additional copies, please contact:
    BookSurge, LLC
    www.booksurge.com
    1-866-308-6235
    orders@booksurge.com

To my parents, Olga and Tibor Zoltai.
When their world was destroyed by war,
they made a journey across
continents, cultures,
and values
to build a future in America.

Preface and Acknowledgements

This book is a re-creation of my parents' lives based on original documents, my parents' memories, and the memories of people whose lives they touched. From much original material, including my father's diary from 1945 to 1948, more than one hundred letters my parents exchanged from 1948 to 1950, numerous other documents, and albums of photographs, their story comes to life. Trying to stay true to history, I only included dialogue when the topic, participants, and points of view were known. I tried to verify facts where possible, but this is not a fact book. It is history as viewed from the lives of two extraordinary people: the challenges they faced and how they adapted to their changing world while trying to stay true to their core.

I would like to thank everyone who assisted with this book. Dozens of people devoted time to share their experiences, track down material, and review the manuscript. A special thanks to my mother who agreed to share her life publically and patiently spent hours telling me details, collecting and translating documents, and reviewing what I'd written. Also a special thanks to my family for supporting me throughout this endeavor.

Timeline of Olga and Tibor's Lives

Tibor Zoltai | **Olga Wagner**

Born 1925

Born 1931

Sept. 1939 World
War II Started

Apr. 1944 Bombed Györ
Jan. 1945 Left Hungary
Oct. 1945 Joined Family in Austria

Dec. 1944 Bombed Sopron
Mar. 1945 Fled Hungary

Fall 1946 Started University

Fall 1947 Started
Convent School

Apr. 1948 Tibor
and Olga Met

Jul. 1948 Moved to France

Apr. 1949 Moved to Canada as
Agricultural Worker

Apr. 1950 Moved to Canada as
Agricultural Worker

Oct. 1950 Completed Agricultural Work Contract
Nov. 1950 Tibor and Olga Married

Fall 1952 Tibor Entered University in Toronto

Fall 1955 Moved to Boston and Tibor Started MIT
Jun. 1956 Son Peter Was Born

Jul. 1958 Daughter Katharina (Kitty) Was Born
Summer 1959 Tibor Became Professor in Minnesota

Dec. 1970 Daughter Lili Was Born
Spring 1971 Olga Began Work at International Institute

Summer 1991 Tibor Retired
Summer 1993 Olga Retired

2001 Story Opens and Ends

Contents

Preface and Acknowledgements   i

Timeline of Olga and Tibor's Lives   ii

Prologue (2001)   1

Part I. The Upheaval of War

  1.   Olga's World Explodes (1944-1945)   7

  2.   Tibor Learns Nothing Is Fair in War (1944-1945)   22

  3.   Tibor Is a POW (1945)   47

  4.   Olga Flees the Russians (1945-1947)   71

  5.   Tibor in Displaced Person Limbo (1945-1948)   97

  6.   That Is the Man I Will Marry (1948-1949)   117

  7.   Indentured Servitude, a Solution? (1949-1950)   142

Part II. Building a Future as Americans

  8.   Canada, We Want to Build Your Future (1950-1959)   169

  9.   Raising American Children, Well, Sort of . . . (1959-1969)   195

  10.   Olga Juggles Family and Counseling Immigrants (1970-1979)   221

  11.   The Harvest of Their Careers (1978-1993)   243

  12.   A Legacy of Cultural Mosaic (1982-2001)   262

Bibliography   289

Prologue
(2001)

Olga and Tibor Zoltai in Summit Avenue Home, 2000.

Hi, Kitty." My mother, Olga, greets me at the door, kissing me on both cheeks in the traditional Hungarian fashion. "We're having coffee in the kitchen."

I follow her down the massive hall, large enough to park three cars, over the soft Persian rugs that blanket the hard wood floor and mute our footsteps. We pass through the dining room that easily seats sixteen at the pseudo-marble table. The cozier kitchen is located at the back of the house. A century earlier the room served as the mansion's pantry. The floor-to-ceiling honey-colored birch-and-glass cupboards make it feel warm and welcoming.

My parents bought this imposing brown stone mansion in St. Paul, Minnesota, in 1982, almost two decades ago. They love everything historic, and this house has 120 years of colorful history.

"Did Mother tell you about her excitement this week?" My father, Tibor, looks up at me through his triple-thick glasses. He's seated at a round Formica table in the center of the room. I bend over to hug and kiss his frail form in the wheelchair. His salt-and-pepper moustache and goatee gently tickle my skin. Although retired, he still has the stereotypical professor look.

"What happened?"

"A young man tried to hijack my car!" Olga's voice is bursting with excitement. "I was taking your sister and a friend to the Minnesota History Center. My friend can't walk unaided, so I got out to walk her to a bench before I parked. I left the car door open and the keys in it, but not running. As I was coming back, a thief was trying to start my car."

She takes a sip of her strong coffee, glancing at me to make sure she has my full attention. She does.

"I read in an article, if you're in danger, start screaming in a different language. 'You dirty thief!' I screamed at him in Hungarian, as loud as I could. 'What do you think you're doing, trying to take my car! Get out of here!!' He jumped out and ran away, the wrong way on a one way street. So I couldn't chase him with the car, although I tried."

I chuckle. I can just picture it; my seventy-year-old, white-haired mother, who barely tops five feet, screaming at him in her native tongue. The fellow is lucky he escaped, or she might have lectured him to death about his rotten behavior.

My parents can always be counted on for a captivating story. It takes more than a thief to intimidate them. I suppose that's a reflection of what they've lived through. A few months back, I sat at the same Formica table and listened to my son eagerly interview Tibor for a school project. It reminded me how fascinating their stories are. They overcame such adversity, adapted to such incredible change.

Both of their worlds were destroyed in World War II. As teenagers, they independently left Hungary only carrying canvas rucksacks. Their experiences, as refugees on the losing side, provide a distinctive perspective on the war, different than what I learned in school as an American. Even once my parents' stories merged into a meandering path, ending here in Minnesota, their adventures furnish an intriguing view of the lives of immigrants and other cultures. Not just their own, but the multitude of foreign-born whose lives they touched.

I find the most valuable part of their story is how they successfully adapted to major upheaval. We all face change, our world transforming or perhaps exploding. Whether it's at work, within our families, with our health, or via technology, change is inevitable. It just keeps coming faster. So how do we successfully adapt? Olga and Tibor's experiences contain gems to learn from.

Let me take you back in time to war-torn Hungary, where their story started. We'll relive their experiences as refugees leaving their beloved homeland, building a new life, language, and culture in a foreign place.

Part I

The Upheaval of War

1

Olga's World Explodes
(1944 - 1945)

Olga Wagner, 1942.

D ear Lord, I'm so young. I don't want to die." Thirteen-year-old Olga Wagner repeated this prayer over and over, her brunette head bowed, tears from her hazel eyes leaving streaks on her cheeks.

As a bomb exploded with a deafening noise, Olga curled up tighter on the stool in the coal cellar of her brick apartment building. Each massive explosion reverberated in the compact space. She repeated her prayer, her body echoing the fierce shaking of the thick plaster walls. Airborne plaster sifted from the swaying walls, mixing with the coal dust in the dank, thick air.

The tiny, coal-covered windows let in only a trickle of diffuse light, and Olga could hardly see the thirteen other residents of her four-unit building huddled near her. But she could smell their sweat and hear their ragged breaths and fervent prayers.

She could make out her mother's voice praying, "Dear Lord, please help us," her mother's shadowy form fiercely embracing Olga's eight-year-old brother. The bombs kept coming, an unending, ferocious, earth-shaking thunder beyond her experience or imagination.

After two hours, the sirens sounded the all-clear signal, a single-solid blessed note.

Olga cautiously emerged from the dark cellar, blinking as she stepped into the blinding light of the early afternoon, her eyes slowly adjusting to the brightness. Explosions still boomed in the distance.

Shell-shocked, she stared through the dusty haze at the devastation.

Her neighborhood was grotesquely transformed. At the end of her city street, the Jewish compound was missing its roof and upper story. The single family home abutting her building had lost all its windows, most of its red tile roof, and part of its brick and plaster walls. The three-foot-thick cellar walls of their neighbor's home, so much like the walls in her building, still shook with the bomb's reverberations. Olga's illusion about the safety of the century-old thick plaster walls was shattered. How easily the bomb could have landed a few feet closer and demolished her building.

"The bomb killed Grandmother," her neighbor moaned. "Dear God, she's dead."

"There's a live bomb!" yelled another neighbor, pointing emphatically across the street to a crater. "I'll notify the military."

It was December 6, 1944. American bombers were targeting Olga's hometown of Sopron, Hungary. This small country in central Europe, with its nine million residents, was only one-hundredth the size of the U.S. and shared borders with five countries. Its size and central location had made it a regular focus for invasion throughout its thousand-year history. It relied on alliances to survive, as vulnerable as Indiana if both Illinois and Ohio had massive, aggressive armies ready to destroy each other and conquer it.

Map of Hungary. Source: CIA. *The World Factbook.*
Sopron located in upper left.

World War II began five years earlier in 1939. Two years into the war, Hungary signed a pact with Germany. It was trying to recover the vast territory lost in World War I; gain a strong ally against the Russians, feared even more than the Germans; and ally with the side they thought would win. But when the Hungarian government took steps to withdraw from the war in March 1944, German troops occupied the country. Allied bombing began that spring, although heavy bombing of Sopron only started in December.

Soon a military crew arrived and meticulously defused the live bomb. Over the next weeks, Olga Wagner walked in the city as

Christmas approached, horrified at the full devastation. So many of Sopron's buildings were destroyed and death was everywhere in the unnatural quiet.

The two-tone howl again pierced the walls of her family's apartment. Olga dropped what she was doing and grabbed her sheepskin jacket. Heart hammering wildly, she ran for fifteen minutes, full-out, alongside her brother and mother, her feet a rapid-fire pitter patter on the dirt road. Their new protection was a cave located two miles from home. Since the destruction of their neighbor's home, the Wagners no longer went to their basement. At the siren's strident screech, they were now conditioned to dash for the cave without conscious thought.

The cave belonged to the textile factory where her father was plant manager. Her father, Eugene Bácsi (Bácsi is a respectful Hungarian form of address for men) arranged for the workers' families to use the underground warehouse space as a shelter.

Olga arrived with her mother, brother, and the families of other workers, out of breath and sweating, and quickly slipped inside. The terror subsided as the safety of the cave washed through her. Whether the Russians dropped their incendiary bombs or the Americans their devastating missiles, the thick walls would isolate them from danger. Here there was no noise, no dust, and no destruction, only a reassuring moist earthen smell. Across the dirt road, a church and a convent, surrounded by trees, stood like sentries guarding her haven.

"I can hear planes," someone near the cave entrance reported. The aircraft thundered overhead without releasing their load. "Headed elsewhere," the look-out added. The built-up tension flowed from the group like the release of a charge after a lightning storm.

Everyone settled in for a couple of hours sojourn. Olga and her mother, Maria Néni (Néni is the respectful address for women), stood near the cave entrance and chatted with others while keeping one eye on the sky. They both wore a jacket over their skirt, blouse, and sweater. Olga's tight French braids had survived the run intact, but wisps of hair had escaped Maria Néni's brunette coif.

Andy, Olga's wiry, brown-haired younger brother, joined other boys in playing close to the cave entrance. The boys ran, yelled, and chased each other in a boisterous game of tag. Andy, trying to escape his pursuer, was oblivious to the mushy ground of his escape route until he stepped squarely on the soft ground of an old outhouse hole. Before he regained solid ground, Andy sunk to his armpits in gooey, odious smelling refuse. After a round of laughter, his friends got help to pull him out. Maria Néni glared at her son, finding no humor in the disgusting mess, knowing there was no water nearby to wash off the itchy, sticky stench. Reeking, Andy waited outside the shelter until the all-clear siren finally sounded. Then Maria Néni marched him home to start the scrubbing—where thankfully they had running water, a wood-burning water heater, and lots of soap.

The only casualty of the day was Andy's rough, irritated skin and a ding in his pride. The day was a success. Would they be as lucky tomorrow?

Almost daily bombing reduced the Wagners' life to the basics. Olga's school had closed months earlier, Andy's school a year before. Eugene Bácsi went to work, but the rest of the family rarely ventured from their one-bedroom apartment. They left for air raid sirens or essential errands like getting fresh food. They had no refrigerator, but a sand pile in the cellar kept buried carrots and winter crops, the pantry stored fruit and vegetable preserves, and the attic was good for hanging food to dry. Olga or her mother went out every day or two for milk and bread, ration coupons in hand, to join the long lines at the neighborhood store and hope supplies would last through their turn.

Christmas with friends before war disrupts their lives, 1940. *L. to r.*, Maria Néni (*second*), Olga (*third*), Andy (*fifth*), and Eugene Bácsi (*sixth*).

At night Olga's family meticulously darkened the two windows in the living room and the one in the bedroom. The window blinds were tightly drawn and a blanket crammed into cracks blocked even a sliver of light from shining through. Total darkness was critical to avoid being a target. Although bombing occurred almost exclusively during daylight hours, the terror revisited Olga and Andy in their dreams. As the siblings tried to outrun the noise and destruction, they would both awake, out of breath and drenched in sweat.

As the months grew, from one to two, to three, and then to four, thousands of people died in the bombing raids and more and more of the city was destroyed. Like the bomb shrapnel tore through the flesh of humans and exposed bone, the raids also destroyed many homes, revealing the skeleton of the city—large stretches of the original city fortification.

Staring at the exposed 400-year-old gray stone structure on one of her errands, Olga remembered an elementary school field trip years before. "In the 1600s, this stone wall was built around the city," the nun had explained to the young girls in Olga's class, "to protect Sopron from invaders." Pointing out an exposed section about ten feet long, she added, "This is the only part known to have survived."

"Could there be more?" a student had asked eyes wide.

"Perhaps. As Sopron grew, homes were built against the inside of the wall. As the city continued expanding, sections of the wall might not have been torn down, but built onto." Now the bombing had uncovered the truth.

Sopron, Hungary.

A half-year before the bombing raids began, the horrors of the war shifted from a tangential impact on Olga's young life. On an innocent summer day, with the sun lazily kissing the houses and streets, Olga left her apartment with her basket on a routine errand to purchase crusty, fresh-baked bread. She had barely stepped onto the sidewalk when the normal sounds of pedestrians chatting, wagon wheels rattling, and birds chirping were overpowered by more than a hundred feet shuffling on the pavement.

With large dazed eyes Olga watched German soldiers, armed with whips, shepherd a line of bedraggled shuffling prisoners. The prisoners each wore a yellow cloth star identifying them as Jews.

Yellow stars bright against their dark clothing, the prisoners were being herded like cattle from the Jewish Ghetto to the railroad station. The ghetto was a recently constructed brick and plaster building down her street, designed for the University; which had become a place to corral Jews. At first Jews were only required to live there, being allowed to come and go while the Hungarian government resisted German demands for deportation. However, once the Germans occupied the country in March 1944, the identifying yellow star became mandatory and voluntary movement ceased. Mass deportation of 440,000 Jews out of Hungary began.

Olga gasped as she recognized her favorite secondary school teacher amongst the herd of prisoners. She could not believe what was happening. The woman was a gifted teacher, liked by all her students, young, energetic, not even thirty years old. Yet she shuffled like an old woman, her eyes downcast and shoulders sagging. Olga's throat went dry. She seemed to forget how to swallow. Her thoughts crashed around in her head. She tried to comprehend the nightmare she was powerless to stop. "Oh my God, what're they going to do to her?" she cried in silence. "Somebody stop them." But nobody did.

A German soldier near her teacher cracked his whip with a loud thwack. Biting leather ripped the teacher's clothes and skin. The teacher edged back into line without even raising her eyes. She trudged woodenly on to the railroad station. Never to be seen again.

Living close to the ghetto, the forced marches weren't the only encounter Olga's family had with the Jewish prisoners. On a spring day in 1944, Andy and Maria Néni cut across the neighborhood park to go to a nearby store. Leafed-out foliage provided patches of shade, and the wood pavilion in the center of the square-block park was encircled by red, white, and yellow flowers. Their sweet fragrance mingled with the meatier aroma of the chestnut trees. Singing birds rejoiced in the warm, sunny day.

As they cruised along the cement path, Andy abruptly came to a stop. A body was sprawled in front of them, a bullet wound encrusted with dried blood visible on the man's chest, close to the distinctive yellow star.

"Watch out!" Maria Néni said. "Give me your hand."

She led him around the body matter-of-factly, and Andy never asked the questions swirling in his eight-year-old brain. Confused by the turmoil of the war, he knew his mother expected him to accept it. Andy came across several dozen dead bodies in the park in the months that followed, usually when the park was still bathed in shadows and the police had not yet cleared the bodies away. The boy learned to detour around them, the corpses part of the scenery like the flowers.

Olga first saw a dead body on an errand to the local market garden. "May I please have four carrots," she requested of the middle-aged garden worker. While she waited for the worker to dig up the carrots, something caught her eye. She turned to look more carefully. A lifeless human form was cradled between the rows of lush, green crops. It was a man in his twenties with dark hair and ashen skin. It looked like the life had been sucked out of his body leaving only a hollow stock. Olga could see the distinctive yellow cloth star pinned to his clothing. She turned away with bile in her throat.

"The police are on their way," the worker said when he saw the agony in her face. Olga hastily paid and hurried home.

"Mother, there's a dead man in the garden!" Olga said, plunking the carrots on the kitchen table.

Her mother didn't look up. "I've seen several too."

"But, Mother—"

"This happens in war. We need to carry on." The flat, emphatic tone of Maria Néni's voice brooked no argument. The conversation was over.

Olga wanted to talk about what was happening, to try to make sense of the horror that ate at her insides like sulfuric acid. As a teenager, she was less willing to just accept things like her mother always demanded. But no one wanted to talk about it.

By March 1945, Russian troops were quickly advancing across Hungary. Sopron was the farthest western city and the last city to shift from German to Russian occupation. The Germans were planning a fierce resistance, defending their last stronghold in Hungary, and heavy casualties were expected.

"Our plant's managers and their families are going to leave Hungary while the Russians fight for Sopron." Eugene Bácsi explained to his family one evening. The twinkle that normally lit his gray-blue eyes was absent. The gravity of the situation held everyone motionless. No one even bumped the embroidered cloth covering the table in front of them. "The plant will provide wagons and horses."

"How long will we be gone?" Maria Néni asked.

"A couple of weeks," Eugene Bácsi said. He touched her hand. "Long enough to avoid the worst of the fighting."

"When do we leave?"

"In about a week."

Every muscle in Olga's body was drawn as tight as strings on a violin. What was going to happen? she wondered. Would her family survive? What about her friends, her beloved city of Sopron? Her seventeen-year-old brother Gene was in Austria. A few months earlier, the family had received a letter; all the students and staff from Gene's military academy were going to Austria to avoid the Russian occupation. They had had no word since.

The Wagner children, 1942. *L. to r.* Andy, Olga, and Gene.

Olga, her parents, and Andy spent their last week in Hungary on their small fruit orchard an hour walk from their apartment. Out in the country, in the one-room cottage, they were safe from the increasingly frequent bombs and fires.

In amongst the fruit tree roots, the family buried a wood chest with their valuables. The chest was big enough to hold a few paintings and several intricate Oriental rug wall hangings, hand-knotted by Eugene Bácsi and Maria Néni. Silver, jewelry, and other valuables had been sold during the Depression to help pay a bankruptcy debt.

Maria Néni's face was etched with determination as she methodically packed a second trunk with food and other necessities for the trip. It reminded Olga of how her mother had protected her the last time Olga had a brush with death. At age two, Olga seemed to collect diseases, first scarlet fever, then diphtheria, then whooping cough. One illness made her limbs swell to three times their size.

"I'm sorry, your daughter's going to die," the doctor had told Maria Néni in the austere hospital room.

"Then I want to take her home," Maria Néni had said, her jaw clenched. With her mother's steadfast care, Olga slowly improved.

Olga watched her father's solemn expression as he made final arrangements for the factory wagon train and remembered their treasured walks through the forests in the nearby Alp foothills. Olga and Eugene Bácsi would hike through the musty, pine scented woods warmed by the patches of sunlight slipping through the leafy canopy. In the spring, they looked for sweet-smelling wild violets; in the fall, the colorful cyclamens. Most often, they searched the pine needle groundcover for earthy smelling mushrooms. The cream colored caps of the Boletus mushroom could grow up to ten inches across. Once, Eugene Bácsi hid a massive, extraordinary mushroom amongst the needles for her to discover. She had been delighted until she realized it was already washed. How she longed for another one of his practical jokes, frightened by his current countenance.

Her parents didn't need to talk about the unjustness that had pushed Hungary into World War II, its alliance with Germany, and their need to flee their homeland. Every day in gymnasium, and even in elementary school before that, her teachers reinforced the unfairness of the Hungarian people being divided, the consummate need for them to be reunited.

On a map, the teacher would show Hungary's border before and after World War I. "Under the Trianon Peace Treaty, our homeland was stripped of two-thirds of its land, and 3,500,000 Hungarians were severed from their fatherland. Hungary lost access to the sea and most valuable natural resources, making economic recovery difficult."

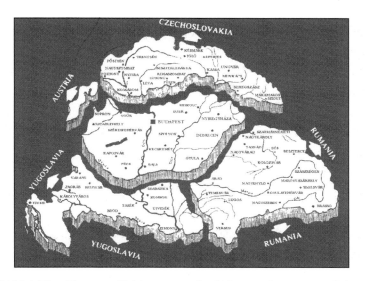

"1921 The Treaty of Trianon & the Dismemberment of the Kingdom of Hungary." *Family Research Austria-Hungary Maps & Atlases.* Copyright the DVHH, Inc.

Daily the class stood and together, with hands on their heart, prayed for those unfortunate Hungarians who had to live in a different country:

"I believe in God.
I believe in my country.
I believe in eternal justice.
And I believe in the rebirth of Hungary.
Amen."

Olga was fiercely patriotic, and she physically felt the pain of exiled Hungarians. For several summers, she spent a month with her aunt and uncle, who lived as an ethnic minority in Slovenia. She saw first-hand their hunger for their homeland. Her uncle, who played the church organ at Sunday services in their small town of Hungarians, even risked imprisonment by playing the outlawed Hungarian National Anthem. Olga knew the Hungarian dream of independence had as much substance as mist under strong sun. The Russians would soon be in control.

Olga packed the rucksack she would carry, there was only room for essentials—clothes and food. Olga's favorite books would have to stay behind. An avid reader from age six, this was hard for Olga to accept. What would happen to her precious stories? she wondered. More important, what would happen to her family? She prayed for the angels to watch over her family on their journey. She shuddered as she thought of the horrible stories she had heard about rape, brutal punishment, and pillaging as the Russians soldiers advanced. She knew terrible things were yet to come. She just didn't know what.

Olga and her family quietly left the orchard on the evening of March 28, 1945. The dark fruit trees, the brown meadow with a tinge of green, and the black sky were all deathly silent. The landscape looked gloomy and barren. What would happen to the Sopron she knew? What would happen to her homeland? Would she really return in a few weeks to smell the wild violets bloom?

Olga was dressed in a dark wool skirt, light blouse, woolen tights, and jacket. With her pack secure on her back, she walked with her family on the paved road to the plant on the outskirts of the city. There they joined other plant employees and their families gathering under the cover of darkness. The families loaded their belongings on fifteen horse-drawn wagons and one donkey cart.

The Russians had been blanketing Sopron with bombs for two days. As the wagon train pulled out around 10:00 p.m., the air raid alarm screeched yet again.

2

Tibor Learns Nothing Is Fair in War
(1944 - 1945)

Tibor's Official Picture taken by the
German Luftwaffe, winter 1945.

Air raid sirens screamed throughout the city of Győr. Tibor Zoltai and his brother Steve did not head for shelter. They hot-footed it out of their ground-floor apartment and ran to get a better view. The fresh smell of new leaves, greening grass, and blooming bulbs that had beckoned them earlier went unnoticed.

Their leather shoes pounded the stone as they clambered up the old stone wall of the original city fortification a few blocks from their home. The large flat area, where years earlier Tibor, Steve, and their cousins had spent many happy hours kicking around a soccer ball, commanded a panoramic view. From here, Tibor could see a fair portion of the city. His gaze barely registered the red and gray tiles roofs, the narrow winding streets, the rich architectural styles crossing centuries, or even the factory towers visible in the distance. He stared at the sky.

It was mid-morning, a crisp, clear day with good visibility. His eyes tracked the American bombers as they flew northward, sun shimmering off their propellers.

There must be 500 of them, Tibor thought, mesmerized by the fast rhythm of the whirring props. But as their loads met earth, thundering booms and earsplitting crashes masked the engine sounds. In five to ten minutes another wave of 500, then a third appeared. The hundreds of roaring metal machines passed 25,000 to 30,000 feet overhead, the bombs ejected from the planes' bellies exploding on impact with earsplitting crashes. Flames burst into life and spread in concentric circles. Buildings collapsed with voluminous roars. Dust and smoke began to obscure the blue sky and fill Tibor's nostrils.

The bombs were more powerful and destructive than anything Tibor had ever seen. In minutes they were destroying what had taken centuries to build. He remembered reading about carpet bombing, but he felt the reality was much more devastating.

The all-clear signal finally echoed through the dust, smoke, and destruction. Tibor and Steve immediately went looking for their family. When Tibor saw that no one in his family was hurt, he released the breath anchored in his lungs. Unfortunately many were not as lucky and needed help. With the first aid and other skills he had learned in Boy Scouts, Tibor went to assist.

Tibor was eighteen, his brother Steve only fifteen. That spring, they spent days helping with the rescue effort in anyway they could; moving cement, brick, and plaster; digging bodies out of the rubble; burying the estimated 2,000 dead. Tibor tried to stay focused on the work, not allowing the gut-wrenching horror and stench of death overwhelm him. The mother and child struck dead on the side of the road. The family buried under the rubble in the building meant to protect them. The smell of burnt flesh from the couple fried in a fire that sprung away from a bomb crash-site. The crisp April air became heavy with the odor of fire and death, the horizon smoky and gray. Tibor heard the wails and grief for lost loved ones permeate every pore of the city.

This first bombing raid occurred on April 13, 1944. In March, Germany occupied the country in response to Hungary's attempt to withdraw from the war. Györ was the first Hungarian city to be carpet bombed by the Allies. It was an attractive target, with an airplane factory that rolled dozens of flying machines off the assembly line each week. But most deaths from the raid were not at the airplane factory, because of state-of-the-art cement bunkers that sheltered workers with backup electricity and a second exit. The deaths were in the city, ordinary citizens, civilians who did not have access to bunkers or other potent protection.

Several members of Tibor's family were intimately involved in the war and politics. One of Tibor's uncles was a bank director, another active in foreign affairs. A third uncle, Jenci Bácsi, was in the Army like his father, although a much higher rank—a major general in charge of the Twentieth Division. Tibor's father, Nicholas Bácsi, was

24

a captain in counter espionage whose assignment was to diffuse sabotage plots in local factories.

As a small boy, Tibor would sit hidden for hours under the wood counter of his grandfather's tobacco shop, eavesdropping on conversations about world developments. The shop was on the ground floor of his grandfather's mustard-colored apartment building. It was crammed with a large assortment of pipes, cigars, and cigarettes; newspapers, magazines, envelopes, and stamps. Tibor loved the strong smell of sweet high-quality tobacco that filled every corner. Customers would linger, discussing the problems of Hungary and the world. The lack of jobs during the Depression, the economic hardship imposed on Hungary by the Trianon Treaty, the growing power of Germany, Stalin's purges and centralizing of communist control in Russia; all were debated.

"Hungary needs to be reunited! The Trianon Treaty's unjust!" was often said loudly with passion. It was one topic on which all customers agreed. Tibor's father captured his conviction in a song: "Righteous eternal god, protect your orphan. The fire is still burning, the flame is protected. A people divided cries for help. Time goes by and destiny unmistakably waits . . . Triumph the strength, the vitality."

The Zoltai Family. *L. to r.* Lili Néni, Tibor, Nicholas Bácsi, and Steve, 1942.

* * *

Despite the chaos of ongoing bombing, Tibor was scheduled to graduate in June from his all-male gymnasium. Run by Benedictine priests, the massive white school building, with symmetrical wood trimmed windows and arched doorways, was in the heart of the city. In the mornings he attended school. In the afternoons and evenings he completed four to five hours of homework and extensive memorization for his finals. To graduate, Tibor had to pass an extremely rigorous oral exam. It covered everything taught during his entire twelve years of elementary and gymnasium education: math, history, science, literature, Hungarian, German, and Latin. Even though Tibor had spent part of tenth grade in a sanatorium recuperating from tuberculosis, he was determined to graduate with his class. Looking the examiner directly in the eye, he did his best to answer the questions on exam day, and he passed on first try.

Tibor gave serious thought to devoting his life to the church. He was attracted to living his Catholic faith as a Benedictine priest and teacher. But after deep contemplation and many conversations with teachers, friends, and family, he decided to enroll in Architecture at the Poly-Technical University in Budapest.

Tibor loved the capital city: the gently flowing Danube River, the inspiring bridges, the fascinating historic architecture, the yellow trams bursting with passengers, the energetic noise. But all the beauty and bustle could not hide the palpable tension as the Russians advanced. Tibor managed to complete a truncated semester before the Red Army with their ground-shaking tanks, booming artillery, and million-strong military force started penetrating the city. Before the bloody destruction and siege commenced, the university closed its doors and he, along with many other students, dispersed.

* * *

As the Russians marched on Budapest, Tibor returned home. The family fled with Jenci Bácsi's wife and her young children to a nearby town where the acrid smell of bombs, fire, and death was only a whiff on the horizon. It was clear that the Hungarian military was no more effective at stopping the Red Army than dozens of sandbags can hold back a massive flood. The military officers' families were congregating to leave Hungary ahead of the Russian takeover of Györ. There were about a hundred wives and children in the group, but no young men near his age of nineteen.

"Mother," Tibor said, a couple of weeks after arriving, "I can't stay here, not when other young men are helping protect Hungary." Clashing, booms, and bangs of the war a couple of miles away could be heard in the background. The fighting had gotten louder each day as the Russian flood spread ever westward. "I'm returning to Györ."

Tibor's deep seated Hungarian patriotism allied with the current government, despite German occupation. Like most Hungarians, he greatly feared the Russians, their communism, purges, and total control. At least under German occupation, Tibor felt a lot of Hungarian culture and values were maintained.

"I wish you'd stay," Lili Néni said softly, shoulders bowed. She embraced and kissed Tibor with tears in her grey-green eyes.

Before he left, she pressed something cold into his hand, her most treasured and valuable jewelry, a round gold broach with a glistening pearl surrounded by sparkling diamond chips and intricate etching. A bar under the pearl turned, opening to reveal pictures of both her sons.

"If you need to, exchange it for your life," she whispered.

"I'll take good care of it," Tibor promised.

"Be careful," Lili Néni said in a raspy voice. "God be with you."

* * *

"Why'd you return to Györ?" Nicholas Bácsi bellowed upon seeing Tibor. "What a stupid thing to do! All the young men are being forced into service by the Germans!"

Even if Tibor had known that on January 1, 1945, the day before he arrived, German occupying authorities had plastered colored conscription posters throughout the streets of Györ, he still would have felt it his patriotic duty to come. The posters stated that every young man over sixteen must register for either the German Waffen SS; a Hungarian division of the army, which was similar to the Waffen SS; or German anti-aircraft defense. There was an implicit fourth choice: not register. Tibor knew if a young man didn't register and was caught, he would be shot.

"We're more likely to be killed in the Waffen SS or Hungarian Army," Tibor and his friends reasoned. "They're more politically risky as well."

"Let's sign up for anti-aircraft defense," they agreed. "That'll still be exciting."

So on January 6, Tibor and Nicholas Bácsi met three of Tibor's friends from the Benedictine Gymnasium under the buzz of the large electric clock in the center of town. They joined the extended procession of parents and youth walking toward the train station. The snow-packed streets muted the sounds of many feet on the sidewalk and street. Their path smelled of wet snow, wool, and cigarette smoke. Hundreds of eyes tracked their progress from the homes and businesses that lined the route. As they passed, voices yelled out good wishes and blessings.

Each boy carried at least one enormous canvas rucksack with clothes, cameras, record players, and lots of food. The youth packed limited clothes since once in Germany, they expected to receive uniforms.

Conscripted Györ youth headed for train station, Jan. 6, 1945.

Tibor walked with head held high, an eager bounce in his step. Even leaning forward to counterbalance his heavy rucksack didn't hide his pride and excitement. He was going to help defend his country. He and his friends had everything needed for an exciting outing, he thought.

"I've never seen Germany," one boy said in a boisterous voice of someone headed on vacation.

"The Austrian countryside is supposed to be beautiful," Tibor said, his breath condensing in the brisk January air.

The procession passed several Russian prisoners. Looking challengingly at them, Tibor said, "We'll never become prisoners!"

"Never!" his friends agreed with absolute confidence.

Nicholas Bácsi, like the other fathers and the mothers, walked beside his son with feet as heavy as stone. The temperature hovering around freezing, the overcast gray day, and the streets covered with dirty, packed snow reflected his mood. He didn't want to send these youth off to be soldiers. His eyes were stained with the sight of blood from too many young men thinking war was an adventure. These boys were so naïve and easily influenced. Would they live through the war? Would they return safely home?

"We love you."

"Take care of yourself."

"God be with you," could be heard throughout the crowd.

The train station clock struck the hour several times. The youth waited for instructions. The smell of steam and coal enveloped them.

"Those eighteen and older form a separate group." The German officer was dressed in a crisp gray uniform and billed cap. The shuffling of boys and luggage reverberated throughout the station.

"You," the officer said to Tibor and the others over eighteen, "will serve in the Hungarian legion in Komáron."

Komáron was on the Russian front!

"Not anti-aircraft defense?"

"The front line?"

"Will we survive?"

Sweat was starting to pool under Tibor's arms. He pounced on Nicholas Bácsi when his father joined them. "Father, please find out more about what's happening."

"They say they're sending you to Komáron," Nicholas Bácsi said a few minutes later. "Don't worry. If it's true, I'll volunteer to be your leader." He had served on the front-line in World War I.

The train clock ticked off the minutes. Then the youth were led to a string of cattle cars attached to a black locomotive spouting steam and particles of coal. The car floors were lined with stiff, scratchy hay, and forty youth were packed per car.

"Dear God, please let us go west," Tibor prayed. A low-ranking officer shouted an order and his crude voice brought Tibor ever closer to the reality of becoming a soldier. It was not like an outing, he thought.

An air raid alarm sounded. "God be with you, boys!" family on the platform cried, and the train pulled away.

Hissing steam and the hoot of the train whistle muffled the yells. The cars gently rocked, the wheels lightly screeching and clanging as it gained momentum. Tibor released a deep sigh. They were headed west; to Germany, not Russia!

A cold rain started to fall. In the fog, the sound of the air raid alarm faded. The smoky towers of Györ slowly disappeared in the distance.

Conscripted Györ youth loaded on train, Jan. 6, 1945.

That dreary, cold January day about 750 youth left Györ, about 150 students, 300 field workers, and the rest factory workers. Over the next few months, new youth came and others left, but Tibor and his friends would stay together, providing leadership for the younger boys.

After four days of gently swaying on the tracks with intermittent stops, the train had traveled 330 miles. Arriving at their destination on the outskirts of Munich, Tibor and the youth disembarked in the dark and marched along an icy, slippery road to the nearby military airport.

The airport was large and modern, Tibor thought, first-class compared to the ones in Hungary. The barracks were solid two-story cement, brick, and plaster structures; the runways and roads smooth and well laid-out; hangers sturdily constructed, spacious, and clean. There was even a dining hall and church on the grounds.

Tibor, like the others, was disinfected and assigned a bunk in the airport barracks. He was provided a worn gray German Air Force uniform, insignia and decorations torn off. His civilian clothes were confiscated while he was out working.

Györ youth digging trenches at the Luftwaffe airport in the outskirts of Munich, winter 1945.

For six weeks, his labor entailed cutting wood, digging trenches, and serving on a human snow-clearing crew. After it snowed, his feet and hundreds of others could be heard shuffling and stamping on the runway until the snow was pressed down, flat enough for planes to land and take off. When he wasn't working, Tibor and his friends played cards, talked, or listened to music that brought the sounds of home into their barrack. They were only to walk within the boundaries of the property, unless escorted by Germans.

*   *   *

"Hitler's my God!" their guard Stabi declared. "You should worship Hitler and the Third Reich, not attend church." Stabi's eyes shot bullets at Tibor and other youth who defied his advice and went to Mass the one Sunday it was available. Tibor found the service very spiritual. The smell of incense and the familiar rhythm of Mass in this little German church reminded him of home.

He sporadically wrote about his experiences in his diary. "Are we going to be forced laborers or soldiers?" he pondered. It took time for the answer to become clear, but the youth never did become anti-air defense soldiers. Officially considered SS apprentices by the Germans, not SS soldiers, and not tattooed, they had merely been pressed into involuntary labor—no pay, only subsistence levels of food.

"Those born in 1924 or earlier form a separate group." A German officer, dressed in a pressed-pristine gray wool uniform and coat, ordered the youth into clusters. It was a cloudy, grey day in early February. The young men stood on the flat snow-covered airport grounds, their two-story plaster barracks a few feet away. Grounded German airplanes were visible in the distance, the sound of their propellers heard less and less due to a shortage of fuel.

Dragging their feet, fifty young men separated from the larger group. Tibor, born in 1925, stayed put.

"Assemble your gear and get ready to leave," the officer ordered, offering no explanation.

"God be with you." Tibor hugged and kissed his friend, who was among the fifty. There was heaviness and lingering to his goodbye, knowing he was unlikely to see his friend for a long time.

Years later, Tibor found out these Hungarian young men were taken to join the SS against their wishes. His friend and most of the others died.

In mid-February, Tibor left Munich with just over 600 youth for their second and more permanent work. They traveled mainly in rail cattle cars, but walked between some towns. For sections of extended walking, Tibor and others with restricted mobility rode in a wagon with their luggage.

Rocking with the sway of the horse drawn wagon, Tibor fingered his mother's broach. It hung in a soft cloth sack around his neck, warm from the heat of his body. He remembered his mother's tender ministrations when he was ill as a six-year-old, the vow she made after hearing the dire predictions of the doctors. In her prayers she had promised that if he recovered, she would give up smoking for a year, the biggest personal sacrifice she could make. She relished the relaxation of the smooth cigarette between her fingers, the silky paper against her lips, the smoky smell filling her nostrils, and the savory taste of tobacco. But when Tibor recovered she fulfilled her vow.

His illness had started innocently enough, an infection of his middle ear. Penicillin or sulpha drugs would have easily cleared it up, but they weren't available yet. The doctors used heated salt packs placed on his ear. The ear drum burst, allowing the infection to drain, but the infection didn't go away. It moved into the bone marrow, so the doctors then chiseled out a piece of his skull, leaving a half-inch hole behind his left ear. They still weren't able to stop the insidious spread. The infection developed into Sepsis, a systemic response to infection which causes organ failure. In 1931, the survival rate given by the doctors was one in one thousand. If Tibor survived, he would not live past forty.

During the course of his Sepsis infection, Tibor had five surgeries, and as a lasting side effect, his left knee no longer bent; it was stiff as a log. At a clinic in Budapest, the doctors used a machine to break a little bit of his knee every day, mechanically forcing the knee to bend. After six months, Tibor had dozens of bone pieces in his knee but was able to bend it about 90 degrees. Although he still didn't walk with ease, this radical procedure improved his mobility and built in him an incredible tolerance for pain.

Throughout elementary school and gymnasium, he was always exempt from physical exercise. This exemption combined with his childhood mop of long curly blond hair, blue eyes, and soft skin, earned him his nick name, Médi, slang for "maiden". He didn't mind the name. His friends had silly nicknames as well, like Dog and Dodo.

Tibor (Médi), Dog, Dodo, and the other youth were waiting at one of their many interim railway stops, soot particles and steam spewing from their locomotive. They pulled out a map to pass the time and huddled around the stiff paper mottled with greens, blue ribbons, and red lines.

"I wonder if we're headed to—" one of youth said pointing a finger, stiff from the cold, to a location in northern Germany. The sound of machine-gun fire cut off his words. As fast as water flows, Tibor and his friends were on their bellies. A plane flew just above the tree line, strafing them and their locomotive.

Once the whir of the plane's engines faded, the youth regrouped. None of them were hurt. Bullets had drawn blood from three guards and pierced the metal hull of their locomotive, incapacitating it.

The next day they resumed their journey with a new locomotive. While they chugged along the shiny rails, the sun set and rose again. In Nuremburg they got off the train to find food. Tibor's stomach rumbled at the thought of savory, warm soup. But the piercing cry of an air-raid siren electrified the atmosphere, the soup forgotten.

Catapulted into motion, Tibor followed his German leader and the other youth away from the station. They crouched, running in a ditch alongside the rail line toward a neighboring park where trenches etched the ground in a zigzag pattern.

The deep hum of the airplanes was soon joined by explosive crashes. Every minute or two a bomb landed on the city, one directly on the train station, its explosion louder than the crashing of two speeding locomotives, Tibor thought. Cars were overturned and fire spread. Another bomb exploded the ammunition car next to their railcar, setting off a violent torrent of bangs like massive fire crackers exploding. A bomb detonated on the rail line next to Tibor. The earth under his body quaked furiously. Pressure built in his ears until they felt like bursting.

Finally after an hour and a half the raid ended. As the youth were marched through the city to another train station, Tibor saw demolished buildings, downed wires, and fires everywhere. The whole city was alight with dancing white, yellow, and red flames. A thick haze from dirt, plaster, and smoke blanketed as far as he could see.

The youth spent a truncated night trying to stay warm in a local barn, then began walking again. When yet again the sirens howled, they took cover in an open field next to a hospital. From there, Tibor saw the lead plane drop its signal bomb a good distance away. Like a spectator, he watched the explosions, the smoke clouds, the fireworks of the phosphate bombs.

Tibor wrote in his diary: "This bombing lasted two and a half hours. In the second hour, a series of bombs fell about 300 yards from us hitting the hospital. There was tremendous air pressure. Flames all over. Dirt. Shrapnel whistled by. A piece of shrapnel flew about eight inches from my head; another piece twenty inches away. The heat was terrible."

When the dust finally cleared, Tibor saw the others struggle to their feet. His whole body was shaking. He looked around to see if anyone needed emergency help and saw ten to fifteen or more Germans near them had died instantly. The tremendous air pressure had caused their heads to explode and spattered brains covered five or six of the boys with blood. He looked around at their surroundings and realized how close they stood to death. Tibor's friend wrote, "I felt I had already passed through death and did not feel anything."

Slowly, the youth began looking for each other. They began to congregate by a broken fence.

"There's a live bomb!" yelled a youth, pointing to a large bowl-shaped crater right next to the fence. In its center was a gigantic bomb. Everyone scrambled away.

Soon over 600 youth had joined the growing group. Only three were missing. The boys started a search.

"I found Szenyor's eyeglasses," one of the youth announced holding up the distinctive heavy glasses mangled by shrapnel. They soon found the soiled hat of another and a recognizable bloodied item from the third. History would later report that during January and February, Nuremburg was bombed several times with the death toll estimated at 6,000.

"I can't see, I lost my glasses," Szenyor said, joining the group not long afterwards. "Anyone see my cap?" came from the youth whose hat they'd found. The third boy soon appeared as well.

None of them had been killed or even hurt. But in their horror, they saw the burning city in the darkness. "Why?" Tibor wrote. "Is there a reason to fight? Germany, regardless of how fanatical they are, can not continue the war for long and worst case was they will be totally destroyed."

Counterfeit butter coupons dropped from American planes, spring 1945.

As their journey north from Munich continued, the Hungarian youth left behind the cities, the human swarms, the almost constant air raids. They entered rough, hilly countryside. On the plateaus were pastures, fields, and forests. Steep valleys of exposed rock dropped away to meandering rivers and lakes formed by man restraining the river's flow. As they neared their camp, they crossed a lake, walking over the hydroelectric power plant dam. The dam was protected by giant balloons tethered with metal cables. Such barrage balloons were used to defend assets, like the dam and power plant, against bombardment by low flying aircraft. The metal cables could catch in the planes and damage them.

Up a steep hill was their camp, encircled by sweet smelling pines, spruces, and firs. Rows of wood barracks were connected by dirt paths covered with patches of snow. The whole camp was enclosed in barbed wire. Tibor went into his assigned barrack, a one-story square that was dark, smoky, dirty, and chilly with a low ceiling and no washing facilities. Frigid winter wind whistled through his building. The stove didn't even work.

Their assignment was to learn how to operate barrage balloons at a training site on the lake, about a mile from their barracks. Even when training was brutal, a part of Tibor appreciated the majestic beauty of the stark gray rock slabs, bare lacy deciduous trees, and evergreens shooting up like arrows to the sky. But these ancient mountains held onto winter several weeks longer than the countryside near Munich, and in the first two weeks, Tibor's extremities literally froze. He had to chip away ice to even remove his shoes. During barrage balloon training, every time he pulled on the ice-cold cables, the metal dug into the flesh of his hands. Days were spent wishing for spring.

Hydroelectric dam near Tibor's camp, spring 1945.

En route to the training site each morning, noon, and evening, the boys stayed warm with strenuous exercises. The trainers commanded them to learn and sing German songs; if they didn't, swift punishment followed. Training exercises lasted until 5:00 p.m., followed by an hour of classroom instruction translated into Hungarian. They learned about barrage balloons, rifles, gas masks, guard duty, even the German language, but beyond a very basic lesson on how to pull a rifle trigger, the youth received no training on handling offensive weapons.

At night, Tibor's muscles screamed in protest, cramping and knotting in his arms and legs. Ferociously hungry, he was repulsed by the mainstay of their diet: boiled, woody, unseasoned white beets. In both smell and taste no better than chewing paper. In Hungary, this kind of beet was used only as animal feed, but Tibor voraciously consumed all of the woody fare provided. His stomach still roaring with hunger, he and the other youth grew obsessed with food, calculating how to get more. They bartered cigarette rations for a loaf of bread, but no amount abated their hunger.

Then the lice came. Soon everyone was itching and scratching. Scabies, caused by the lack of washing, infested the barracks. Although Tibor regularly washed, he still had limited success staying clean due to the lack of soap or clean underwear. Many boys didn't wash in the numbing, frigid water.

It seemed so long ago that they were enthusiastically walking to the train station in Györ. "The insufficient nourishment, the bad living arrangements, the difficult training, and the knowledge we are only barrage balloon operators is bad enough," Tibor wrote in his diary, "but our trainers also treat us like dogs. Promised food never materializes. The trainers eat twice as much, and better food, than we do. They laugh and yell at us if we complain. They consider us a barbaric people and make sure we know it. They even blame all the war losses on the Hungarian military."

Their German captain had a tendency for sadism, enjoying torturing the boys. "He's a nervous, fanatical, double-dealing man who promises everything and delivers nothing," Tibor wrote. Once for punishment, he made the boys lay down in the mud and walked back and forth on their backs in his boots.

After finally accepting the Germans discarded their concerns like rotten food, the youth developed a philosophy of passive resistance. They did everything expected of them, but where they could, they didn't work. When two youth decided passive resistance was not enough, they snuck out of camp and headed home. The captain shouted that they would be shot. Tibor hoped the two runaways made it home. He knew the captain's threat was not an empty one.

When the three-week barrage balloon training was over, fifty youth left to become barrage balloon operators at the power plant. Those remaining constructed tank barricades out of long, straight pine logs piled up between wood poles on each side of the road. By late March, Tibor was ill and exhausted from the training and work. The doctor declared him unsuitable for heavy labor due to his defective knee, so he was assigned kitchen duty, a good job since kitchen workers didn't starve as much as the others.

Pieces of war news filtered to the youth. Each time Tibor heard anything about Hungary, it was about another city fallen or another military loss. His head bowed when he heard the Russians had taken Győr on March 28. He prayed his family and friends were safe.

The front crept closer every day. By April 1, the Americans were only eighty-five miles from the camp. Bombing and strafing became more frequent. Crashes echoed in the hills as the barrage balloons were shot down and the dam damaged.

Tibor was standing next to the latrine when the camp was directly hit. With a thunderous roar, the air pressure from the exploding bomb lifted him off his feet and threw him into the bursting latrine. With the lack of soap and only frigid water, getting clean was near impossible. The harder he scrubbed the more red and raw his skin became. The obnoxious odor lingered, but at least he was alive.

By April 12, the Americans were only five to ten miles away. At 2:00 a.m., soldiers and recruits were ordered to abandon camp and began to flee the Americans on foot. The order was to head eastward toward Dresden, but the swarm of retreating men and youth went in whatever direction the Americans pushed, like cottonwood fluff in the wind. They would walk at night and then rest for a period in a barn or a school before again kicking up dust.

They traversed mile after mile of dirt and paved road, passing farmland, pastures, and villages, reaching eastern Germany and moving into the far western part of Czechoslovakia. There were no wagons, except for supplies. Tibor kept walking, hoping somewhere along the route he could hop a wagon or a train. At first he walked with the slower-paced older German officers, pushing their baggage cart. But after tens of thousands of steps he was unable to even push the small cart. By the second day, the officers refused to allow him to accompany them. Tibor's request to put his rucksack on a wagon was also denied.

Tibor had a very high tolerance for pain from all his childhood illness, but his mental discipline only went so far. The extended walking was like continually stabbing hot pokers in his leg. In his physically weakened condition and with lack of nourishment, his body revolted against the pain. He wrote about the second day of fleeing: "With my rucksack and despair, I started to walk. After the first mile, I fell. I asked in vain to be able to put my rucksack in the wagon following us. When I was afraid I would fall behind, another wagon passed me and allowed me to put my rucksack on it. This way, it was easier, but still quite difficult for me to make the twenty miles that night."

"During the following nights," Tibor wrote, "I was always able to smuggle my rucksack onto a wagon. Then, finally, I received official authorization to do it." But, as the days went by, Tibor's health got worse. He became jaundiced, and his stomach hurt so much he was barely able to walk. For several days he had nothing to eat. On the third day a farmer took pity and traded a slice of white bread and a pint of milk for ten cigarettes. Tibor was unable to swallow the bread. With the help of his friends stealing some life-giving milk and eggs, Tibor survived the next week and even gained back a little strength.

As they got further from the front, their pace slowed. Supplies shrunk, rations were reduced to one potato for one meal and soup for a second, and the youth longed for food, their bellies always empty and nagging.

Tibor's group fleeing Americans, spring 1945.

One night, Tibor and his friends decided to sneak out under the cover of darkness to a neighboring village to beg for food. The farmers were generous that night, so they tried two more times. The evening of their third foray they were near the Czechoslovakia-German border. Another pair of young men went begging as well.

Tracked to a nearby Czech village, the other pair was marched back to camp at gun point. The guards faced them toward the wall for forty-five excruciatingly slow minutes, cold steel of a barrel in their backs.

"The law states deserters can be shot on sight," the guard proclaimed, reinforcing his point by increasing the deadly cold pressure in their backs. Sweat drenched and shaking, the pair was finally hauled off to the police for the night.

Tibor and his friend were luckier. They talked their way out of punishment. Because they went to a German village, not a Czech one, and had snuck back into camp rather than being caught off-site, the officer was more sympathetic.

Tibor's group fleeing Americans, spring 1945.

On their evasive march from the Allies, the Germans took the Hungarian youth on a winding path, traveling about 220 miles. Finally, the Germans turned the group around so that when the youth surrendered, they would not become Russian prisoners of war;

Russians were known to be much harsher on their prisoners than the Americans.

It was May 6, a sunny day with the vibrant green and clean scent of new growth hinting at new beginnings. Tibor walked toward the Americans with a light, quick step, his hunger, weakness, and tiredness forgotten. He thought of going home soon, convinced the Americans would release them.

He and the other youth took a short-cut through a forest. "The Americans are close, just on the other side of the village," town locals told them as they passed through. And soon American vehicles became visible on the horizon.

Suddenly the German officer in charge went up to a canvas-covered wood wagon. It had looked innocent, like all the other wagons. Now, uncovered, it revealed a deadly load of rifles. "Pick up the guns, move to the front, and fight," the officer ordered.

Tibor and the others stood transfixed, not knowing how to escape their certain death. But after a few seconds, Tibor became aware that the German guards had vanished. He and the others hastily found some white cloth, picked up a rifle, and attached the cloth to the butt. They prominently displayed their improvised flag and waited.

The rumble of engines and a dust cloud grew as the Americans approached. A large vehicle in camouflage colors, with multiple machine guns mounted on top drove into view. Four muscular Americans in battle gear jumped out, each aiming a machine gun at the Hungarian draftees.

"Arms up." Deep thuds reverberated around Tibor as the American soldiers shot into the earth.

The youth raised their arms.

The Americans hastily broke the guns in the wagon then searched the boys, removing both their weapons and wrist watches, claiming the latter as spoils of war. As he watched, Tibor still felt hopeful, a pressing weight lifting from his shoulders. The war was over, he thought. The four months since he left home seemed an eternity. How naïve he had all been, thinking they were going on an adventure.

Now they were prisoners of war without ever having been real soldiers, without fighting in the war, without even carrying a gun. How ironic that the real soldiers, the Germans that guarded them, got away.

Tibor now knew that nothing was fair in war. He had learned a lot. Now he could go home, he thought. He was about to find out the truth: his war lessons weren't nearly over.

3

Tibor Is a POW
(1945)

Wood carving Tibor whittled in POW camp, 1945.

Tibor and one hundred other men were corralled in a thirteen-by-thirteen-foot room that served as their cell. Whatever direction Tibor faced, he was only inches from another body, close enough to see the pores on his neighbor's skin and inhale the sour breath. The night lengthened and the smells of sweat, dirt, and urine accumulated in the room. Tibor alternated standing and squatting, trying to relieve the pressure and pain in his knee.

In the morning, his group walked to an empty glass factory. There they joined hundreds of German POWs in the large yard of a production complex with a stream trickling through the middle. As they waited, Tibor used the icy-cold stream to wash off layers of dirt and the foul smells that had accumulated during the last few days. Tibor and his friends foraged for food, found a few potatoes in a building abutting the yard, and roasted them over a crackling fire. Tibor savored every bite of his share.

Herded onto trucks a few hours later, they joined more prisoners in another city. Like small tributaries flowing into a river, their numbers continued to grow. At midnight, Tibor and the others were again shepherded onto military trucks.

Bangs, shuffling, and grunts accompanied the loading. The Yanks shoved and pushed until they had squashed sixty-four prisoners onto Tibor's truck, then threw the luggage up into the air above the men's heads. Anything the POWs didn't catch crashed to the ground and was left behind as the trucks rumbled away.

It was difficult to even stand during the five-hour ride. Whenever the truck slowed down, speeded up, or changed direction, the full weight of sixty-four people crushed those hanging onto the sides. With nothing to hold onto, those in the middle became airborne. Men crashed into each other, threw up, and passed out. The motion, combined with the smell of sweat, vomit, and urine, made Tibor nauseous.

It was still dark when they stopped. Only a few could find their bags in amongst the mixed-up mess at their feet. In the truck's headlights, Tibor could make out water covering most of the ground, dry islands here and there. His feet still numb from the crushing ride, he stumbled off the truck, laid directly on the wet clay ground, and promptly fell asleep.

In a few hours, the sky began to lighten and birds announced the arrival of a new day. Tibor got up and tried to put his wet, dirty clothes in order. He made a fire to get warm. As the morning fog cleared, a barbed wire fence and machine gun towers came into view. Tibor saw thousands and thousands of prisoners—a gray sea of bedraggled men. It was a POW camp. The enclosed area was no more than 650 by 450 yards. Apart from an administrative office, there were no buildings. No tents. No structures of any kind. No protection from the wet ground, the cold air, the mist. No grass. Just bare wet dirt with man-dug ditches.

The lifeless men behind the barbed wire shivered and stretched as they awoke in the cold May morning. Tibor heard Hungarian.

"Where are we?" he asked a Hungarian POW.

"Janahof," the muddy man answered.

Janahof, a village in the lowlands of southeastern Germany, was close to the Czechoslovakian border.

"What's it like?" Tibor asked.

"We've been here five days," the POW whispered his face and voice void of expression. "There's almost no food."

Before allowing Tibor and the new POWs to enter camp, the Americans searched for weapons again, their fifth search in thirty-six hours. The new arrivals waited in a long line, snaking around the perimeter. Suddenly, rifle shot cracked the air. A German POW dead as he ran toward the water. Another was shot later as he approached the barbed wire fence.

With the new arrivals, camp numbers swelled. Tibor estimated there must be 15,000 to 18,000 prisoners. And not nearly enough food for all of them, he discovered over the next few days. Tibor was already emaciated, his total food consumption for the past week had been one potato, a small tin of pureed meat, and water. Even before that, in training camp and during the 220 mile march, food had been scarce.

Food in the POW camp, mainly clear vegetable broth, would be just enough to keep him from dying.

Tibor passed his days lying down to conserve strength. If he tried to stand up, he usually fell back five or six times before he could even sit. His muscles, already wasting away from hunger over the past five months, continued to disappear, leaving loose skin with angular bones. He even lacked the energy and coordination to easily follow his brain's basic instructions. Sun burned his skin during the day and the penetrating cold made him shiver at night

Each day Tibor wrote a card. By the sixth day, the stiff cream colored tag-board was illegible. His hand no longer capable of the fine motor control needed to smoothly guide pen on paper.

"You'll be in Janahof a few days," the Americans had told the Hungarian youth when they arrived. But day, after day passed. Even though the Americans had specifically promised the Hungarian major that the apprentice soldiers would soon move on, only time moved on. Tibor's hopes of going home melted away with his muscles. The noise from the masses of POWs crammed together subsided as time drained their energy reserves. The smell of foul bodies, diarrhea, and urine grew stronger. Tibor and his friends got weaker and weaker.

A black fog took up residence in Tibor's brain, suppressing coherent thought. In this semi-sleep state he passed the bulk of each day. When his mind was clear enough to think, he obsessed about food and home. He fretted about what had happened to his family. Were they alright? He hoped they were faring better than he.

* * *

After several days, the Americans found a stockpile of German military canned food. Each prisoner got one can. The cans were only labeled with a number. The youth shook their cans, trying to guess what was inside. The cans were fairly heavy and didn't slosh or move when shaken.

After clunking sounds from pocket knives prying open the cans, they found that each Hungarian in Tibor's group had received a can of pork fat. The heavy, savory smell made Tibor salivate, but he knew if they devoured pure fat after starving, they would become very ill.

"Just one spoonful a day," Tibor advised. "Mix it with broth, then your body will be able to digest it."

Five days passed, and the food situation improved. Peas and potatoes were added to the clear onion broth soup. Within two weeks, the prisoners were receiving half a liter of soup twice a day. But still many died.

With hollow eyes, Tibor watched the foul corpses pile up. "More than a thousand gone, bloody stomach," Tibor heard from another prisoner. Bloody stomach was slang for severe dysentery.

Serious food shortage was compounded by poor sanitary conditions. One faucet served all 15,000 prisoners. Because there was hardly enough water to drink, washing was difficult. The camp reeked of sweaty men, diarrhea, and death.

Lice quickly spread from one man to the next. The parasites in the German training camp were like a light drizzle compared to this torrential rain. The lice infested the whole body.

In mid-May, Tibor and the youth were put on a truck and driven less than a mile to a POW camp in Cham, Germany. En route, they stopped to wash in a bracing creek and be disinfected, which gave them some relief from the lice.

The new camp was similar to Janahof, but here the bare dirt was divided into compartments by wood fences. As he surveyed his new home, Tibor's eyes kept being drawn back to the fences, their depressing height representing long-term imprisonment. When he was fleeing, he thought he would soon be heading home. He and his friends joyously planned their journey along the Danube River on their way to Györ. Now they faced bare dirt and high walls, their only foreseeable future, a stark reality of war.

The 1,200 Hungarians were segregated, allocated one of the eighteen fenced-off compartments, but Tibor didn't stay long. Before even coming to Cham, he had suffered from an ear infection, difficulty with balance, and fever. He hadn't wanted to be separated from his group in case they left for home, but now he gladly went to the infirmary with its protection from cold spring downpours.

In the infirmary, Tibor was able to barter for food, a few white potatoes, milk, eggs, and crusty bread. He began to feel a little stronger and returned to the Hungarian compartment.

Each prisoner received cigarettes as part of his weekly rations. If Tibor and his friends pooled theirs, they could get fifteen German marks. For fifteen marks, they could buy a pail of potatoes to make tasty potato puree. If they had canned meat to add, the meal was heaven itself. Tibor was even able to get a tent for thirty-five cigarettes. He and his friends thoroughly appreciated watching the next day's downpour from inside their dry canvas shelter.

"You'll temporarily be assigned to labor camps," camp leadership finally announced. "After a month, you'll be sent home."

"We're going home soon," the boys rejoiced. This wasn't just a rumor, camp leadership had announced it! They could leave behind the illness and death, be reunited with their families at last.

But in early June, assignments came: the friends were separated, some sent with a group of POW's going to build barracks, others traveling to different POW camps. "God be with you," Tibor said, with a heavy heart, as he hugged and kissed his friends. They had stayed together through trying times for five long months.

"I'll see you soon at home," he promised them, trying to reassure himself.

Tibor headed to the American Labor Camp in Plattling, Germany, an hour southeast of Cham. Even though the weather was dreary and rainy, Tibor enjoyed finally seeing the world beyond a prison fence. Through the rain, he watched the grass, the trees, the streams, the houses, took deep breaths of sweet smelling air. Life seemed hopeful again.

But the Plattling Camp was worse: much smaller than Janahof or Cham, surrounded by electrified, barbed wire fence and guard towers. A loud, unharmonious buzz emanated from the mass of prisoners as he jumped off the truck, and a jeering welcome came from a group of German SS POWs.

Tibor saw that the camp was divided into partitions: one for the Ukrainians, one for the Hungarians, and one for the Germans. The Ukrainian camp had American tents, the German camp had German tents. Because the Hungarians had arrived last, when there were no more tents, most slept on the ground. Tibor was glad that he had brought his own tent, good protection from the rain and wind.

Assigned labor started the next day. It varied between digging, carrying lumber, and construction. Mostly the POWs built the barracks they would ultimately live in, their hammers keeping a steady melodious rhythm. As at the other camps, Tibor received medical exemption and was assigned cleaning duty inside the camp.

At the end of each shift, the guards almost always allowed prisoners to take a few 2 x 4 boards into camp. Hammering sounds soon added to the din as POWs built cleverly constructed shacks. Tibor and his tent mates used boards to make their tent more like a home: a plank on the dirt for a bench (with a hole for their feet so they could sit like in a chair), a little table, and boards as platforms so they didn't have to sleep directly on the cold damp earth.

"As long as we were building our tent, and even afterwards," Tibor wrote in his diary, "we found joy in it and forgot the horrible circumstances. Slowly the problem due to the shortage of tents abated, and we got used to our situation. We accepted the wire fence and the machine guns in the towers, but some incidents made us bitter. For instance, when a Hungarian passed our camp and shouted one or two words to us, the guards shot toward him, warning him to move on quickly."

Tibor still struggled with how the Hungarians, and especially the youth, were viewed by the Americans. "Were we so guilty in the war?" he wrote. "We're considered the same as SS soldiers. Such misery have we fallen into! Earnest people are jumping after discarded cigarette butts and would even fight if there was an opportunity for better work." He understood why initially the youth were mixed in with the German soldiers. After all, they were wearing old gray German uniforms and there were loaded rifles in the wagon next to them.

But once the Americans understood their situation, he thought they would send them home. He couldn't comprehend how their crimes matched the German SS.

* * *

The rich emerald of spring slowly faded to the more mellow colors of midsummer. One month of captivity passed with no further mention of going home, and time dragged. Hours moved slower than honey in January. After each workday, Tibor enjoyed chatting with fellow prisoners and gave architecture lessons to an interested POW, but there were still countless hours to pass. Like many others, Tibor began crafting objects out of raw material scrounged in camp: a ring out of copper, a cigarette holder from colored sections of discarded toothbrush handles surrounding an aluminum tube.

The project that meant the most, Tibor worked on for weeks. Using his pocket knife, he carefully whittled out of wood a likeness of Jesus nailed to the cross. He lovingly carved Jesus's face, meticulously capturing the intricate details of muscles, loin cloth, and crown of thorns. His faith in God gave him strength, and he was glad to have a likeness of Jesus by his bedside.

Cigarette holder Tibor crafted in POW camp from discarded materials, 1945.

When they first arrived at Plattling, Tibor and the other prisoners received warm soup and bread three times a day. Once or twice they even got some warm oatmeal, rice, or noodles. Slowly, Tibor's digestive system began recovering. But after a month, the food supply deteriorated. The prisoners no longer had morning soup. Instead they got a pat of butter. Supper soup was then omitted, sometimes for weeks. The gnawing hunger began again.

Potatoes in a nearby field were ready for harvest, their branched leaves beginning to yellow, and Tibor and his tent mates planned an escape to get some. A few friends served as lookouts, while others prepared an exit route through the electrified barbed wire fence. But at the same time, the guards noticed Ukrainian POWs outside the fence stealing potatoes, and shot into the ground near the escapees forcing them to return. "Guards have received orders to shoot all escapees," camp leadership announced the next day.

But Tibor's hunger was stronger than his fear. That very night, when the guard adjacent to their secret exit walked away, Tibor and a friend escaped carrying an empty scratchy burlap sack. The two dug up the fertile earth around the plants, hurriedly filled the sack with the young tubers, and snuck back into camp. Their timing was lucky. A few minutes after their return, the guard was back in his tower, vigilantly scanning the fence and yellowing fields.

Tibor knew the escapade was dangerous. But he felt if the Americans caught him, they wouldn't kill him, only put him in an isolation cell a few days without food or water. He didn't think they were as disciplined soldiers as the Germans, and wouldn't follow through.

Even though they were prisoners, the POWs still had occasional visitors. A visitor of a friend offered to deliver a letter for Tibor to his maternal cousin and roof-top playmate, Charlie Kováts-Szabó, informing him where Tibor was being held. During the war, Charlie was in Germany for medical school and was still on campus a few towns away.

"God delivered you!" Tibor exuberantly hugged and kissed Charlie when he came to visit.

"I was so relieved to hear from you!" Warmth radiated from his cousin's eyes.

It was wonderful to see family again. After they caught up on each other's lives, Tibor asked, "Do you have any news from home?"

"Nothing," Charlie said. "You?" Charlie looked around the group of Tibor's friends. But no one had news.

Charlie did everything he could to get the young men out of the camp, but to no avail. While he wasn't able to sate their desire for freedom, he brought a bag of crusty bread. The yeasty, familiar flavor brought back normal life, the world outside the fence. "If there's any way," Tibor and his friends promised Charlie as he was leaving, "we'll find you when we get out, then travel home together." The cousins exchanged fierce hugs and teary good-byes wondering where and when they would meet again.

The one month promised stay in the Plattling Labor Camp was moving into its fourth month. Gold and browns began replacing the green of summer. Tibor reluctantly accepted he wasn't going home soon. Despite this, it always seemed there was a new rumor that gave him hope, then another that quashed it. A new group of U.S. soldiers arrived who registered the prisoners yet again for discharge papers, but nothing came of it.

Tibor often wondered how his family was surviving. Where were they? How sad they must be, not knowing what had happened to him. The news filtering in from Hungary was only bad, often about severe shortage of food. "What're the victors going to do with Hungary?" he and his friends debated as they lounged in their tent. "Everybody blames the fallen powers, but are the new ones going to be any better?" They heard good and bad things about the Russians. They dearly wanted to go home, but also feared returning to their country under Russian occupation.

"Will it be communist? Or perhaps a new kind of government?" Tibor asked the others.

"Forced new ideas often have a bloody beginning," said one of the youth.

Could Hungary end up with a better social order? Could anything good come out of communism? They talked into the night, hungering for more information.

The new wood barracks were finally complete. Construction was solid, keeping out rain and the cold wind that ushered in fall. There were even beds and tables with chairs.

Tibor was pleasantly surprised by the quality of life in the new barracks. They were in closer proximity to each other so there was always someone to spend time with. In addition to interesting discussions, they amused themselves with a bowling alley, ping-pong tables, table bowling, soccer, and card playing.

On Sundays, an ethnic German Hungarian priest from the nearby town arrived to give Mass. Hearing the Catholic priest recite the familiar scriptures in Latin and sprinkle the air with the sweet smell of incense felt like home to Tibor. Later, the Hungarians even got a small organ to accompany their voices as they rose in praise to God. The organ was used for Hungarian folksongs and popular music more often than hymns, but that too brought a taste of home.

With better food and all the activities, Tibor thought it was almost like the vacations he had had as a child. None-the-less, he longed to be released.

* * *

One morning, the camp leadership announced that all prisoners would depart for Regensburg, where they would be freed. The news was unexpected and should have been welcome. But instead of rejoicing, a large pit lodged in Tibor's stomach, something was wrong. His friends felt it too.

It was mid-September. They left the Plattling Labor Camp in a truck headed northwest, and when they arrived in Regensburg, Germany, the oft-repeated promise of freedom evaporated.

Tibor wrote in his diary, "Our premonition was not wrong. They have taken us to a well-fortified camp with windy barracks and no beds. The bad barracks, the insufficient food, and the way they treat us make us despondent."

The youth were used to surprises, but this was a blow. Many became depressed. The camp was definitely a former SS camp, with wire bulwarks and reflectors between the double fences. There was no contact with the outside world. No letters. No parcels. No visitors.

"The days are more boring," Tibor wrote. "Winter is approaching and we're cold."

For the past nine months, Tibor had been grateful for the skills he learned as a Boy Scout in Győr. Leadership, discipline, survival, and first aid helped him stay alive during his long captivity. He often thought of his favorite teacher and Scout master, Father Gácsér, but it was quite a surprise when the Father showed up in Regensburg to hold Mass.

"Father Gácsér! Father Gácsér!" The boys joyously hugged and kissed the stocky man in his flowing black robes and stiff white collar. He was about twenty-five years older than them, with wavy brown hair.

"How did you find us? Any news of our families? How are things in Györ? How's Hungary faring?" Father Gácsér was inundated with questions.

They talked for hours. He explained that he had spent the last nine months looking for them. While he didn't have a lot of current news about their families, he was able to give the youth a much better understanding of the political situation in Hungary: the current devastation, the hunger, and the increasing Russian control. Father Gácsér left with a promise to visit again and to work on their release.

In the barrack that night Tibor lay wrapped in his blanket, not even aware the cold autumn wind whistled around him. His mind was racing, digesting all he had learned about Hungary. He'd been planning to return to his homeland upon his release, but now he wasn't so sure. Based on what Father Gácsér had shared, it was most likely that his family was outside of Hungary to escape Soviet control and his father's imprisonment for derailing communist plots.

Sleep remained elusive. A kaleidoscope of thoughts about home and family scurried through his brain, including memories of Scouting. Scouting in Hungary, had a strong nationalistic element with history a major underpinning. Active in Scouts from sixth grade until the end of gymnasium, Tibor had loved that focus, as well as the camping, hiking, and earning merit badges on fascinating topics. But as the night deepened, thoughts of Scouting were pushed out by other memories, then yet others, until finally sleep took over.

The next time Father Gácsér visited, he had astonishing news. "I've secured your release!" he told the twelve former Benedictine students, his eyes alight.

"We're really going to be freed?!"

"Yes!"

G 0450442

51647

CONTROL FORM D.2.
Kontrollblatt D.2.

CERTIFICATE OF DISCHARGE
Entlassungschein

LEVENTE

> ALL ENTRIES WILL BE MADE IN BLOCK LATIN CAPITALS AND WILL BE MADE IN INK OR TYPE-SCRIPT.

I
PERSONAL PARTICULARS
Personalbeschreibung

> Dieses Blatt **muss** in folgender weise ausgefüllt werden :
> 1. In lateinischer Druckschrift und in grossen Buchstaben.
> 2. Mit Tinte oder mit Schreibmaschine.

SURNAME OF HOLDER ZOLTAI
Familienname des Inhabers

DATE OF BIRTH 17.10.25
Geburtsdatum (DAY/ MONTH/ YEAR
—Tag/ Monat/ Jahr)

CHRISTIAN NAMES TIBOR
Vornamen des Inhabers

PLACE OF BIRTH GYOER
Geburtsort

CIVIL OCCUPATION STUDENT
Beruf oder Beschäftigung

FAMILY STATUS—SINGLE † Ledig
Familienstand

HOME ADDRESS Strasse MICHELSDORF
Heimatanschrift
Ort CHAM
Kreis
Regierungsbezirk/Land/.
N'BAYERN

NUMBER OF CHILDREN WHO ARE MINORS
Zahl der minderjährigen Kinder NONE

I HEREBY CERTIFY THAT TO THE BEST OF MY KNOWLEDGE AND BELIEF THE PARTICULARS GIVEN ABOVE ARE TRUE.
I ALSO CERTIFY THAT I HAVE READ AND UNDERSTOOD THE " INSTRUCTIONS TO PERSONNEL ON DISCHARGE " (CONTROL FORM D.1).

Ich erkläre hiermit, nach bestem Wissen und Gewissen, dass die obigen Angaben wahr sind.
Ich bestätige ausserdem dass ich die ,, Anweisung für Soldaten und Angehörige Militär-ähnlicher Organisationen " u.s.w. (Kontrollblatt D.1) gelesen und verstanden habe.

SIGNATURE OF HOLDER
Unterschrift des Inhabers

TIBOR ZOLTAI

II
MEDICAL CERTIFICATE
Ärztlicher Befund

DISTINGUISHING MARKS SCAR BEHIND LT EAR RT KNEE AND FOOT
Besondere Kennzeichen

DISABILITY, WITH DESCRIPTION JOINT RHEUMATISM
Dienstunfähigkeit, mit Beschreibung

MEDICAL CATEGORY TEMPORARY LIMITED DUTY
Tauglichkeitsgrad

I CERTIFY THAT TO THE BEST OF MY KNOWLEDGE AND BELIEF THE PARTICULARS RELATING TO THE HOLDER ARE TRUE AND THAT HE IS NOT VERMINOUS OR SUFFERING FROM ANY INFECTIOUS OR CONTAGIOUS DISEASE.

Ich erkläre hiermit, nach bestem Wissen und Gewissen, dass die obigen Angaben wahr sind, dass der Inhaber ungezieferfrei ist und dass er keinerlei ansteckende oder übertragbar Krankheit hat.

SIGNATURE OF MEDICAL OFFICER
Unterschrift des Sanitätsoffiziers

NAME AND RANK OF MEDICAL OFFICER IN BLOCK LATIN CAPITALS
Zuname/ Vorname/ Dienstgrad des Sanitätsoffiziers
(In lateinischer Druckschrift und in grossen Buchstaben)

CAPTAIN MC

P.T.O.
Bitte wenden

† DELETE THAT WHICH IS INAPPLICABLE
Nichtzutreffendes durchstreichen

Wt. 11216/67326 2,001M BPL 51-6097

Tibor's POW Discharge Papers, Oct. 1945 (two pages).

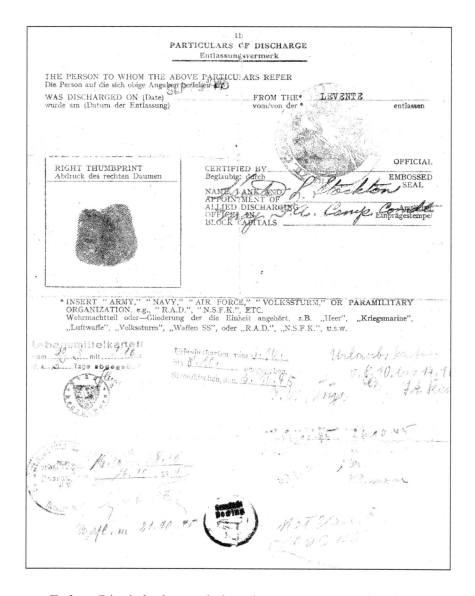

Father Gácsér had appealed to the camp commander for their release: "There are twelve youth in your camp from my Benedictine High School," the Father had explained to the commander. "I was their teacher and Boy Scout leader for years."

At the words Boy Scout, the camp commander had set down his pen and met the Father's gaze. "Boy Scouts in Hungary?"

"Yes, it's popular. Our troop was very active."

"I was a Scout master back home." Memories had softened the commander's eyes. "Boy Scouts helps build character."

"These youth earned lots of merit badges and rank advancements, served as officers in the troop. They're good young men and were never in combat." Father Gácsér had held direct eye contact and added, "I'd like to arrange their release."

The bond of Scouting helped the officer in charge see beyond the old German uniforms to the youth underneath. The commander gave the twelve Benedictine boys their release papers, an authorization document to travel to Michelsdorf, and ration cards for two days.

At the Benedictine Catholic Church in Regensburg, a large Romanesque Church with massive stone walls, round arches, and decorative arcading, Tibor knelt in the solid wood pew and gave thanks to this miracle. The familiar smell of stone mingled with the lingering smells from throngs of people was welcoming and serene.

Father Gácsér went on his way. The twelve youth eagerly traveled on to Michelsdorf to find Tibor's Cousin Charlie. But Charlie had already returned to Hungary. Tibor's companions believed their own families remained in Hungary, so they also arranged to be shipped back, joining 800,000 to 1,000,000 Hungarians in Germany and Austria making their way home.

"God be with you." Tibor said his heartfelt good-byes to each of his friends, hoping they would soon be reunited with their families. He had chosen not to return and wondered how to begin looking for his parents among the millions of refugees. Combat, ethnic cleansing, genocide, and general fear had uprooted so many. Officially called Displaced Persons (DPs), roughly fifteen million roamed Western Europe when Tibor was pounding boards in Plattling. By the time Tibor obtained his freedom, several million remained. The large majority were persecuted Jews or, like the Wagners and Zoltais, from areas of Europe that were now Communist dominated.

The homeland they loved no longer existed. They were not welcome there.

His family could have gone to Austria, Italy, Germany, or any other country in Europe. Even if they were in Germany or Austria, they could be in the American, British, or French occupying zone. Where should he begin? Tibor remembered a visitor at one of the POW camps who thought the Zoltais might have gone to a refugee camp in Bavaria. He decided to start there.

He used some of the precious money he still had from home to buy some black market food for the journey. Train tickets were inexpensive, so he decided to ride the rail, to conserve his minimal strength and speed up his search.

He chugged along from town to town, stopping to check at each Red Cross station for information on Hungarian refugee locations. The International Red Cross and national Red Cross groups were the major tracing organizations, having registered millions of displaced persons. By June 1945, merely a month after the war ended, the Hungarian Red Cross had already registered 130,000 of the estimated 400,000 official Hungarian displaced persons.

Tibor knew his father's surname, Zoltai, improved his odds of finding his family. Tibor's father had been born a Mersich, a name from a Croat ancestor. In the early 1940s, when all military officers were required to have Hungarian family names, Nicholas Bácsi applied for a new surname. He was granted his second choice, Zoltai. Zoltai was the name of a fictional hero in a very famous Hungarian novel set during the Hungarian-Turkish war in the 1500s. Because Zoltai was less common than Mersich, Tibor was only looking for a needle in a haystack, rather than a needle in a field of haystacks.

At the eighth or ninth train stop, Tibor found his first clue. In a Red Cross office, as he read page after page after page of Hungarian refugees living in various DP camps, he came across, "Zoltay, Nicholas, Lieutenant" registered in a camp in Feffernitz, Austria. The spelling wasn't quite right and the rank was off, but it was close. He had his first lead!

With no mail or phone service, Tibor set out for the camp to see if it was truly his family. He would need to travel about 230 miles southeast, cross the German-Austria border within the American zone, and then the American-English zone border within Austria. Tibor had heard from fellow travelers that zone borders were as challenging to cross as the country frontiers. Thankfully, his discharge papers listed Michelsdorf, a common town name. But it would not be sufficient authorization to cross into another zone.

Tibor explored options: first he tried to cross the border river east of Munich. Then he tried to obtain official crossing documents. Next he made arrangements to accompany a legitimate official across the border. None of these plans worked.

Studying his maps, he decided to try Passau. Here, the tip of Germany extended slightly southeast of the Danube and Inn Rivers, long stretches of these rivers served as the actual border with the swift water a natural barrier to crossing and the limited bridges mercilessly guarded. In Passau, Tibor nonchalantly crossed the river bridge within Germany during daylight, alongside the purrs, whirs, and chatter of regular traffic. He then slipped off unobserved into the silence of a nearby forest to await the cover of night. Staying in the shadows, he surreptitiously crossed through the forest into Austria. No more than a ghost to the armed border guards.

Tucked safely in his rucksack, Tibor carried a letter to a colonel from his troops in Germany. For this delivery, the colonel rewarded him handsomely, a month of ration cards. For the first time in a long while, Tibor ate until he was full. As his journey continued, he could eat whenever his stomach rumbled. He savored this incredible luxury. The ration coupons also authorized him to buy one hundred cigarettes. These he purchased, but saved to surprise his parents.

A ration card,
Oct. 1945.

On the road, Tibor met many Hungarian refugees. Some were going his direction, others the opposite way. With each group, he would trade advice.

"Cross into Germany by Passau," Tibor said. "Your best chance is if you . . ."

"Take this train, getting off at that stop," a traveler advised Tibor pointing at a map. "Then you'll avoid the checkpoint at the next station."

In this way, Tibor traveled extensively by passenger railcar, without being discovered by the authorities. He even got sound advice on how to cross from the American into the British zone.

"Take the regular train to the last stop, then transfer to the local line, it'll take you a few more miles. From there hike across the pass into the British zone."

Tibor followed the advice, boarding the local train. It was old, worn, and in poor repair due to a shortage of parts. When the train approached an incline, he and the other passengers got off to walk. With a strained chugging from the steam engine and an unnatural clunking on the inclines, the train finally reached its destination.

From the end of the rail line Tibor hiked up through fir and spruce forests, across dormant meadows, and over craggy rocks. As he approached the top of the pass, lights from a shelter beckoned. There he joined other Hungarians, also looking for their families but crossing in the reverse direction. He spent a memorable night in this cozy, one-room cabin filled with the scent of burning pine logs. In front of a crackling fire, he swapped stories, laughed, and shared food. While the snow gently fell through the night, covering the meadows and trees with a pristine white blanket, Tibor stayed warm and dry. The next day, he waded through the fluffy white, down the other side of the mountain into the British zone of Austria. His skin became icy and numb with no jacket over his worn, thread-bare German uniform. However in his excitement to reunite with family, he barely registered the freezing cold.

He hiked to the nearest town and went by train to his destination of Feffernitz.

From the train station, he could see the camp. It was in a large fertile river valley nestled between steep forested mountains. Among a series of wood barracks, the camp office was clearly marked.

Feffernitz DP Camp, late 1940s. Source: Luke Kelly's private collection from when his grandfather was stationed at Feffernitz.

"Is there a Zoltai family here?" he said, excitement and worry causing his stomach to churn.

"Oh yes, Zoltay, Lieutenant, barrack nine."

His feet devoured the ground to barrack nine. Like all barracks in the refugee camp, there were temporary walls made with blankets or the like separating family cubicles. He knocked as best he could on a door frame.

"Hello?" When no one answered, he cautiously walked in.

"How come you walk in without knocking?" said a young woman he had never seen before.

It turned out he had the wrong Zoltai. With slow steps and sagging shoulders, Tibor made his way out the door and back to the office. A month wasted. Now he needed to start the search all over again. Where to begin? They could be in Italy, even Northern Germany.

"Even though our name's unusual," he said to the officer in the camp office, "it looks like there's an unrelated Zoltai family."

"That's too bad," the man in the office said, "but it happens daily."

"Is there a spot I can roll out my blanket?" Tibor said.

"Sure. The kitchen will open soon if you're hungry." Tibor gladly accepted. While he waited, he shared the story of his search with someone else who entered the office.

"Zoltai?" said the newcomer. "Zoltai. Yes, there's a Zoltai in Camp B. Go half a mile that way," he said pointing. "Ford the brook, then on the right you'll find the office."

Tibor almost ran to Camp B. His feet, wet from the brook, left dark prints as he entered the small wood shack serving as the office. He joined the line for new arrivals, planning to share his story and seek help. While he waited, he realized Nicholas Bácsi was the man sitting behind the desk. He had a second to lovingly devour his father's strong classic features before his thoughts were interrupted.

"Next," Nicholas Bácsi said, not looking up.

"Csókolom," Tibor said in a choked voice, giving the Hungarian greeting for elders.

Nicholas Bácsi's head rocketed up. They were both frozen in place—overcome with emotion. Then his father jumped higher than Tibor had ever seen.

"Take over!" he shouted to the young lieutenant. He grabbed Tibor's rucksack, barreled through the office door, and started running with Tibor up the hill toward their family's quarters.

"Lili! Lili! Come!" he yelled the whole way up the alpine hillside. Just the day before, Lili Néni had told him, "If Tibor finds us, he'll come to you in the office. Call me right way."

Lili Néni heard the yelling. She ran out the door of their one-room cabin, fearing something had happened to her husband. The family dog followed at warp speed. His tail wagging, he began wildly jumping all over Tibor, trying to lick off his face.

The old German military uniform and his scrawny frame were no disguise. Lili Néni knew her son had found them. Tears running down her face, she fiercely embraced him.

Tears, laughter, great joy, jubilation don't even begin to describe how incredible their reunion was. To know the other was truly alive. To be reunited, after ten months of wondering if it would ever happen. To be holding each other in person, not just in their dreams and prayers. To again inhale their loved one's distinctive smell. There was nothing in Tibor's past to compare to this moment. It was emotion so intense, it was overpowering.

As they later sat together around the rough-hewn wood table in their cabin, Tibor lifted the pouch from around his neck. He carefully removed the pearl broach. "Here," Tibor said, placing it in Lili Néni's hand, the metal still warm from resting against his body. "Thank you, but I didn't need to use it." Lili Néni hugged him hard, her eyes wet with joy.

When Tibor's brother Steve returned to the cabin that evening, there were more rounds of hugs, kisses, and stories. The Zoltais feasted on the stash of special food Nicholas Bácsi and Lili Néni were saving, including a small British canned ham, an extremely rare delicacy. Tibor passed around the treasured cigarettes and the celebration lasted long into the night.

Their prayers were answered. They were together once more!

4

Olga Flees the Russians
(1945 - 1947)

Caricature of Olga drawn by her brother Gene, 1946.

Eyes down, Olga trudged alongside the wagon train. The roads of Sopron were covered in glittering shattered glass, which rattled and crunched as she plodded next to the wagons. Even in the shadows of night, Olga could see the shells of the buildings lining the road, many missing walls and tile roofs, many with windows bare of glass.

Fire and smoke obscured the horizon and filled her nostrils as they passed through the decimated city.

On the city's outskirts, the wagon train joined throngs of people traveling the main paved highway to Austria. Olga climbed atop one of the wagons, sitting next to the driver on a hard wood bench. The wagon gently swayed to the clip-clop rhythm of the horse's hooves and the clickety-clank of wood and steel wheels.

It was peaceful, almost sleepy, until the roar of aircraft roused her. Above the road, Russian planes appeared, dropping flares. Each flare provided a burst of light, falling in a shape like a lit Christmas tree, and the night sky was suddenly bright as day. Then the low flying Russian planes swooped in, strafing anyone visible on the highway.

Olga and the others dropped down from the wagons, frantically running for ditches or other shelter. Screams pierced the air against the fast paced rat-a-tat-tat of the machine guns.

Slowly the hum of the airplanes receded, and the travelers began to search for their loved ones. Andy had gotten separated from the family in the chaos. As other families were reunited, Olga, Eugene Bácsi, and Maria Néni searched every ditch, looked among the injured, checked the milling people. They pictured Andy hurt or dead, but after an hour they found him.

Andy, young boy that he was, stood in a group of soldiers, eyes wide, mesmerized by their every move, oblivious to the activity and dangers around him.

Her mother ran to hug Andy, and Olga's tense muscles relaxed. They were all back together. No one was injured. She silently prayed her family would make it through the rest of their journey.

*   *   *

The caravan drove through the night, still rolling when the first rays of light crept over the hills. During the darkness they had crossed the Austrian border without fanfare. They were now out of Hungary, although the countryside had not changed from the low foothills of the Alps where pastures, forests, and farmland showed the earliest touches of spring.

In the lightening sky, houses and a church steeple became visible at the crest of a steep hill. The horses' muscles bulged as they strained to pull the overloaded wagon in front of Olga's up the incline. As it started to slip and gain backward speed, the rhythm of the rotating metal wheels accelerated. Rapid clanks pierced the still morning air.

The wagon began barreling toward Olga. In a panic, she stuck out her foot to stop it.

The wagons collided with a deafening crash, her leg crushed between them.

"Aaaah!" she began to scream at top volume. The pain was excruciating. Vomit rose in her throat, the feeling of stupidity compounding her pain.

With the effort of many hands, the wagons were pried apart enough to pull her out. Her leg quickly swelled to twice normal size and when she tried to stand, she almost passed out.

Baggage from the flat donkey cart was transferred to other vehicles, so Olga would have a place to lie down. The caravan proceeded to the open meadow on the far side of the village to rest.

"Is anyone a doctor?" Maria Néni said once they settled in the field. "No," was the reply.

"Is there one close by?" Eugene Bácsi said. No one answered.

Maria Néni and Eugene Bácsi applied a wet compress to Olga's forehead, helplessly watching the pain on their daughter's face. "Where can we find a doctor?" Maria Néni said. "I think it's broken—"

"THE RUSSIANS ARE COMING! THE RUSSIANS ARE COMING! THEY'RE ON THE OTHER SIDE OF THE VILLAGE!" A man was yelling as he wildly flew toward the group.

In a burst of confusion, people leapt aboard wagons, whipping up the reticent horses, forcing wheels to turn. The caravan sped away as fast as the horses could be coerced to go. Soon, the clearing was empty.

Empty, except for the Wagners. Eight-year-old Andy, thirteen-year-old Olga with her broken leg, their parents, the very slow, plodding donkeys, and the donkey cart were left in the meadow. In their rucksacks, they had a snack and a change of clothes. The rest of their food, clothes, blankets, cookware, and other supplies were gone, packed on the horse-drawn wagons. The Russians were only minutes away.

There was no time to allow for terror, panic, hysteria. They had to act quickly or be in the hands of the advancing Russian soldiers, soldiers known to brutalize and rape fleeing Hungarians.

Eugene Bácsi saw a small dirt path leading away from the clearing and climbing steeply through the forest. They quickly gathered themselves and drove the donkeys toward the bumpy, rutted dirt path up into the foothills. Olga lay on the cart, the wood and steel wheels transmitting every rut into a harsh jarring of her leg, making it feel on fire. She bit her lips to try to keep the pain inside. Andy walked alongside the cart. Maria Néni leaned her full weight into pulling the slow-moving donkeys. Eugene Bácsi pushed the cart from behind. They made it out of the clearing just in time.

The first day they traveled all day and all night. Straight up the dirt path they went, through mixed forests of evergreens and deciduous trees bare of leaves. Even without resting during the night, though, the Wagners fell behind Russian lines.

Russian troops advanced speedily on the highway, their big roaring tanks and automobiles eating up the miles. But because the Russians didn't stray from the main road, the Wagners avoided capture.

Not long into the first day, their food was gone. They kept pushing forward for three more days. There were no switchbacks or crossroads. The pine-scented path just kept climbing toward the heavens, ascending at close to a 40-degree angle.

The family wasted no energy talking. The only sound was the occasional bird, wind in the trees, and metal wagon wheels striking rocks. With nothing to eat, the Wagners ran on sheer determination. They lacked even a dish to water the donkeys. Eugene Bácsi improvised, using his hat to get water from the icy mountain stream.

When they stopped the second night, Andy and Olga cuddled up on the cart to sleep. Eugene Bácsi and Maria Néni slept sitting upright on the hard bench in the front of the cart. With no bedding or blankets, the cold mountain air penetrated to the bone, but sleeping on the cart was warmer than sleeping on the ground where the freeze of winter still lingered. While deeply chilled, Olga still preferred the night to the harsh, jarring pain that accompanied daylight and movement upward on the rutted path.

By the third day, their worn bodies trudged along in an oblivious fog. They focused only on their next steps, consumed with placing one foot in front of the other over and over again. As they approached the summit, the path widened into a clearing. There before them was an enormous steel gun.

They had neither heard nor seen any signs of humans before stumbling onto this massive weapon. Fear and shock froze the

Wagners in place. Within seconds several soldiers emerged from their camouflaged positions dressed in full battle gear.

"What're you doing here?" demanded a voice in German.

"Fleeing the Russians," Eugene Bácsi said, talking slowly but picking up speed. He spoke German fluently. "We were in a caravan, but when my daughter's leg was crushed we got left behind without supplies. Since the Russians are on the highway, we took the hills. We haven't eaten in three days."

Slowly the soldiers approached, lowering their weapons. They saw Olga injured on the cart, the exhausted animals, the starving family. One came over to Olga, gently feeling and moving her leg and ankle. "The swelling's starting to go down, your foot will be OK," he said. "When it stops hurting, start to put weight on it."

The soldiers offered them a half loaf of black rye bread. It was the color, shape and weight of a black brick, so dense and hard, Olga could not bite or cut it. Eugene Bácsi whittled off a piece with his pocket knife and gave it to her. She sucked on the piece until it was soft enough to chew.

That bread was the most treasured food Olga ever ate. Having the dense, earthy taste in her mouth, after three days of no food, was like heaven. She knew nothing in her memory, or in her future, would ever surpass the taste of that bread in the mountain clearing.

After resting, the Wagners began their descent through the forested hillside. The trip down was faster since the donkeys struggled less. About halfway down the mountain they saw a town and a paved thoroughfare. The early-morning light illuminated a throng of people and wagons traveling on the road.

As the family got nearer, they could hear the clumping of hoofs and shuffling of feet, but Olga was struck by the absence of chatter. People's faces were drawn, their voices silent.

The Russians had not arrived ahead of them. The troops had gotten caught up in fighting in lower Austria, and these villagers were fleeing the advancing Russian front.

Against this exodus, one wagon was moving toward them, huge, pulled by two dark muscular horses. Eugene Bácsi deliberately stepped in its way, forcing the driver to reign in his team.

"Where are you going?" Eugene Bácsi said.

"I'm headed home—done with coal deliveries," the driver replied. He pointed toward his village, behind them.

"The Russians have taken your village," said Eugene Bácsi. "You can't go back!"

The driver's eyes darted back and forth. Everyone was indeed traveling away from his village.

"My daughter's hurt," Eugene Bácsi said. "I'll pay you to take us to the next town."

The driver slowly nodded.

The two huge powerful work horses, harnessed to the sturdy wood wagon with rubber tires, were soon drawing the Wagner's small donkey cart. And atop the coal wagon platform, riding in comfort, was the burly driver covered in coal dust, the four depleted Wagners, and the two weary donkeys.

With donkeys, the pace was slower than walking. The muscle-bound horses went faster than anyone else on the road, galloping for a whole day with the donkeys on top, the Wagners were able to gain many miles. Their good fortune lasted until the next town where a policeman stopped them.

"When people are escaping on foot, without even a wagon, you have donkeys on a platform wagon?" he shouted. "This isn't fair!"

The driver tried to explain what the Wagners had been through. The policeman would have none of it. He took out his gun.

"Get those animals off the wagon. You'll only take people—not these ones."

The Wagners got down, uncomplaining. The interlude on the wagon had been a miracle. Now they were almost a day-and-a-half ahead of the Russians. With the help of the burly driver covered in coal dust, the Wagners and their plodding donkeys were able to cross the Steyr River ahead of the Russians, safely moving into what would become American-occupied territory.

For several weeks, they continued to walk alongside the donkeys.

"Have you seen the wagon train from Sopron?" Eugene Bácsi asked travelers and locals they met along the road.

"Oh yes, it passed through here," they frequently heard, but the wagon train remained elusive.

Olga's leg slowly healed. Soon she was able to hop along with a stick. Then walk with a limp. Just as the soldier said, it was going to be OK. But even though she was in much less pain, the break healed crookedly. One leg was now a half-inch shorter than the other. After many months, she did learn to walk without a limp, but her injured leg would always remain shorter.

The family had no food, no ration cards, not enough money to buy food on the black market. When there was nothing for Maria Néni to cook for the next day, Olga and Andy would sneak into a farmer's field. They would look for moonlight reflecting off white potato flowers, and dig up any tubers beginning to bulge. Raised not to steal, it soothed Olga's guilt that even the Pope recognized the dire hunger of many in Europe, or so her father heard from fellow travelers.

"The Pope decreed it's not a sin to steal to keep from starving," Eugene Bácsi told the family. In truth, Olga realized she would have done it anyway. Staying alive came first. If she lived, then she could worry about her soul.

The family stayed in many barns on their six-week journey through hilly farmland, meadows, and forests dusted with occasional villages. Olga felt the cattle barns were the best, much warmer than horse barns. But any barn with livestock was warmer than an empty one. And any shelter was preferable to passing a cold spring night cuddled together shivering on the donkey cart.

Picture postcard of hospital town where Olga's family spent the summer, 1945.

The large hospital town was nestled amongst rolling farmland, church steeples dominating the skyline. The Wagners had heard the town would be taken over, not bombed, so they arranged with a local estate to stay in one of their outbuildings. The estate's green fields of wheat, corn, and grass were gaining height with the warmth of the early-May sun. The family slept soundly in the fresh smelling hay of the estate barn, and awaited the Americans.

What will the Americans be like? Olga wondered, sheltered in her hay nest. She had seen firsthand their destructive bombs, and the memory made her shiver. But other refugees told stories about the Americans helping to bring peace, which was encouraging. There were no stories about rape and brutal punishment like those preceding the Russians.

Walking along the paved highway near town, Olga saw ditches full of gray German uniforms. "No man wants to be found dressed as a soldier," her father said. They'd only been in town one day, but she'd already seen men frantically trying to obtain civilian clothes before the Americans arrived.

They heard the rumble of vehicles in the distance. "The Americans are coming!" someone shouted. "Everyone off the highway. Line up by the ditches."

The Wagners quickly did as instructed.

Soon Olga saw her first Jeep, a sturdy green metal automobile with no doors or roof, but a machine gun mounted on the back. American soldiers sat in the jeep, in camouflage uniforms and fighting helmets, looking ready for combat. One man was black, the other white. Olga remembered the only black-skinned men she'd ever seen, several years ago, when black missionaries visited her school.

The soldiers jumped down, demonstrated they wanted arms raised, and the civilians complied. Olga assumed they would check for weapons, and was shocked that the Americans didn't even look for weapons but took their watches! As more American troops arrived, they told all adult males to go to the village square. The men were kept there in case they'd resist American occupation. After a day, the men were allowed to return to their families.

A few days later, Olga and her father were leaving the hospital after visiting a friend. An American soldier stood on the sidewalk, inhaling the last puff of his cigarette. He casually dropped the smoldering butt on the sidewalk. An elderly man eagerly reached for it, hoping to eek out another smoke, but the American thoroughly scrunched the butt with his boot. The soldier looked directly at the old man as he did this, and Olga wondered if Americans were used to so much that they had no compassion for those who had nothing.

Olga's official refugee papers, 1945.

After six weeks of constantly being on the move, Olga and Andy cherished life in the barn. It was sturdy, its gray, weathered wood keeping out the wind and rain. In two-thirds of the huge building, hay still reached the ceiling. But in the third where they lived, it was down seven feet. For Olga, the hay was a safe, sweet smelling haven. Andy saw the barn as a giant playground. He particularly loved to climb the wooden beams in the loft and jump down into the cushioning hay.

Since the Wagners were planning to stay a while, they no longer felt they could steal food. Their neighbors would never let them remain if they behaved so poorly. The dilemma of what to eat was again upon them.

"If they can eat it so can we," Maria Néni said, as she watched the donkeys rip and munch the readily available green grass. She proceeded to make grass soup.

One of the estate's servants allowed Maria Néni to use her wood-burning stove. In a borrowed pot, she boiled water. To the boiling water, she added fresh green smelling grass, and a little salt. Then she simmered the mixture, softening the stiff grass and turning the water light yellow-green. An earthy, cooked greens smell rose from the kettle.

The soup had a terrible, bitter taste, and provided no nourishment, but a kind local farmer seeing their predicament gave them some fresh, creamy milk instead, and Olga savored the delicious gift.

Eugene Bácsi registered the family at the town's government offices. Within a few days, they began to receive government-issued ration cards. Each ration card let them buy a little bread, a little jam, a little lard, and some cigarettes at very low cost.

Without ration cards, food was only available on the black market at exorbitant prices or bartered for other goods. What made the biggest difference in keeping some food in their bellies was Eugene Bácsi's success at bartering and at fishing. He first bartered their extra set of clothes, then the low-cost cigarettes. Each day Eugene Bácsi would recount his day's trades. Olga kept a family log.

"Today I bartered our cigarettes for a loaf of bread." Eugene Bácsi reported, head held high, to his family gathered in the barn.

"Then I traded the bread for almost double the cigarettes. These cigarettes I exchanged for two loaves of bread."

Soon Eugene Bácsi traded for a bicycle to expand his trading radius. He also began to fish. Austria required a license to fish, but the government would issue no licenses to refugees. The only option was to fish illegally. Olga hiked into the hills with her father, and stood guard on the path nearby, attentively listening for human sounds over the babbling of the stream and the rustling leaves. Her father, a city boy, had never fished in his life, but he soon became adept at catching delicious river trout in the cold mountain streams. The succulent, tender fish was particularly valuable in bartering since any form of protein was very scarce.

On one bartering trip a good distance from the barn, Eugene Bácsi learned of a vacant cabin. It was in a camp made up of a hundred prefabricated units originally built for Austrians bombed out of their homes. The camp's current occupants were mainly Hungarian car-factory workers.

When the grass near their barn was knee-high, the family left for their new home. The cabin was made of unfinished planks of sanded wood preassembled into sections. The sections fit together to form outside walls, a room divider, and furniture. It was simple, sturdy, and snug.

An outside door led into the main room. It had a table with two benches, an eye-level bunk bed with a storage closet below, a shelf, and a stove. The second room was smaller, with an upper and lower bunk bed and space for storage.

Each room had a pane glass window with functional shutters. There was even an outhouse.

The family moved in, happy to have a home at last.

The Wagner family in their prefabricated cabin. *L. to r.* Andy, Eugene Bácsi, Olga, and Maria Néni, late 1940s.

"Olga," Maria Néni said shortly after they moved into their new home, "I was able to buy some horse meat, enough to share with our old neighbors. Please deliver it."

Meat of any kind was a rare treat. Olga maneuvered her bicycle out of the smaller cabin room where it was stored.

She was proud of her bicycle, a recent acquisition from Eugene Bácsi's bartering. Soon she was pedaling the ten miles to their friend's home near their old quarters in the sturdy weathered barn. The day was beautiful and Olga was pleased to deliver the rare treat.

Hours passed, and Maria Néni began to worry. It was not that far to the neighbors. Suddenly, she saw her daughter, accompanied by an old neighbor. Olga's clothes were dirty. Her arms were scraped and bandaged. She had a stunned look.

"Olga, what happened?" Maria Néni let go of the two pails of water she was carrying from the communal pump. The pails overturned with a thud, the water splashed out, cascading in every direction. She started running toward Olga. The sight of Maria Néni frantically running toward her, the feel of her mother's crushing embrace, triggered Olga's long-term memory.

Strangers had found her on the side of the road.

"Are you OK?" they had asked. She only stared at them.

"Where do you live?" No answer.

"What's your name? What are your parents' names?" With each question, her eyes got larger and she became paler. She didn't know.

They had taken her to the local hospital where someone remembered seeing her at the barn. Once at the sturdy weathered barn, a neighbor knew her family had moved to the prefabricated camp and took her there.

The family speculated she was hit by a car, but Olga never knew. She had no memory of the accident. After many months, she was once again able to climb on a bicycle.

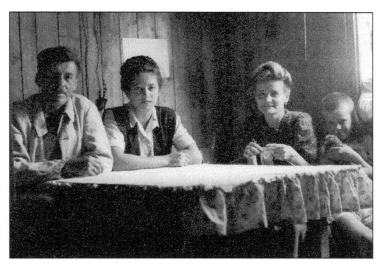

Wagner family in their cabin. *L. to r.* Eugene Bácsi, Olga, Maria Néni, and Andy, 1948.

* * *

Olga sat on the cabin bench helping Maria Néni clean potatoes for their dinner of paprika-seasoned sautéed potatoes. The fire in the stove was already crackling, filling the room with the familiar husky smell of burning wood. While she peeled, Olga thought about how much more normal and stable their life was now. For the last six weeks they cooked in their own kitchen, ate at a table, and slept in beds. Recently, when the Austrian government put the cabins up for sale, Eugene Bácsi was able to buy their unit with money from bartering.

Despite their better life, Olga always dreamed of going home. Eugene Bácsi had already sent back their borrowed donkeys and cart with soldiers headed that direction. Olga knew her dream to follow the donkey's path could not happen as long as Hungary was under Russian occupation. Her father had helped diffuse a few Communist sabotage plots in the plant he managed and the Russians dealt harshly with returnees. The family later learned that he would have been arrested, the Communist government had concocted a case against her father, saying that cigarettes Eugene Bácsi had given each employee as a goodbye gift were actually a bribe to lure them to join the army, an offense against the Hungarian people.

Talk on the street said the Americans would continue their advance, and the Russians would be pushed back to the eastern border of Hungary and other recently occupied countries. These rumors gave Olga hope they could return soon.

To be prepared, her family planned. They would move from their hospital town in the center of Austria, closer to the Hungarian border. They would hire a truck to take them and their cabin. Just like a snail carries its shell, the cabin's unique prefabricated design gave the family the flexibility to move with their home. The unit could be dismantled within a few hours, moved, and reassembled.

Olga hadn't made it home in spring. She hadn't seen the wild violets bloom like her family had originally planned. Yet perhaps she would still collect mushrooms in her beloved hills.

Olga was collecting mushrooms sooner than she dreamed, but not near Sopron.

In the small town of Gniebing, near the border with Hungary, an Austrian farmer let the Wagners set up their cabin. The green meadow that served as their yard was bordered by a railroad track, a dirt road, and a forest similar to the one by Sopron with majestic spruce, firs, oaks, and maples, excellent dark, damp habitat for mushrooms.

Olga and Andy spent hours in the forest, collecting. When younger, Olga didn't like mushrooms' wild, musty flavor. But with the scarcity of food, she had learned to appreciate having them for dinner. The family also dried them for winter and for bartering.

Andy loved playing on the abandoned portable anti-aircraft gun in the meadow forty yards from the cabin, his private merry-go-round. The camouflage colored metal vehicle had two rubber wheels on the front, tank tread on the back, and an anti-aircraft gun mounted on top. The gun had two handles: one made it elevate and lower, the other made it spin. Andy sat on the smooth steel barrel and made the gun whirl and whirl, until a mechanic dismantled it for parts.

Now that life was more settled, Olga and Andy began attending the local school. It had been almost a year since Olga attended school and even longer for Andy. Olga liked being back in the routine of school. Even with her classroom lessons in German, she found the

Folk Schule quite basic compared to the gymnasium she attended back home.

Outside of the farmer whose land they stayed on, most locals resented refugees and were not friendly to the family. They did not greet them. They even turned away.

"There go the damned refugees," the "Verflüchte Flüchtlinger", locals would often comment in a harsh accusing voice.

No one had enough to eat. The millions of refugees were consuming the residents' precious supplies. However, Olga wondered, was there no place in the world her family was welcome? They couldn't return to Hungary. The Austrians didn't want them.

Was there no country she could call home?

Eugene Bácsi's bartering skill kept them clothed, with food on the table. In addition to bartering with locals, he would pedal his bike many miles over the dirt roads and rolling hills to the closest Hungarian Refugee Camp where anything was open for trade. Eugene Bácsi traded the succulent fish from a nearby mountain stream, rolled cigarettes bought using ration cards, baked goods Maria Néni made with supplies from previous trades, pungent dried mushrooms, or anything else he could find. He traded tobacco for leather, gave the leather to a shoe maker, and allowed him to keep the extra in exchange for making them shoes. The Wagners slowly got food, clothing, and even toys.

"Why would you trade for a puppet?" Olga and Maria Néni asked when Eugene Bácsi came home with a wood-and-cloth clown. "We don't have young children."

"I didn't trade for it," Eugene Bácsi said, humor sparkling in his eyes. "I bought it—in a store. This is the only item I've seen in a store since we came. I bought it because I could!"

"Heaven help us," Maria Néni sighed.

Near Christmas, Eugene Bácsi was able to trade for ingredients to make szalon cukor, the traditional sweet fondant, decoratively wrapped, and hung on the Christmas tree. Sitting at the wood table in the cabin, Maria Néni, Andy, and Olga molded miniature versions of the candy to stretch the ingredients. Rather than using six-inch squares of white tissue paper, they made the candies small enough to be wrapped in white cigarette paper squares. They fringed the edges of the paper and covered the center in foil like in prior years. In the nearby forest, they found two foot-and-a-half tall evergreens they covered with the miniature szalon cukor.

Having one Christmas tree in their home, and being able to gift the other to their generous landlord, made the holiday very special.

In the fall, Eugene Bácsi had paid a smuggler to get a letter to his sister in southeast Hungary. Regular mail, like many services after the war, didn't function, and this letter was the first news the Wagners were able to get back home. They let their family know they were alright and were temporarily living in Gniebing, Austria.

Olga's older brother, Gene, heard the news from his paternal aunt. He immediately made arrangements to smuggle a letter back to the family. He wrote that at war end his school disbanded in Austria. He had made his way home to Sopron where the neighbors told him the family all perished in the bombing. Thinking he was an orphan, Gene traveled to the southeast side of Hungary where both his parents had siblings. There he stayed with Maria Néni's brother and his family. His aunt was a gymnasium teacher and tutored him. With her help, he successfully passed his high school graduation exam.

The letter arrived on a crisp autumn day: Gene was alive! The Wagners decided to take advantage of the well-developed smuggling system across the Austrian-Hungarian border. They would bring

Gene out of Hungary. They smuggled another letter to Gene. The letter instructed him to go a specific town on the western border. There he was to meet up with the smuggler. They paid the smuggler handsomely out of funds Eugene Bácsi earned bartering.

Then they waited. The leaves turned brilliant colors. The foliage lost its grip and crunched under foot. The family's footprints became visible in the snow. The snow began to pile up against their cabin.

Crossing the border was dangerous. Armed guards were instructed to shoot trespassers. "Dear God, please deliver Gene safely to us," they prayed daily.

In the middle of a dark, cold February night in 1946 there was a loud rap on the door. Eugene Bácsi carefully lit the wick of their kerosene lamp, opened the door, and shone the light on two shadowy figures outside. "Gene!" he shouted as his eyes honed in on his son: tall, lean, with wavy brunette hair.

The entire family scrambled out of their bunks. They descended on Gene, smothering him in kisses and hugs. Each member had to touch him, to hold him. Reassure themselves that Gene was truly with them.

"Thank God," Maria Néni said, bowing her head and forming the sign of the cross. "Our family's together again! We're blessed."

They celebrated the whole night through. Like farmers in a life-destroying drought who finally received a gentle rain, they were eternally grateful. They were back together after more than a year! Their prayers were answered.

Through ice and snow, and past the armed guards, Gene had smuggled in a steel water-can full of aromatic, moist tobacco. Selling it gave them funds to continue Gene's studies, and he enrolled in the Poly-Technical University of Graz and moved into the city.

With his natural talent to draw cartoons and craft witty captions, he soon got a job as a sports cartoonist for a local paper. Gene thrived in this new open, creative environment, so different from the regimented military school he had grown to hate.

Seeing her brother so happy, Olga began to dream of independence and adventure. "Will you look into a boarding school for me?" She asked him.

"You think Mother will let you live in Graz?" Gene's eyebrows rose so high they almost reached his brown locks.

"She knows how little I'm learning in Folk Schule." Olga's face was etched with determination. "She always wanted me to get a good education." Maria Néni had been insistent Olga attend a gymnasium in Hungary, not a school with lower academic standards. Attending gymnasium had been Maria Néni's childhood dream, but the family could only afford to send her brothers, she was apprenticed in a sewing shop with mind-numbing work.

"If she knew you're keeping an eye out for me it might help," Olga added.

"I found something Mother might agree to," Gene said a few weeks later.

"What?" Olga said, her eyes sparkling.

"The Urseline Convent Boarding School. It was converted to a military hospital during the war. The nuns were sent to the Netherlands and Belgium," he said. "But they're back now. The school's reopening!"

"What kind of school?"

"A finishing school," Gene said. Cooking, sewing, embroidery, raising children, and similar topics were covered, not very challenging material Olga thought. But still, it was an exciting prospect to go away to school. So with Gene's help, Olga persuaded her parents to let her go, a major victory. Maria Néni believed in a very strict, controlled upbringing, especially for girls. Fifteen-year-old girls were not usually allowed such independence.

Maria Néni took an orange-patterned crepe dress Olga had outgrown, transformed it into a slip and made a two-piece suit from an old gray German uniform they salvaged from a roadside ditch. With careful planning, cutting, and intricate stitching, Olga had the clothes for her new school.

Eugene Bácsi sewed together burlap potato sacks and stuffed the large bag he created with straw. It was the ugliest, scratchiest, oversized, and most embarrassing mattress Olga ever saw, but it was functional and allowed her to have the required items to attend the convent school.

She traveled with Gene in the back of an uncovered truck, her mattress and new clothes safely tucked behind other passengers who also paid for a ride to Graz. The strong, warm wind was refreshingly cool against her cheeks. It barely disturbed her long brown hair, tightly braided and coiled around her head like a crown. Olga felt like a runner on the starting block, every fiber of her being ready to move forward.

The Urseline convent was a two-story square light gray building constructed from thick brick and plaster walls and red roof tiles, similar to other buildings in Graz. It abutted the street, with a courtyard in the middle and a park in back full of trees and walking paths. A fountain in the center courtyard caught Olga's eye immediately as they unloaded her bags, the flowing water glistening in the brilliant sunshine. Windows surrounded the courtyard letting natural light brighten the adjacent hallways.

Her dorm room was on the second floor, facing the street and the life of the city. Most of the girls were a few years older and Austrian.

They arrived with real mattresses and clothes not made out of discarded uniforms, and Olga felt like a donkey among black stallions, the only refugee. Her clothes were limited, her mattress ugly, her German broken. But nothing could dampen her joy. The five Austrian girls assigned to her dorm-room were friendly and didn't focus on her differences. They soon became friends, chatting, laughing, and sharing confidences.

A feeling of freedom pervaded the school. The nuns rejoiced because their building had been returned to the church, no longer belonging to the Nazis. Olga also felt free. While the nuns were very strict, she was not living under her mother's constant scrutiny, was surrounded by teenage girls, and the curriculum was new.

By late fall, Eugene Bácsi, a fairly well-known textile expert, was able to find work in his field. He got a job in Stainz, not far from Graz, making a decent salary as a Master Weaver, responsible for keeping fifty weavers and their wooden looms operating efficiently, the thread shuttles rocketing back and forth to produce finely woven cloth.

The family packed up their cabin to move to Stainz. With permission, they reassembled it on the shore of a small lake, fed by a clear stream and surrounded by apple trees, an idyllic spot. Croaking frogs even provided nightly concerts when the weather warmed.

For the rest of the school year, Andy joined his siblings in Graz attending a Catholic boarding school. He and Olga traveled home to Stainz every few weeks by train, with Gene sometimes making the trip.

"Thank you, God," Olga prayed, "for all our blessings." Money was still scarce, but her family was blessed compared to many refugees. They had all lived through the war, were together, never went to bed with totally empty stomachs, and had the luxury and privacy of their own cabin in a nice setting, not crammed in with a dozen other refugee families in a barrack. Her father had work and she and her siblings were in school. She was indeed grateful.

Maria Néni and Eugene Bácsi with their chickens, 1948.

Olga graduated from finishing school in June and spent the summer holiday in Stainz with family. On a lazy, late-summer day, Olga peeked out of the cabin, eying the golden meadow and the apple trees laden with fruit. Her eyes scanned for Pityu, a rooster Eugene Bácsi had purchased alongside chickens to supplement the family's diet with protein-rich eggs. Pityu's multicolored feathers, with their beautiful iridescent glow, hid five pounds of explosive belligerence. He had free reign in their meadow and would peck at anyone wearing skirts, although he had soon learned to fear Maria Néni's kicks.

Not seeing Pityu, Olga dashed for the outhouse, her skirt lifted over her head to protect her face from the sharp beak. Alerted by her rapid foot steps, the rooster scrambled after her, fluffing his feathers, crowing, and flapping his wings, but Olga slammed the outhouse door before he arrived.

Pityu stationed himself as outhouse sentry, and Olga was finally forced to call for Andy's help. "Shoo! Get away!" Andy said, waving his hand to force the bird to move.

"I'll tell Pityu on you," Andy later teased, when Olga turned down his request for her apple.

In fall 1947, Olga returned to Graz as a convent boarder, but now she went across town by street car to her new school, a business vocational institution with a mixture of men and woman studying bookkeeping and secretarial skills. Gene also remained in Graz, continuing his studies at the university, but Andy chose to stay in Stainz to attend the local public Catholic school.

The family settled into a daily routine of work and school. But the future was anything but routine or predictable, with fear of a third world war pervasive. Tensions were building between the Allies and Russia. The term 'Cold War' was coined to refer to the growing animosity.

It had been two years since the Wagners moved closer to the Hungarian border, hoping the Americans would invade the Eastern Bloc countries and free their homeland. But President Truman's policy towards the Soviet Union was containment, preventing Communist electoral victories in Greece and Turkey, not truncating the Russians' existing occupation.

As long as Hungary remained under Russian control, returning was not an option. What should they do? This question occupied their minds. Would it be best to stay in Austria? Eugene Bácsi spoke German well and had a good job.

However, Austria was overcrowded, food was scarce, and war loomed. There were limited opportunities for Gene, Olga, and Andy's future and most Austrians resented the "damned refugees." Should they try to emigrate? With so many million refugees, perhaps it would be best to leave. But where could they go? There was no systematic immigration available for families. There was no country where they belonged.

5

Tibor in Displaced Person Limbo (1945 - 1948)

Feffernitz DP Camp, 1945.

Tibor joined his family, living in Camp B of the Feffernitz Displaced Person Camp nestled in the wide alpine valley by the small village of Weissenstein, less than a mile from the main camp. Each day when Tibor awoke, a beam of sunshine radiated from his heart to every cell in his body. To see his mother, father, and brother, knowing they were all safe, was pure joy. It had been almost a year.

He learned what happened to them while he was drafted into service. Lili Néni and Steve remained with the officers' families congregated to leave Hungary. As the Russians streamed into western Hungary, Nicholas Bácsi, his uncle Jenci Bácsi, and other military officers joined their families. Together they fled in a wagon train. Like Olga's family, they knew their wagons had to keep rolling west until they left Russian control. They joined thousands of refugees crowded into the British-run Displaced Person Camp.

Camps like Feffernitz had been created to meet the needs of millions flooding into Western Europe during the war. In Austria alone there were over a hundred camps, averaging 3,000 DPs each; food, water, shelter, and sanitation always pressing problems. From all the DPs Tibor had talked to on his journey, as well as what he had seen, the British zone was the best. British troops had vast expertise handling mass numbers of people with limited resources. The Americans had the best of intentions, but just weren't prepared. The French had the experience, but didn't care. The Russian zone was dramatically worse.

The camp air was now filled with hardwood smoke from the many campfires burning to stave off the chill November wind. The men Tibor passed were dressed in typical DP fashion: coarse pants and gray soldier's jackets. The women were more traditionally outfitted in skirts, knit stockings, and wool coats from home. While gaunt, bony features abounded, no one looked like walking death.

The camp had grown from an empty grass field in the alpine valley, quickly becoming rows and rows of cookie-cutter barracks housing the DPs in the main camp, with more barracks under construction for refugees staying in Camp B. Temporary shelters sprawled across the meadow and hillside of Camp B; tents made from a blanket or bed sheet and a stick, with piles of dry leaves or compressed snow for insulation from the cold ground, as well as shacks built out of logs harvested in the nearby forest or using materials from home.

Tibor walked the camp each day, shivering as icy gusts blew through his threadbare German uniform, his feet chilled from leaky boots, happy to return to the sturdy, wind-proof log cabin his father and brother had built. His family had one of the nicest spots, looking down into the valley. Sheltered among large pine, birch, and oak trees, the cabin had one room with a place to cook, a table, a bench, and make-shift beds. The smell of wood burning in the stove, mingled with the aroma of Hungarian cooking, welcomed him. After POW Camp, he felt like he was entering a luxurious, spacious mansion, a blessed man, with books to read and his mother's delicious cooking.

"Your new barracks are complete at the main Feffernitz Camp," camp officials announced in mid-December. "Prepare to move. Camp B's closing."

Feffernitz Camp, late 1940s. Source: Luke Kelly's private collection from when his grandfather was stationed at Feffernitz.

The Zoltais and the 1,000 other DPs at Camp B packed their belongings. Wood sleds made earlier for the youths' pleasure easily transported their household goods over the snow and frozen brook. But during the move there was a lot of grumbling.

"Our new quarters are tiny," one man said.

"I wish we didn't have to move," another said, looking back toward Weissenstein.

"With the snow cover it's hard to tell one barrack from the next," Tibor added, gazing at the rows of uniform barracks.

But the move was not optional. The camp was shut down.

The new barracks each followed the same design, roughly twenty-four-by-ninety-six-feet, they were subdivided into a communal cooking area and units for about twenty families, with blankets, sheets, canvas, or whatever families could scrounge for partitions. Thin walls barely dampened noise, so sounds traveled and echoed around the units. Conversations, arguments, foot steps, scraping chairs, and clanging pots all loudly reverberated. Smells also permeated. Families knew what their neighbors were cooking, if a child was ill, or if a fire was burning.

Tibor's family was assigned a thirteen-by-thirteen-feet corner unit. Tibor helped hang blankets to cordon off their unit, carefully arranged their table, bench, and beds so everything fit into the considerably smaller space. Lili Néni put up Hungarian lace curtains, spread a Hungarian cloth on the table, and covered the beds with traditional spreads to give a touch of home. In his youth Tibor had taken her loving touches for granted, but no longer.

"Everyone gets almost a pound of bread per person per week," Tibor wrote in his diary, "which is satisfactory, but there is hardly ever any meat." After starving in POW camp, Tibor's standards for "satisfactory" were very low. Rations were a small fraction of the 2,500 calories an average male adult burns daily. A few months later Jenci Bácsi wrote in his own diary, "They have decreased our food so we receive about 800 calories. That means besides the morning coffee and bread, we receive food only once daily." A medical survey of camp adults in early 1946 documented the seriousness of the undernourishment, finding an average weight loss per person of 31 pounds, or almost twenty percent, in just a three month period.

Tibor's family was fortunate, able to supplement their food. For three months before moving into the barracks, Steve and Nicholas Bácsi had collected mushrooms in the dark, damp undergrowth of the forested hills. Not just a few, but enough to start the winter with three large sacks of earthy dried fungi. Nicholas Bácsi also bartered items from home in the black market for a sack of dried beans. Unlike in POW camp, Tibor never went to bed with a totally hollow stomach. Through the black market the family also filled other basic needs. For Tibor, they obtained solid leather boots to keep his feet dry and used wool fabric which Lili Néni transformed into a warm coat and hat through the magical whir of her foot-powered sewing machine, brought from Györ.

The days passed without life threatening physical hardship with the extra food, bartered items, and heating fuel chopped from the neighboring forest. Tibor had ongoing health problems, digestion difficulties, and a long-lasting infection in his knee, but he tolerated these reasonably. The real challenge was staving off the despair common among DPs due to the aimlessness and uncertainty of camp life. Tibor longed to know what would happen to them. Where would they live? How would they earn a living? There was no control over their lives; they couldn't move forward, only pass time.

Every evening, Lili Néni used her needle and thread to weave together the unraveling edges of the holes in the family's socks, so each person had warm protective covering for their feet the next day. As the day progressed, their walking would wear through the mending and the original yarn to make the holes reappear and grow in size. Again and again she would darn, never getting ahead, having to work a little harder each day as more of the original yarn disintegrated. Their lives were like darning socks, Tibor thought, watching his mother at her endless task.

Tibor and his family's philosophy was to stay busy. Many of the DPs shared this idea. A school started within weeks of their barracks being finished. One barrack housed the high school, sub-divided into classrooms using blankets, with a separate classroom for each of the eight grades. Steve attended Form VII, the second to the last grade, picking up where he had left off in Hungary. Tibor audited math and physics classes in Form VIII to refresh his knowledge. The teaching style was the same as back home, with lots of memorizing and oral testing. However unlike back home, there was only one school. Not a separate school for college bound and laborers, not even separate schools for boys and girls. Despite the deafening noise of all the classes in one barrack, despite having no textbooks, Tibor cherished being in a classroom and learning again.

Lili Néni on errand to get milk from local farmer, 1946.

* * *

Neither Jenci Bácsi nor Nicholas Bácsi ever considered returning to Hungary. As a Counter Espionage officer, Nicholas Bácsi had sent numerous Communists to jail. If he returned, he would be thrown in jail or killed. As a major general, Jenci Bácsi's risk of death was even greater. The families feared both men might be forcefully turned over to the Hungarian authorities. Jenci Bácsi was especially vulnerable due to his high rank. Their dread was well founded. The Allies forcibly repatriated tens of thousands of Soviet citizens, as well as citizens of the Ukraine, Slovenia, Yugoslavia, and other countries under Soviet control, to ensure the Soviets honored agreements to promptly return Allied citizens liberated from Nazi camps, as well as to establish trust to enable successful joint government in Germany across the zones.

On May 30, 1946 their fear was realized. The British military police conducted their first raid in the Feffernitz Camp, looking for high-level Hungarian officers.

The day started out like any other: the clanking of dishes, the chatter of people, and the smell of coffee. When the British announced the raid, a deathly silence descended. It was as if the color in the green meadows and the vibrant wild flowers was abruptly sucked out, Tibor thought, shocked at the potentially deadly consequences to his father and uncle for having tried to defend and reunite Hungary. He knew British soldiers had the right to search their quarters, but his skin felt like it was being bombarded by piercing ice pellets.

Tibor's eyes carefully tracked the soldiers as they marched from barrack to barrack, taking some men into custody, the men forcibly separated from their families. When it was his family's turn, the soldiers rifled through their belongings, scrutinized Nicholas Bácsi's official papers. Finally, they moved on.

Then they were in Jenci Bácsi's quarters. Thankfully, he was not in the camp, but at his construction job, so the soldiers left.

By the end of the day even those detained were released, but the raid brought to the fore the real and menacing risk of Jenci Bácsi being turned over to the Russian authorities for his role in the war.

A few weeks later, the situation turned grave. Jenci Bácsi's name showed up on a publicized list of war criminals. No specific crime was cited, but he was accused of helping to extend the war. This discovery made Nicholas Bácsi's nerves sizzle.

That very night he swiftly walked the eleven miles through pounding rain to the village where Jenci Bácsi worked, banging on the door of the room Jenci Bácsi shared with coworkers.

"Who is it?" Jenci Bácsi called out, awoken from a deep sleep. It was 2:00 a.m.

"Zolti," Nicholas Bácsi said in a voice as strident as an air-raid siren. "Thank God, I found you! Let me in."

"What's up?" Jenci Bácsi opened the door, slowly, tempering the alarm in Nicholas Bácsi's voice. He knew his brother routinely worried over minor things.

"Yesterday the English came looking for Cornel Mesko and you." Water splattered off his clothes as if to emphasize the turbulent nature of his comments. "They found Mesko. They took him! You need to disappear."

Jenci Bácsi realized his brother's alarm was fully justified, and a war raged inside his heart for long minutes. Honor demanded he face the charges and defend himself. Duty to his family demanded he hide. Hiding won: his wife and young sons needed his help to survive.

His brother helped him gather his belongings and make a plan. Once Jenci Bácsi was safely away, Nicholas Bácsi returned to camp to help arrange fake papers.

*   *   *

For Tibor, helping to start a Boy Scout Troop served as a powerful counterbalance to the threat of his uncle being repatriated, ongoing health challenges, and the stress of aimlessness. He thought it was important to keep the youth in camp occupied and out of trouble. He wanted to give the boys the same energizing experience and moral compass he had received. The group first formed in late winter. Tibor served as a youth patrol leader, but then his leadership expanded to troop-wide activities.

Any boy over ten years old was welcome. Initially thirty were interested, then fairly quickly sixty joined. Most of the youth were novices, so Tibor started with hikes, scout games, and meetings focusing on the mental discipline and learning needed for the first rank advancement. The British officers encouraged it, familiar with Boy Scouts since it was founded in England about forty years earlier. The camp commandant even provided half a barrack for meetings and activities.

Tibor in Boy Scout leader uniform, 1946.

"We should have a summer camp," Tibor said to other leaders at a planning meeting. Daylight hours clung longer to their mountain valley now, and school teachers discussed a brief summer recess.

"Camping is the best part of scouts!" another leader agreed.

"The boys' nutrition is so poor, we'll need to make sure to get enough food," Tibor said. Conversation then dove into the details of planning.

"I've found a few possible camp sites," offered a leader a few days later.

"Let's go check them out. We'll stop at neighboring farms, see if they're willing to donate food."

Some farmers were receptive, others were unfriendly, but enough promised to donate food, mainly potatoes. Eventually they had over 400 pounds of potatoes and other items from farmers. Combined with camp rations, a donation from the Red Cross, and a contribution from a Hungarian Engineer, it was enough to take thirty of the older Scouts camping for two weeks.

The camp was held on the summit of a large hill circled by towering evergreens. Pine scent filled the air. The sounds of the wind whistling and the nearby creek gurgling were often masked by the chatting, singing, and laughing of the campers. The boys worked on survival skills, played Scout games, and sang Hungarian songs around a crackling campfire. One popular game was Capture the Flag.

One patrol planted the flag on the hill. Boys in the other patrol tried to steal the flag. If the number pinned to the player's shirt was yelled out, the player was 'dead'. The team with the flag and last player 'alive' won.

"Our sons each gained several pounds!" beamed the mothers after hugging and kissing their returning Scouts. Muscles had appeared on their scrawny, starved frames. "They're in so much better health! This is amazing. How'd you do it?"

With the success of this first camp, Tibor immediately began working on another for the younger Scouts. He wrote to the largest landowner in the area, a Count he met during the first camp, asking for permission to use his land.

When the Count's reply arrived, Tibor audibly caught his breath. The Count, a former Scout, not only agreed, but volunteered to provide all the food! There was nothing he could have done that would have been more appreciated. Just like at the first camp, the boys devoured their refugee camp rations along with the two sacks of potatoes and other food the Count and Red Cross provided. Once again the boys came home looking meatier, less like strung-together bones covered with skin.

While the troop had started with few experienced Scouts and lack of discipline, the boys had learned new skills, the values of Scouting, and self-discipline. Tibor treasured the experience, and before the greens of summer faded, he wrote a novel about Boy Scouts set in a DP camp.

Feffernitz Hungarian Boy Scout Troop's summer camp, 1946.

Boy Scouts in line for food
at summer camp, 1946.

As the first tinge of gold touched the forests, Tibor became anxious to continue his university studies. He wanted to shift his life into forward gear, not just continue idling. Over the summer, he had explored options and found the nearby Poly-Technical University of Graz was the only feasible one, it accepted DPs and he could afford the registration.

On Tibor's first visit to Graz, he was delighted with the bustling town: the inviting squares, the narrow streets, and the historic old buildings in the city center near the university. The noise of countless footsteps pounding the sidewalks, wagon wheels clomping on the cobbled and paved roads, and church bells ringing reminded him of Györ. The old town had survived Allied bombing with minimal damage.

On his second visit, he completed all the details of registering, enrolling as an architecture major just as he had at the Poly-Technical University in Budapest.

But Tibor had no success in finding a room or apartment in the city. With the vast number of refugees, housing was as scarce as water in the desert. Without a room, how would he be able to attend the university? He had exhausted all his options. He would have to return to the camp. After a couple of days tracking down dead-end leads, his steps no longer had much bounce as he climbed the stairs to a university building.

"Hi," Tibor greeted a young man he recognized from the Feffernitz DP Camp.

"Are you going to the university?" the young man asked.

"I'd like to," Tibor explained. "I've registered, but don't have a room."

"I couldn't find a room last year and commuted from Feffernitz, only coming in for exams."

Determined not to give up on attending university, Tibor decided to try commuting as well. Another Hungarian student offered help, Gene Wagner, Olga's brother. Gene was also a first-year student and they had several classes in common. Gene offered to take Tibor's student identification lesson book and get the mandatory professor signatures. The two young men found they had interests and experiences in common. They became fast friends.

Tibor flourished with the mental stimulation of his coursework. Even though he was attending university, most of his days still passed in the Feffernitz Camp. But now the camp had a small library, its own magazine, even a theater. Many barracks had gardens around them, muting harsh angles, adding splashes of sweet fragrance and color. As DPs left for outside employment or returned to Hungary, the vacated barrack space was often used to open small stores.

When Tibor walked around camp he could hear the pounding of a shoemaker, laughter from a bar and barber shop, and the whirring of a seamstress's sewing machine. There was fresh-baked pastry from one shop, fresh vegetables from another. Even Lili Néni joined in the entrepreneurial spirit, jointly operating a seamstress shop with another woman.

In mid-November 1946, a tsunami of change hit the camp. "Effective immediately, the Feffernitz Camp is closing," announced a British officer to assembled DPs. "You'll move to the Camp in Kellerberg."

Tibor immediately began packing the Scout equipment.

"Why are you packing?" another British officer demanded, when the officer walked into the Scout barrack.

"A British officer ordered us to move."

"Put everything back."

"I can't obey both orders. They conflict," Tibor said.

"Stop your packing. You're under barrack arrest." A vein in the officer's neck throbbed. But that evening, another British officer released Tibor from barrack arrest and ordered him to resume packing.

Conflicting British orders threw the whole camp into chaos. The DPs didn't understand the rationale, only felt the whiplash created by the British officers' power struggle. They demonstrated that night.

This led to several days of mayhem, screamed threats, and intimidation. Finally packing resumed, the DPs moving with cement feet, pandemonium an unfortunate end to the reasonably well-run Feffernitz Camp.

Two weeks before the camp was shut down, Nicholas Bácsi was hired by a factory in the town of Wietersdorf that produced pipe and roof tiles. The factory mixed crushed rock, asbestos, and water into viscous slurry which was poured into moulds and allowed to cure, yielding sections of hard pipe and slabs of tile. Jobs were scarce in the battle-scarred countryside. Pay at the factory was minimal, but Nicholas Bácsi was a proud man. Not being able to support his family had been eating away at his insides. The job was too far away to commute daily from Feffernitz, so he was living in a room on plant property with other refugees.

When Nicholas Bácsi heard the Feffernitz Camp was closing, he was able to make arrangements for the family to join him. The Zoltais were fortunate. Most DPs who moved to Kellerberg became despondent. The weather was freezing, yet they hardly had any firewood for heating, food was much more limited, their quarters cramped.

Tibor visited friends at Kellerberg two months later in January. He painted a dreary picture in his diary. "Everybody was cold and tired. Life seemed horrible. Most people were hungry. In the family where I stayed overnight, the five children were all starving. The little food I brought I shared with them. It didn't help very much. The cultural organizations have ended, the Boy Scouts as well. I tried to encourage my friends to keep the Boy Scout organization alive, but it's hard with no energy." Tibor had also been trying to help the Scouts long distance, but the camp sucked their life blood dry. As much as he wanted, Tibor wasn't able to rejuvenate them with a transfusion of hope and purpose.

The Zoltai family adjusted fairly quickly to their new home in Wietersdorf. Steve got a job constructing barracks and later a job inside the factory helping his father mix slurry. The smell of crushed rock permeated their work area. Airborne rock and asbestos particles irritated Steve's eyes, nose and throat, but he still preferred his new work to hammering the whole day in the hand-numbing cold. The family received ration cards but their salaries barely covered the cost of food.

It was uplifting to again be earning a living, but the family had no premonition of the high price they would pay, breathing the needle-like asbestos fibers.

With the tough conditions in Kellerberg, Hungarians were now even more anxious to live outside the DP camp. Soon seventy-three Hungarians worked at the plant, including Jenci Bácsi. His family was able to leave the down-trodden DP camp and live in the factory barracks.

"Foreigners are taking jobs that belong to Austrians!" the union complained to management. But most workers were not directly unpleasant to the "damned refugees."

Tibor planned to again hop the rail to Graz, this time to register for spring semester. Part of his brain kept mulling over the problem of how to get his brother Steve a university transcript. Steve had successfully completed his high-school exams shortly before the Feffernitz Camp had shut down. While Austria recognized the DP Camp diploma, his family fretted it would not be accepted in the country where they would eventually settle.

If Steve could show a University transcript, his high-school diploma would not be challenged. But two sons attending university was not a luxury they could afford.

"I think I can get Steve a transcript," Tibor announced to his family as they relaxed one evening in their two-room barrack unit, one of the barracks Steve had helped build. Tibor's eyes sparkled, "I'll register Steve for my physics class and take the exam first as myself, then later as Steve."

"How will you take the exam as me?" Steve asked.

"I'll get a student identification book in your name, but use my picture."

"It's worth a try," Nicholas Bácsi said. It would solve Steve's further education problems, wherever they ended up.

At the end of the course, Tibor first completed the oral test with his identification book. Two weeks later, Tibor returned to the musty-smelling hall to complete the colloquium using Steve's book.

"Weren't you here before?" the Professor said, looking Tibor over.

"Oh no, sir," Tibor said holding his book with an iron grip. "It must've been my brother. We look very much alike."

A close call. Tibor successfully got Steve his transcript. Years later, when Steve applied for college, the transcript fulfilled the purpose of removing any question Steve was a high-school graduate.

Tibor (*front*) and friends, spring 1947.

As Tibor entered his sophomore year, he was forced to change majors to physics and math. Architecture majors had to purchase a slide rule. The intricate mechanical calculating tool was only available on the black market, at a cost as out of reach to Tibor as world peace. With his new major, all he needed was fountain pen and paper.

But classes were only half way through, when Tibor sought medical help for his digestion. His intestines still hadn't recovered from starvation in the POW camp. Two years of persistent hunger since then only compounded his problem. In the last few months his digestion had taken a turn for the worse. He had lost weight, was weak, and frequently dizzy.

At the hospital in Graz, the doctors did a thorough examination. "The vegetative nerves in your digestive tract no longer function properly," they told him. For three months, he stayed off and on in an austere, disinfectant smelling hospital ward while the doctors tried various treatments. Nothing helped. As the months dragged on, Tibor became scrawny and exhausted, his belly bloated.

Finally, a Hungarian doctor came to see him one evening in the ward. "Smoke five of these a day." He handed Tibor a pack of cigarettes. "They'll help your digestion, stimulate the vegetative nerves."

Tibor took the pack. He was willing to try anything. "I already feel better!" he told the doctor the next morning.

From that day forward, Tibor smoked after every meal. Not only did cigarettes help his digestion, but the smell and feel of them between his fingers was soothing.

Years later, even when research showed smoking cigarettes were harmful, Tibor still smoked. Without the cigarettes, his digestion shut down. When the surgeon general's health warning came out that smoking is hazardous to your health, he liked to tell people: "I started smoking under doctor's orders." He enjoyed watching their disbelief.

* * *

As the days got colder and shorter, letters from Hungary added to the Zoltai's conviction they could never return home. Relatives wrote in code using terms that wouldn't trigger police censorship. "Someone is fully occupied at this time," was code for family or friends in jail.

The secret police still wanted to snare Nicolas Bácsi and Jenci Bácsi. Their mother's mail was closely scrutinized. They even barged into her home in Györ to question her once.

"What are your sons writing to you?" they demanded, towering over the old woman.

"Why ask me? You always read it first," she said, looking straight into their eyes. Atypically, the secret police allowed this spunky old lady her disrespectful reply.

Nicolas Bácsi and Jenci Bácsi's deep-seated fear of persecution if they returned was well founded. Those who opposed the Communist state were arrested, tortured, tried, and imprisoned in concentration camps, or executed. In the early 1950s, the Hungarian courts dealt with about 650,000 political crime cases and decreed one in every twenty-five Hungarians guilty. The family later learned Nicholas Bácsi and Jenci Bácsi were both tried in their absence, found guilty, and an effigy of them hung. Had they returned, the rope would have tightened around their necks.

Tibor and his family discussed where to make their new life. They wanted to stay in Europe but dreamed of finding a country with less overcrowding, less hostility to refugees, away from the impending world war.

"There's a Hungarian company in Alsace Lorraine looking for miners," Nicholas Bácsi announced to the family one chilly November evening.

"You and I could do the work," Steve said.

"There's training we'll need to pass," Nicholas Bácsi said. Within a few weeks, he and Steve were on their way to France.

Their friend Father Gácsér, now in Paris, sent a letter of recommendation which helped them find someone willing to rent to strangers. The Father also offered Tibor a job in his office and suggested Tibor continue his studies at La Sorbonne in Paris.

As Tibor and Lili Néni tried to get papers to join their family, the brown meadow, visible when Nicholas Bácsi and Steve left, became hidden under a blanket of white snow. The snow eventually melted, again revealing the brown grass. Fresh new grass shoots sprung to life turning the meadow brilliant green. But still the papers did not come.

The newspapers reported of the growing conflicts between the Western Allies and the Soviet Union. Nicholas Bácsi and Steve saw frequent movement of American troops between France and Belgium. They feared the rest of the family wouldn't be able to join them before another war erupted.

6

That is the Man I Will Marry
(1948 - 1949)

Olga Wagner and Tibor Zoltai, 1948.

I don't feel well. I've a fever."

Istvan, a Hungarian university student, was staying in an apartment with Tibor and others. Tibor had noticed Istvan's breathing was shallow and fast, and the youth radiated heat like a stoked stove.

At the hospital, the doctors were grave. "He has pneumonia," one said, his brows drawn together. "He'll need to stay here overnight."

But when Tibor went to visit the next day, the doctor told him Istvan had died.

What a blow! This was the second friend Tibor had lost within a few days, the other to suicide. Istvan must have gotten infected during his medical school studies, Tibor thought, and he began notifying Istvan's friends about the funeral.

The next morning he stopped in at the Urseline Convent to tell a mutual friend, Emma. A nun greeted him at the front entrance of the two-story gray building. The nun, in her black habit, politely informed him that Emma was not in. Tibor asked to speak with the only other Hungarian he knew who lived at the convent, the sister of Gene Wagner.

"Please wait here," the nun said, escorting him to a reception room. The room was painted white and had a well-worn wood table and several chairs. Tibor sat, waiting.

Olga, an attractive sixteen-year-old, entered the reception room. Tibor explained Istvan had died. "Would you be kind enough," Tibor said, "to tell Emma about Istvan's funeral?" Olga nodded.

"Would you like to come to the funeral tomorrow?"

"No, thank you. I'm busy then and I didn't know Istvan, not even by name."

There was a pause. Then Tibor asked, "Would you like to go to a movie?"

Olga's hazel eyes studied the handsome university student. He was two hand-widths taller than her five-feet-two-inches, with dark blond wavy hair, a warm smile, and sparkling gray eyes. "Yes, I would," she said.

The next day, Tibor met Olga at the street car station near her business school. Together they went to see *Caesar and Cleopatra* in living Technicolor. The 1945 American film was dubbed in German. With TV sets an unknown luxury, the theatre was packed with young and old. The pulse of the audience collectively rose and fell as the drama unfolded on the big screen.

Afterwards, the two rode the rocking, gently buzzing electric streetcar back to Olga's boarding school. Getting off at the stop directly across from the convent, Tibor waited in the cool evening air to make sure Olga was safely inside before catching another street car.

Olga floated up the stairs, bubbling with excitement, to the room she shared with several other girls. She pulled her closest friend to the second-story window, overlooking the street car stop.

"See that young man waiting at the corner?" She pointed to Tibor illuminated by a street lamp.

"Yes."

"That's the man I'll marry," Olga said in a matter-of-fact tone.

"What?!" Her friend's eyes grew until they took over her face.

"Yes," Olga said, her expression dreamy but certain.

And so it was to be, but a lot of days, miles, and uncertainty lay before them.

Both Olga and Tibor's family were trying to leave Austria. Tibor was no longer taking classes at the university since he was expecting to depart shortly for France. A few days after his date with Olga, he joined Lili Néni at the Kitschdorf Refugee Camp and began working on why their travel papers were stalled.

Starting in 1947, Olga's family had begun closely watching for opportunities to emigrate. Immigration programs moved slower than a lizard baking in the sun. The early openings were all for singles, not families. Then the Wagners got word that Chile was interested in healthy, experienced tradesman and their families. Eugene Bácsi's textile expertise fit the bill!

Eugene Bácsi had Maria Néni and Olga train for a week at his plant to be loom operators, so they could claim the occupation with the Chile Commission. Olga learned how to properly operate the semi-mechanized looms: how to refill the thread shuttle, when to switch thread color to generate the desired pattern, where to adjust the speed alternating vertical strands raised and lowered, and how to make the thread shuttle rocket side-to-side to yield finely woven fabric.

For most of the week, the rhythmic chorus of zooms, thumps, and creaks from fifty wooden looms filled the production floor. The process saturated the air with cotton dust.

Olga's new skill didn't come without unexpected excitement. She almost crushed her hand in the loom one day, incredibly lucky to only end up with a few colorful bruises. Another day, the loom next to hers caught fire. A spark from a speeding shuttle landed on the frame igniting the dried-out wood. The smoldering soon grew to a crackling blaze. The flames leapt to her loom before it was finally extinguished.

Although the Wagners registered for Chile in the fall of 1947, weeks grew into months. Each week there were rumors that the Commission would be arriving shortly, but they still hadn't been interviewed nor had their physicals, both required for final approval.

Olga received a letter from Tibor in early April, shortly after their date. "Would you like to become friends via correspondence?" he wrote. "We could share our hopes and frustrations through letters, since we probably won't meet again." Olga sighed, thinking about how far away Tibor was going, how even farther away she would travel. But she longed to correspond.

Every few days they exchanged letters. At first, Olga's letters were written in the teasing style she used with her father and brothers. "Please forgive my scratchings. I haven't written in Hungarian for a long time. I'm not used to conversing seriously with anyone, for fear of being considered a sentimental fool. I don't know if you'll find my letters interesting, but please don't give me too much grief about them."

Tibor, not used to this kind of light-hearted banter, responded seriously. "I considered your letter very well written. I don't understand your concern. I wouldn't make fun of you." After a few attempts at a light tone, Olga dropped the teasing.

Tibor followed his heart and made an unplanned visit to Graz to see Olga before his planned departure to France on May 5. Since Olga wasn't allowed to receive male visitors at the convent, outside of family, Tibor knew he would have to arrange a clandestine meeting. He told her he'd walk past the convent at 7:15 a.m., April 28. If she wanted to see him, she should wave from her window.

Positioned by her window on the morning of April 28, Olga carefully scanned the street bathed in early morning light. The city was coming to life. The number of people on the sidewalk and in the buzzing street cars multiplied as she watched. Her heartbeat echoed in her ears as she waved to Tibor walking past. He eagerly waved back.

At 2:00, Tibor was waiting for Olga outside her business school. Together they hopped a streetcar to Schlossberg, the castle mountain with its historic castle ruins and garden atop a massive tree-covered, craggy hill in the center of Graz.

As they approached the park, the brilliant spring green of the trees and grasses became interspersed with white, yellow, and blue wildflowers. They paused to admire the blooms and pick a few, then continued up the winding path and stairs to the peak, through the gardens and ruins, admiring the still-standing bell and clock towers.

Schlossberg, Graz, Austria. Copyright Graz Tourismus.

At each delicious hour Olga and Tibor spent together, the oldest bell in Graz joyously rang in the hour. Each time Tibor reached out, Olga shyly let her cool hand be enclosed in Tibor's warm fingers. They gazed out over the panorama of red rooftops with varying angles and heights, leafy green canopies, and church steeples. Olga held the small bouquet of wildflowers she collected, the fragrant Lily of the Valley sending its sweet aroma through the afternoon air.

The next day, Tibor again met her after school. This time they went to Lake Hilmteich, a small man-made lake half the size of a soccer field. Sunshine played on the leaves and the water reflected the brilliant blue of the sky as they walked around the lake hand-in-hand. As they shared their frustrations, hopes, and dreams for a better future, Olga gently secured a Forget-Me-Not in Tibor's lapel. Its vibrant color captured the hope in their words. Tibor gifted Olga with the copper ring he had handcrafted in POW camp. Tibor rowed them around the lake, the oars gently swooshing the water and the boat silently gliding forward.

Near the end of an idyllic day, Tibor kissed her. It was a lovely, gentle kiss.

On the way back to the convent, Tibor and Olga brushed shoulders in the softly rocking street car. Tibor talked in sad tones about the hopelessness of their future relationship. Olga was quiet. Tibor thought she was reflecting on how far apart they were moving, but her thoughts were still on the kiss.

Their attraction blooming, Tibor went from addressing his letters to "Dear Olgi" to "My dearest little Olgi." They wrote each other about what was happening in their lives, observations about the times, and their beliefs.

Exploring their mutual struggle with faith and religion was core to their deepening friendship. Even though both Tibor and Olga had a Catholic and a Lutheran parent, Catholicism had dominated their lives just like it dominated Hungarian society. The Church had not allowed Maria Néni to wed Eugene Bácsi until he signed a document that any children would be raised Catholic. Because Lili Néni and Nicholas Bácsi wed in Lili Néni's Lutheran Church, the Catholic Church didn't even recognize their union. The Church was going to declare Tibor illegitimate until Nicholas Bácsi's mother, who was influential in the Church, avoided the disaster with the couple's commitment Tibor would be raised Catholic.

In Hungary, Tibor and Olga were both devout Catholics. Tibor admired many of the priests who ran his Benedictine school. When he finished high school and later in DP camp, he seriously considered joining the order. He even completed an application in Austria to become a Benedictine priest and teacher, ready to forsake earthly pleasures and commit to a life of God's work, but his application was turned down, most likely due to his health problems.

Olga strived to be a good Catholic as well. She often stopped to say a prayer at churches she passed on her walk to school. No matter how hard she tried though, there was always something to feel guilty about. Once in elementary school she had wished Maria Néni would be sick so she wouldn't have to help her clean their apartment every day. Guilt shredded her insides that she had wished her mother ill.

Tibor's keen probing of spirituality began in POW camp. At first he found tremendous peace and strength in his Catholic faith. It helped him survive imprisonment and starvation. However after a couple of years in DP camp, an unsettled feeling developed in his soul as his inner scientist continued to search for truth about the meaning of life, spirituality, and God.

He struggled to understand: why would God help some suffering in war, some who were praying for assistance, but not others.

One rainy spring day, Tibor sat at the table in his and Lili Néni's Kitschdorf DP camp unit, hammering away on his portable typewriter. His fingers could hardly keep pace with his torrent of ideas on faith and religion. He was so immersed in his theories, the pounding of the rain on the roof and the cacophony of barrack life didn't impinge on his consciousness. That day, Tibor sent Olga many pages. He wrote (in synopsis): I tend to believe there is a God, although not a humanized being like most religions teach. He would not behave like humans, who would judge a person's soul and send it to heaven or hell. If there is a God, he is concerned about the existence of the world. So why do many religions believe in a God who divinely intervenes in the lives of individuals? Human nature is built on desires. Desire is the power that motivates people's activity and goals. Most goals are oversized and can not be reached, which causes frustration. Religion helps reach a certain peace through an ever powerful God that will help provide if one observes his rules. The mystics of religion give into the hands of God the random happenings occurring due to the complicated, uncontrolled laws of nature. We accept both the happy and unhappy incidents in our lives as God's will; and accept that God will eventually make us happy in afterlife.

Outside the rain poured, Tibor wrapped up in his words, continued writing: My brain has led me to believe there is no such God as an independent power that would be worried with the individual person; that would be influenced by religious regulation. Destiny is nothing more than the laws of nature unfolding. We should think about the fantastic progress man made in the past centuries to understand more of the laws of nature. How we comprehend more mysterious happenings, with less and less remaining secret and supernatural. Our religions do not satisfy the age we live in nor answer the questions of our times. While ethics and morals are essential, they can exist separate from religion.

A nun delivered Tibor's letter to Olga a couple of days later. Olga sat at one of the scarred wood desks in the convent study hall. Cloud filtered sunlight streamed in the many windows of the light, airy room where other young women sat quietly in similar school desks. She read through the pages, mulling over Tibor's ideas.

Over the next few days, Olga thought about how she had begun questioning the divine nature of the Catholic dictates in her mid-teens. How her mother crackled with anger if Olga ever verbalized any hint of the churning in her soul. Yet here was someone who questioned as she did—a free thinker who embraced new ideas.

Again sitting at one of the scratched study hall desks, her fountain pen scribed to Tibor her recently crystallized beliefs: "What made me first question religion was that the church considers things sins that I do not," she wrote. "Also some of the things we have to believe seem like fairytales. I have a difficult time to accept that non-baptized children can never go directly to heaven, but have to go to purgatory. How the bread and wine turn into the body and blood of Jesus. I have a hard time understanding the mysticism of religion."

"I did not yet get as far as you, Tibi, that there is no God above us that intercedes in our daily lives. That I can not ask for help. That I have to trust only myself and I do not need to thank heavenly help. Up until now, if something happened I explained to myself that this was destined. But if there is no divine intervention in daily events, then our whole life is a line of haphazard happenings.

"I should not have asked if you believe in God. I should have asked if you believe in religion. I don't doubt the existence of God, but that religion has announced so many regulations as God's words. If I would tell someone I do not believe in religion, they would think 'such a young girl and already a lost soul.' They would consider me immoral, because I do not have religion to protect me.

"I believe one has to have beliefs to guide her thoughts and life. Otherwise she is lost. One has to be able to distinguish between good and bad. One has to do things out of conviction, not out of fear of the wrath of God."

As ink flowed out of her fountain pen onto the thin parchment paper, Olga began to sit up straighter. Reaching this point in her thinking was one of the happiest days of her life, like the throwing off of a heavy, constraining yoke and embracing freedom.

Tibor found these topics so enthralling, he began voraciously reading about religion, philosophy, and human motivation. This helped pass the endless hours waiting for travel papers, since lack of official papers had prevented their May 5 departure.

Sometimes he read in his barrack. More often he found a spot in the woods where the only sound was wind rustling leaves overhead.

In the leafy shade, he contemplated changing his major to religion and philosophy when he enrolled at the university in Paris. A career writing and teaching philosophy appealed to him, even though it would pay much less than the engineering career path he was on.

He wrote to Olga about this idea before sharing it with anyone else.

When her reply arrived in a few days, his hands were not quite steady slitting open the light-weight paper. "You should change your plans," she wrote. "If your happiness depends on a field that does not pay well but interests you, by all means you should follow your desires. I have an utmost belief in you and that you'll succeed."

Her response was all important. He had found a life partner with similar goals.

Tibor and Lili Néni *(seated)* with Austrian home owner friend, 1948.

Even though Tibor and Lili Néni were delayed in their emigration, the Wagners' plans finally began to progress.

Olga and her family got their physicals, a critical hurdle. If a person failed, they could not emigrate; countries only accepted the young and healthy. If a family member got rejected, the family had to decide: Should some go forward, earn money, and bring the rest of the family later? What if they could never get entry? Or should they all stay where they were, even if jobs, food, and opportunities were scarce?

Many faced gut-wrenching decisions, ripping apart the fabric of a family based on one exam.

The Wagner family's first day of the physical screening was uneventful. However when they returned to the crowded Graz clinic a few days later to have their Tuberculosis skin test read, Olga ran into trouble. She was seated with the healthcare worker in one of the clinic's clean-smelling, tiny examination rooms.

"It's red and swollen," the worker said, frowning over the site of Olga's TB injection. A reaction to the injection meant either latent or active TB.

"The doctor will check your X-ray," the worker explained. A clean chest X-ray was essential because people with latent TB were approved, but not those with an active infection. Olga had had TB in fourth grade, which could have caused the skin reaction. But when the doctor examined her chest X-ray, it was not clear. He could not eliminate active TB. Olga repeated the X-ray and failed again. The circles under her eyes grew darker, her voice became flat, and she tried the test one more time.

Everyone anxiously awaited the results of the third X-ray. What if Olga couldn't pass? Her family wouldn't leave without her, but Olga didn't want to be the reason they couldn't go. If she couldn't pass, that didn't just eliminate immigrating to Chile. No country would take them. Would she yet again derail her family's escape plan? she fretted. Just like when she was thirteen and broke her leg.

But the third X-ray was conclusive. The doctor approved her. The TB was not active.

Now things seemed to really be falling into place. Not only had the entire family passed the physical, but with their training, Olga and

Maria Néni were able to intelligently answer the questions on loom operation, and the Chile commission approved them to emigrate.

"Be ready to leave in late July," the commission told the Wagners. "We're on schedule to complete screening, load the transport, and be ready to depart then."

Lili Néni finally got her papers in mid-June, but Tibor's didn't come, the hold-up appeared to be his inability to do hard physical labor. The two decided Lili Néni would definitely leave for France on July 14.

If Tibor didn't get his papers in time to leave with her, he would find an illegal way to cross the border.

The bushes in the convent garden gained their summer fullness. Olga awaited departure.

She struggled with feeling her life had no goal, no meaning. Sitting at a scarred study table, she captured her thoughts in a letter to Tibor, telling him how deeply her internal compass had shut down.

"We have to find our own happiness," Tibor wrote back. "We need to get pleasure out of the little things, a walk, flowers, playing sports, a funny story, or a friend's smile. We need to work on being happy. Concentrate on whatever is good, no matter how small." She knew how often Tibor was in pain, and how he focused on the joys. In forced labor and POW camp, he had to look harder for the good things, but found enough to keep him going.

Olga took his advice to heart. But when he wrote, "The heart is the treasure of a woman; you should look to the future and focus on seeing your happiness in loving and caring for your husband and children," she wasn't sure she agreed. Olga did dream of having a family someday, but she questioned if that would ever happen. She also felt a woman should have an intellectual purpose.

As summer days lengthened, their love grew. Olga cared deeply for Tibor, and he for her. But neither felt they could make any commitment to the other. Would they ever live in the same country again? Blown about like dandelion fluff in a tornado, the two young people resented not being able to plan their future.

Olga decided to send Tibor a symbol of her love, a pressed Lily of the Valley from their Schlosberg outing. The sweet scent of their day still clung to the petals. Tibor sent her back three fragrant rose buds sealed in a little glass bottle with wax. Even though they had to wait, he hoped they would someday be together.

He was able to squeeze in two trips to Graz before his planned July departure. The couple took long walks along the Mura River, hand-in-hand, admiring the historic buildings and nature's beautiful mosaic of light to dark greens. But most of all, they admired each other. The couple knew they were in love and savored every moment they had together. They may never meet again.

One day, Maria Néni made an unplanned trip to Graz. When she completed her errands in preparation for the Chile trip, she visited Olga.

The nun at the front desk greeted her. "Olga's in the reception room. You're in luck, your son's here. Not the dark haired son, but the fair haired one."

Maria Néni followed the nun to the reception area. Olga was sitting in one of the worn wood chairs, chatting amiably with a blond young man who Maria Néni had never seen before. Either she could acknowledge him as her son, or get Olga thrown out of the convent for having a male visitor who wasn't family.

"Hello, son," said Maria Néni, stiffly embracing Tibor and kissing him on both cheeks.

Despite the awkward beginning, Maria Néni thought Tibor was polite, respectful, and charming. In every letter to Graz after that, Tibor always sent his greetings to Maria Néni.

Tibor and Lili Néni left as planned on July 14, 1948, but French immigration officials refused to allow Tibor to enter the country. He argued that his father and brother were already working in France, a job was waiting for him in Paris, but the officials didn't care. They told him to return home.

Tibor and Lili Néni stayed in the nearby Bad Salzburg DP Camp with other Hungarians that evening. On Tibor's behalf, the local DPs enlisted the help of an influential Hungarian Countess. The Countess took up his case with the immigration officials. She got a commitment that if the proper paperwork came from Paris, Tibor could enter.

While Tibor appreciated the Countess's help, he wasn't satisfied with this arrangement. He decided to enter France illegally after Lili Néni left. But just before Lili Néni's departure, Tibor's paperwork came.

On July 24, both he and Lili Néni climbed aboard a passenger train headed out of Austria. Spewing a large cloud of steam and coal dust, the train chugged and rocked through the night, arriving the next day in the town where his father and brother worked in the mines. The family enjoyed a week together, then Tibor traveled on to Paris where his employer anxiously awaited his services.

The conditions in France differed from Austria. Comparatively, there was no food shortage, although they still had ration cards for lard, bread, and sugar. The people were better dressed and healthier. Their homes were in decent repair. The people actually became kinder when they realized he didn't speak their language! Tibor felt they weren't as overwhelmed with DPs and appreciated the foreign-born more.

Arriving in Paris, Tibor started his new job as personal assistant to Father Gácsér. The office was involved in local politics and helped arrange immigration for Hungarians to Argentina where the Benedictine Order had a mission. Tibor was excited to be in a hub of Hungarian activity, to have an opportunity to learn a side of politics that only came from direct involvement.

Father Gácsér *(left)* and Tibor in Paris, 1948.

He began classes at the University of Paris, Sorbonne as a philosophy and religion major. La Sorbonne was in the heart of Paris, in the Latin Quarter on the north bank of the Seine. Each corridor, arch, pillar, and frontage told a page of its seven-hundred-year history. The entire Latin Quarter, with its vibrant intellectual and artistic life, Bohemian lifestyle, and rich past, emanated excitement and mystique, the antithesis of the fleeting existence and slow-paced DP camp life he left behind. Tantalizing smells came from the cafes, welcoming notes of musicians, and the robust discussion of students and artists beckoned him.

Tibor filled every minute with activity, getting by on only a few hours of sleep. His full-time job with Father Gácsér didn't pay enough for school, his small quarters, and food, so he found a position as a security guard for the City of Paris working a few hours in the middle of the night. In addition to his two jobs and classes, Tibor made time to help the Catholic youth organization and to write for a Hungarian magazine targeted to DPs, *As You Can*, an appropriate title for the times.

Olga passed her days in the Stainz meadow. Devastated when Tibor left, knowing it was unlikely they would meet again, she realized he was the only man she ever loved. She stumbled around, listless, a flower stripped of its colorful bloom and energy-generating leaves.

After a while, she decided she needed to accept the situation, move on, hard to do when each letter she wrote him brought her feelings to the fore. So she wrote less and less frequently.

All five of the Wagners were living in their cabin now, anxiously awaiting departure for Chile. Their paperwork was in order. They were assigned to the second transport leaving in early August. The family completed their series of typhoid shots. The children's school year was over. Eugene Bácsi resigned from his job, and a goodbye mass was held for all the departing Hungarians.

Gathered inside a thick-walled church in Graz, they were cocooned from the sounds of city life. "No healthy Hungarian man should leave," the priest giving the sermon said from the pulpit. "You should stay and fight for Hungary." His voice shook with emphasis. "There is clearly going to be another war. It's just a matter of days or months. Soldiers will be needed to free our homeland."

Olga found it ironic that two weeks later they were still in their meadow, but the priest had left for Canada.

The first Chilean transport had sailed away on schedule but upon arrival in Chile, many of the DPs did not have the expertise they had claimed. They were not mechanics, engineers, tailors, bakers, or other craftsmen, just people desperate to leave, mostly officers and intelligentsia, not the artisans Chile wanted. False representation created a scandal, and the Chilean government put a hold on further transports. The family felt like they were already at sea without any oars. They decided if their Chilean transport didn't sail by the time school started in September, they needed to take their lives off hold.

The start of school came and went. The family sold their cabin and got a one-bedroom furnished apartment in Graz. The children returned to school, Eugene Bácsi found a job in a Graz textile mill, and the Wagners kept looking for a way out of Europe; scanning every posting, listening to every rumor; investigating every lead.

The food shortage had eased some with the advent of the life-saving U.S. Marshall Plan, which infused $13 billion in economic and technical assistance to Europe over a five-year period, starting in 1947. But tension was high. On June 24, 1948, the Berlin Blockade began. The Soviet Union blocked rail and road access to the three Western-held sectors of Berlin, deep within the Soviet zone of Germany. Their goal was to gain control of the two-million-strong city by cutting off supplies. Allies responded with an incredible, unprecedented airlift of supplies that kept the entire city of West Berlin operating. Originally only expected to last three weeks, the airlift was already in its third month, providing coal, food, clothing, and everything else the city needed by plane. Even candy bars and bubble gum for the children came from the sky.

Planes were landing every three minutes, twenty-four-hours-a-day, seven-days-a-week. The tension from the boiling crisis was expected to explode any moment.

In Hungary, early in 1948, the Communist party with the support of Soviet troops seized total control. Horror stories spread about imprisonment, labor camps. Just the act of writing to people in the West put individuals at risk. Despite this, Olga's namesake cousin wrote regularly, using cryptic words to pass the censors. They learned Olga's cousin Margit had been killed, stalked by a Russian soldier. Returning home was clearly not an option.

More opportunities to immigrate and resettle were becoming available. The Wagners learned of a chance for singles to go to Canada and decided Olga should go as a domestic servant, Gene as a laborer. They didn't want to split up the family, but this was the best alternative. The two young adults would later sponsor the rest of the family. But before Olga and Gene departed, Eugene Bácsi learned of yet another opportunity.

"Canada is accepting families as agricultural workers!" Eugene Bácsi said. The family had just finished dinner, the smell of fried potatoes still lingering in the apartment.

"We could immigrate together?" Maria Néni asked.

Eugene Bácsi pushed aside his plate. "We'd have to pretend to be farm workers." His brow furrowed.

"Couldn't we do the work?" Maria Néni said.

"You don't need specialized training," Gene said, pausing in his doodling. "You just have to work hard."

"We can do that," Maria Néni and Eugene Bácsi said, the unfocused look leaving their eyes. "Yes, we can make the commitment."

Olga and Maria Néni dressed up in borrowed dark, coarse peasant frocks, aprons, and head scarves. The three male Wagners put on peasant trousers, shirts, and work boots. Dressed for the part and nerves aflutter, they rode the street car to their interview on a crisp Friday morning early in November.

"In exchange for a two-year commitment to hoe sugar beets," the Canadian officials explained, "the Canadian government will loan you money for passage." They outlined more details.

"We understand," Eugene Bácsi said, nodding decisively. "We'd like to go."

In March 1949, they received notice that they'd been accepted. In a flurry of activity, the family sold larger belongings, packed bags, and said teary goodbyes to friends.

A week later they traveled by rail to Salzburg to join several hundred other DPs congregating for the trip. From Salzburg, the family boarded a northbound train for Bremerhaven, Germany.

"Look, look!" yelled Andy, bouncing up and down as they approached Bremerhaven.

Olga joined Andy, her face plastered against the glass, eyes round in wonder. There before her was the ocean, its vastness extending as far as she could see. While she had seen pictures, the reality looked so much more infinite. The monstrous ocean liner docked in port was larger than a tall building.

The family joined thousand of DPs from other host countries and awaited departure in a nearby camp. To pass the time, the Wagners went into the city center each day. Its brick and plaster buildings reminiscent of other city centers Olga had explored, but the hour walk there was more foreign than the far side of the moon. The streets were desolate, block after block of homes flattened in the bombing raids years earlier. While the stench of death had long ago rotted away, Olga found it eerie walking through the area. There were no trees, no plants, and no intact buildings, no smell of life, just cement, brick, and plaster. It was a sad, but apt place to say goodbye to Europe.

Olga's emigration certificate, 1949.

* * *

The waters of the Seine were the heart and soul of Paris. Tibor walked along its banks away from the Latin Quarter and La Sorbonne toward the Eiffel Tower. The smell of fresh bread and espresso filled his nostrils, the chatter of French filled his ears. Tibor made time on Sunday afternoons to explore Paris, its incredible beauty, architecture, and history fascinating him.

It was early fall, the days still warm, the evenings crisp. Just over a year ago he had arrived here. He enjoyed his university classes, he liked stretching his mind studying philosophy. However the rest of his life was no longer fulfilling.

A few months after his arrival, Church leadership asked Tibor to take on running the Hungarian Catholic youth organization. It was a fantastic opportunity, but Tibor declined. He felt he lacked the strong Catholic faith it required. But he kept helping the youth organization.

Interest in his leadership continued until he began formal philosophical debates about Catholicism that winter. The Hungarian community was invited to attend, but mostly students and priests sat in the wood chairs arranged in the colorless room. A Hungarian priest, a leader in Catholic philosophy, argued pro-Catholicism. Tibor argued for lack of blind acceptance of church doctrine. While he felt he didn't express his thoughts eloquently, the debate laid out in the open his philosophy about Catholicism.

After the debate, Father Gácsér tried to help him see the error in rejecting century-old truths.

"The most compelling reason to have faith is the proof before your eyes," Father Gácsér said, his hands sweeping the wood-lined walls of his office. "All the wonderful miracles occurring in the world around us."

"A lot of things 500 years ago were considered miracles, yet today we have medical explanations," Tibor said, and he continued the debates.

One on predestination laid bare the root of Tibor's problem with Catholic doctrine.

"If God knows everything then he knows what was, is, and will be," he argued. "He also knows if a man will make it or not."

"God gives you the free will to choose between good and evil," the priest said.

"But if God knows everything, then he knows what I will choose."

"Logic stops here, but we have to believe in God and the church," the priest said.

After the first public debate, Tibor's Catholic friends and coworkers prayed for his soul. When he didn't reform, they began to ostracize him. Eventually he was asked to withdraw from all activities, even the Boy Scout camp he was helping to plan. In the heat of the summer he formally severed his tie to the Catholic Church, then he resigned from his job with Father Gácsér.

Tibor now lived a more solitary life, he wrote Olga. But at least he could hold his head up high knowing he stood true to his convictions. But his normal optimism had become buried under the way his life was unfolding.

He no longer believed in the spiritual foundation that was his compass since a small child. He had lost most of his Catholic friends. He had a consuming drive to write down his philosophical thoughts, yet the writing devoured his energy, optimism, and spirit, leaving him drained.

When he studied human behavior, he saw the crushing burden of humanity continuing to repeat the same mistakes. If he pursued a career writing philosophy, he would have to give up his dream of a wife and children. His philosophies were not popular, and he clearly could not make a living writing and teaching about them. But it was more than his own situation that weighed heavily on his shoulders. He worried about his father and brother working in the harsh, dangerous conditions in the Alsace Lorraine mine.

A fair number of Tibor's friends had chosen to end their lives in the aftermath of the war. Despair over the postwar world overwhelmed them. Although Tibor thought about suicide, even kept a gun in his apartment in case it ever got to be too much, his natural optimism would not allow pessimism to drag him below the muck's surface. He did not cock the gun to silence the despair.

The weeks crept by. Tibor continued to struggle with dark thoughts. He filled the void with writing. He felt a burning obsession to write.

He moved out to the suburbs of Paris, renting a small three-room house, expecting his family would join him shortly. Nicholas Bácsi already had a fair paying job lined up and Steve an apprenticeship.

Bright spots in his days were the letters from Olga. She was in Canada. She wrote how she felt more certain and happy about life than since she had left Hungary. While work was physically hard, it helped give her life purpose.

Canada offered a haven from war, the dream of being accepted as part of a community, making a decent living, and advancing through hard work.

When Olga offered help if his family wanted to immigrate as agricultural workers, Tibor immediately went to talk with his parents and Steve, too impatient to await their arrival. All the Zoltais wanted to immigrate, excited by what Canada offered. Tibor was the least motivated to leave, he loved Paris, but being near Olga again was a powerful attraction.

Zoltai family in Paris just before leaving for Canada, 1949.
L. to r. Steve, Lili Néni, Nicholas Bácsi, and Tibor.

Departure could not happen soon enough for the Zoltais, anxious to leave Europe before war broke out. The cold-war tension had not ended with the resolution of the Berlin blockade. After almost a year, the Soviets opened Allied land access to Berlin, but this only ended one stressful episode. Other power struggles continued to feed the upward spiraling tension.

Any day one was expected to ignite into war, like a spark in a drought-ravaged forest.

7

Indentured Servitude, a Solution?
(1949 – 1950)

Picture postcard of Wagner's ocean liner to Canada, 1949.

In early April 1949, Olga, her family, and two thousand others boarded the Scythia ocean liner headed for Canada. This steam-powered transport carried soldiers during the war. Its new load was displaced persons.

The ship was the size of an enormous building. Even leaning her head way back, Olga couldn't see the top. The black hull itself was many stories tall, and it was topped with several more stories of white deck. The black-and-red chimney extended even farther into the sky.

With a deafening bellow of the ship's horn and a large puff of steam, their journey from Europe began.

Olga and Maria Néni followed a mass of women into a large room densely packed with rows of triple-deck bunk-beds that spanned most of the deck. Their ship level was exclusively for women; other levels were devoted to men. Not much privacy, but Olga was delighted to have a real mattress, not a lumpy burlap bag stuffed with straw.

Ocean liner berthing card, 1949.

The dining room offered a buffet table covered with an assortment of salads, savory soups, meats, steaming potatoes, vegetables, drinks, and desserts, more food than Olga had ever seen, and she got to eat as much as she wanted!

In the recreation room, was a Ping-Pong table. Olga and her brothers had never heard of the game, so they attentively watched. Ping-pong was the sound the small white plastic ball made as the players paddled it back and forth across the green wood table. The Wagner youth quickly picked up the rules, although sometimes they struggled to control the ball when the boat dove or climbed a large swell. Each day of their weeklong journey, they paddled hours away.

Olga, Gene, and Andy had fun on the ship. They were delighted to be leaving Europe, were hopeful of a better future, and saw the change as the harbinger of better things. Maria Néni and Eugene Bácsi didn't share their enthusiasm. They had spent more than four decades, their entire lives, in Europe. Maria Néni was particularly distraught to leave the continent for an unknown country. Traveling up and down the ocean swells made her nauseous, and she was unable to keep down even a bite of the generous food.

The afternoon sun illuminated the western sky as the ship docked in the port of Halifax. The refugees were welcomed by the Salvation Army with live music, the beat of the drum and bright brassy sound exhilarating. Volunteers served donuts, apple juice, and coffee. Olga had never seen a donut before and delighted in the pastry's tantalizing aroma. She and Andy used the introductory English they had learned in Austria to help translate for their parents. To go from being "damned refugees" to such a welcome was incredible!

Within a few hours, they were shepherded a short distance to a string of railcars hitched to a black locomotive. When they reached a passenger car with sleeping births, their guide waved them to board. A loud whistle, a hissing cloud of steam, and the clankety-clank of the iron wheels declared their journey was resuming. No one offered any explanation where they were going.

One day extended into two, then three still thundering along the tracks. Day and night, they rolled westward along the Canadian Pacific line, trailing the locomotive's belching plumes of steam. All they could see from their rail car was lush green and brown marshland, then prairie. They passed mile after mile of no forests. No buildings. No people. The only signs of civilization were the train stations.

Occasionally the whistle and screeching of brakes announced they were approaching one of these outposts of humanity. Olga remembered how in central Europe, it was unusual to go thirty minutes without passing through a town. How different her new country was!

"What kind of godforsaken land is this?" one of the experienced farm workers said. "This looks like the surface of the moon. There's not even a regular tree. Where do people live?"

The landscape's desolation heightened the Wagners' fear. They knew so little about Canada, farming, their farmer. What awaited them?

On the fourth day, the Wagners were instructed to get off the train. They had arrived in Lethbridge, Alberta. A Hungarian farmer named Jula Horvath was waiting for them on the station platform. He was a thin, middle-aged man a few inches taller than Olga, his leathery skin topped with a mop of blond hair.

When he saw them, his face lit up.

"Welcome to Canada!" Jula said in Hungarian. He shook everyone's hand vigorously.

"Thanks for sponsoring us," Eugene Bácsi said, returning the smile.

"I'm happy to have workers." Jula's tongue stumbled over the Hungarian words, but the grin never left his face.

Jula noticed their hesitant look and tense stance. "This is really a good country," he reassured them in halting Hungarian. "I've been here twenty years and found plenty of work. You really shouldn't be afraid of making a living." Jula, like a number of farmers in the area, had emigrated from Europe during the economic downturn of the 1920s. He told them he had a better life here than he would have ever had in Hungary.

"My truck's this way." Jula pointed and picked up some luggage. "It's an hour drive to Raymond, to my farm." His face glowed with pride. "I rent forty acres and am going to plant sugar beets."

Years ago wheat dominated the prairie since it survived on the sparse rainfall. But the area had acquired systematic irrigation and the highly profitable sugar beets had become an option. Jula had worked as a farmhand for years and this was his first year to venture out on his own. As he later explained, a farmer could make a living on forty acres of sugar beets instead of needing more than ten times as much land for wheat. He praised the government's new agricultural worker program, which provided much-needed workers for the labor-intensive crop.

Jula led the Wagners to his pick-up, despite dings and scraps from years of farm use, the brown truck looked sturdy.

"We should celebrate your arrival. Let's go for a beer!" he said, putting their luggage in the back of the truck. He motioned for Maria Néni and Eugene Bácsi to sit in the cab, the youth in back. In a few minutes, he pulled up to a painted wood building with a bright, lit beer sign, several cars and pick-ups parked out front.

"You'll have to wait here," Jula said to Olga and Andy when they began to follow. "You're not old enough to come in the bar."

Olga watched people come and go, mesmerized by her new surroundings. Everyone here was so different. Their coloring, hair styles, and clothes were strange. Some women looked bald, their hair in tight little curls bobby-pinned against their head. Many wore trousers, not dresses! Automobiles were not painted dark but stood out in their bright colors. The houses and other buildings were not constructed of brick and plaster, but wood, their design flimsy compared to anything she'd ever seen. The distances between homes and between villages were vast, the farm fields enormous.

Jula didn't have any living quarters for them on his rented land, so he arranged for the Wagners to stay on a Dutch farm a few miles from his fields. He stopped the truck next to a one-room shack, their living quarters. The shack was made from a single layer of weathered boards, gaps between them and fist sized holes visible where once knots had been. The half hung door creaked as they opened it and stepped inside. Chill wind blew through the gaps and holes.

"In Hungary, this shack wouldn't be fit for housing horses or cows," Maria Néni said. She sat down abruptly on the hard wood bench in the center of the shack, tears streaming from her eyes. "Yet this is our new home."

They gazed around the room, with its table, bench, and a cast iron stove vastly undersized to dissipate the April cold. How were they going to cook? Olga wondered.

Eugene Bácsi walked outside. From their conversation in the bar, Eugene Bácsi knew Jula was a life-long bachelor and had no idea what a family needed. "Jula," he said, looking straight into his eyes, "This shack isn't going to work. A family needs to have a place that will keep out the cold and rain. A stove with burners for cooking."

"Oh," Jula said, looking down. "I'll find something better."

That evening, the Dutch farmer invited the Wagners into his home for supper. In the wavering light of a kerosene lamp he prepared scrambled eggs in the friendly, spacious farmhouse kitchen. Olga closely watched every move, trying to learn more about her new country. The farmer didn't fuel his cast-iron stove with wood but opened a valve allowing gas to flow from one of four large tanks located behind the stove. She watched as he quickly cracked and threw the eggs in the cast-iron pan. He didn't even pause to scrape the inside of the shell for the last bit of adhering egg. Did he have so much it didn't matter?

Within a week, Jula was able to arrange better accommodations. He had a sturdy wood cabin delivered to the farm neighboring his land, owned by a second-generation Hungarian. The whole Wagner family was on hand to watch in amazement when the fully-assembled-wood house, painted red, arrived. With a few creaks and thuds, their new home was slid off the trailer and ready for use.

Like their first quarters, their new home didn't have electricity or running water. But this cabin had a main kitchen and two bedrooms. A small shack was even set next to the cabin as a bedroom for the boys. Both buildings were well constructed, with solid wood planks that kept out the weather. The cabin had two small windows in each bedroom and a large one in the main room. The smooth inside walls were painted light green. The place had a good sized wood stove for cooking, a table, chairs, beds, and shelves. Close by was a fresh water well and outhouse. The Hungarian farm family even provided a washing machine they no longer used.

Maria Néni and neighbor girl using the Wagner's first washing machine, 1949.

Olga was awed by the washing machine. She had never seen one before. It was a large wooden tub constructed similar to a wood barrel, with metal reinforcing bands holding the wood shape.

Mounted on top was a wide metal bar with an agitator that extended downward. The metal bar raised and lowered to allow access to the tub. On the top edge of the tub was a metal unit with two wood rollers that clean clothes could be run through to squeeze out extra water. Olga pushed and pulled the handle to power the agitator, then gave her brothers a turn.

The outhouse they shared with the farm family was designed so the whole family could go out together in the winter: a large hole for father on one side of the wood structure, a medium hole lined with soft-silky fur for mother on the far side, and a small child-sized hole in the middle.

The Wagners had promised each other that they would not be surprised by their new world. However, the promise was quickly abandoned as they realized the magnitude of the differences. When they left Hungary and moved to Austria, the major change was the language, the culture was similar. But here the culture, the language, the buildings, the machines, the land, and even the food were all distinct.

The grocery store was a particularly fascinating place for Olga. She wrote to Tibor, "Imagine being in a huge store covered with large shelves having all kinds of food. Sometimes you don't even know what an item is. The food is quite cheap. One pound of bread is fourteen cents. Sugar is the same price and flour is a few cents more. The bread is beautiful, white and very fluffy, but it has no taste. We wish for the wonderful old bread from Graz."

Clothes are also inexpensive, Olga wrote. This was fortunate since the youth all needed to buy jeans for farm work. Jeans stood up better than what they had brought with them. For Olga, this was the first time she ever owned, much less worn, any sort of trousers. It was odd to feel the thick, stiff jean material between her legs.

Their work was hard, unlike anything they had ever done. Hoeing the sugar beets made their backs ache and burn, rubbed their hands raw, created blisters. Neither Eugene Bácsi nor Maria Néni was able to bend over for the long workdays, so the work fell on the three youth.

Gene and Olga were able to chop and scrape the dry earth at a steady pace, back and forth across the flat rows of fresh-smelling green shoots. Andy could work at an incredible speed when he chose. He was short, and with legs spread out, he could go along without even bending down.

But, at twelve he wasn't interested in working long hours, day after day. "Why so early?" he said each morning in his sleepiest voice when it was time to get up. The first rays of sun were only starting to lighten the sky.

"We need your help," Eugene Bácsi said. "If you're willing to work hard, we'll buy you something special. What do you want?"

"A cowboy hat, gun, and gloves." With a dreamy look, Andy added, "I want to be a real American."

The family took Andy to the general store in Raymond. He bought a straw cowboy hat painted silver, a metal bee-bee gun, and brown-leather Roy Rogers's gloves that went up to his elbow. The gloves had a big silver star on the cuff and lots of great fringe. Together with his jeans, he was sure he looked like an American cowboy.

The bribery worked: in this outfit, he came to the fields and he would hoe. His little silver cowboy hat could be seen just above ground, going up and down in a rhythmic pace as he worked better and faster than his siblings.

Sugar beet field being irrigated in Raymond, Alberta, 1904. Same process used in 1949 and 1950. Source: Notman/Library and Archives Canada/C-020310.

"The Japanese workers next door are always out earlier than we are," Gene said one morning.

"Let's start a half hour earlier tomorrow. See if we beat them." Olga thought it was fun to make a game out of their job, even though each worked ten to twelve hours a day.

They went out a half hour earlier, the Japanese couple was already bent over their hoes. The youth decided to start working earlier each day, until they were in the fields before 5:00 a.m. when night still blanketed the fields. But still the couple was already stabbing at the earth.

The game ended. "They must work fourteen-hour days!" Gene said. "Or maybe they sleep in the fields," Olga said.

Instead of matching their hours, the Wagner youth decided to just admire how hard the Japanese couple worked. They went back to their regular schedule, hoeing only as long as the sun shone.

To stay hydrated under the burning summer sun and clear their dust-coated throats, the youth kept a gallon glass water jug at the edge of the field. After an hour or more heaving the hoe, the lukewarm liquid was as refreshing to them as the irrigated water to the beets. The only problem was Olga had no experience drinking from a heavy jug.

"Eighteen-years-old and you still don't know how to drink," her brothers teased as the water dribbled down her chin onto her blouse. They didn't let up until she mastered how to swig without spilling.

Olga described the work over several letters to Tibor so his family would be prepared when they came. Unlike when she first starting to write to Tibor, she now felt comfortable using her natural teasing style. She wrote: "I have to tell you working in the field is rather difficult if you're not used to it. You get to enjoy the sunrise and sunset out in the field every day without rest until the work is done. One worker can usually manage ten acres. There is about two months of actual hoeing and one month of harvesting.

"You asked: 'How do you hoe? How often? By hand or machine?'

"When we arrived here I asked a number of people how to hoe. They laughed. They really couldn't explain it; you just have to do it. You hold the hoe tightly, with the right hand in front of you and the left hand behind you. At about a seventy-five-degree angle, you stab it in the earth. You repeat this practice several times being careful to leave a few plants intact. It's really very simple.

"In general you have to hoe three times, but the first one is the most difficult because the beet plants need to be thinned. The main thing you have to watch for is to leave plants approximately 16 inches from each other. It could of course be 16.5 inches (she liked to tease Tibor about his precision). After that, you hoe to remove weeds. The second hoeing is to calm your conscience that weeds won't weaken the plant. The third is to calm the conscience of the farmer. Of course if the fields are very weedy, it's different. You don't have to be afraid of this, because your farmer sponsor is famous in the village for his clean fields. I expect your work isn't going to be too difficult.

"There is the use of a machine called a cultivator that really makes the work much easier because it cleans away one-quarter of the weeds. At home, I believe this has to be done all by hand.

"Between the third hoeing and the harvest there's about two months. Harvest is the most difficult work. The beets grow up to 18 inches long and weigh 3 to 4 pounds. A tractor plow loosens the beets. You follow carrying a razor-sharp machete with a hook on the end. You snag a beet, knock off the dirt, whack off the crown, and toss the root onto a truck."

Post-World War II contract workers harvesting sugar beets. Source: the Timmerman Family Collection of the Pier 21 Society, Canada's Immigration Museum, Halifax Canada. Copyright 2009 Pier 21.

The youth were glad when the beet harvest came to an end. They were tired, their jeans and hands bore the scars of their less-than-perfect-whacks, and their backs ached. It was a relief to put away their hoes and machetes, to leave behind the musty smell of earth. They were still city people at heart.

Gene followed the beets to the steel and cement processing plant in Raymond where he worked as a day laborer. The processing of the beets emitted a strong sour odor from blocks away. In the first step, the beets with small clumps of dirt still clinging to their surface were washed. With a series of gurgles, swooshes, hisses, and clangs; the sugar was extracted, purified, concentrated, and crystallized. The dirty gray, lumpy root vegetable was transformed into pure white crystalline sugar sold in stores and used in candy and pastries.

Ten months earlier, thousands of miles away, on a Graz street lined with sturdy brick and plaster buildings, Eugene Bácsi had committed the family to the farm work. How much their world had changed.

At that time, the official had explained in detail the family's obligations: "Your contract will be with the Canadian government. You commit to complete the farm work on your assigned farm for two seasons and repay the government's loan for travel expenses."

"Yes," Eugene Bácsi nodded.

"The farmer directs your work, provides housing, and pays the contracted amount after harvest . . ."

With pleasure, Eugene Bácsi committed to the obligations the official had outlined. It wasn't until decades later that his family even realized the actual contract he signed once in Canada, written in English, only specified one year not two. Signing his name, Eugene Bácsi committed the Wagner family to be indentured servants.

An indentured servant is, by definition, a laborer under contract to work for a defined employer, for a specified amount of time, to pay off passage to a new country or home. While technically they met the criteria, the Canadian system did not allow for the abuses notorious two hundred years earlier in the U.S.

Form 1949

ALBERTA CASH LABOR CONTRACT - SUGAR BEETS
Contract for Hand Labor for the Season 1949

Memorandum of Agreement made this _____ 20 _____ day of _____ June _____ 1949,

by and between _____ Julius Horvath, Raymond _____ hereinafter called the Grower,

and _____ Eugene Wagner _____ of _____ Raymon _____ hereinafter called the Contractor.

WITNESSETH: Whereas the grower has entered into a contract with the Canadian Sugar Factories Limited, hereinafter called the Sugar Company, for the growing of beets during the season of 1949 and is desirous of contracting with the Contractor for the doing of handwork on said crop.

NOW THEREFORE in consideration of the covenants hereinafter set forth, it is mutually agreed between the parties hereto as follows, to wit:

1. The Contractor hereby agrees to do the handwork on _____ — 25 — _____ acres, more or less of sugar beets

planted or to be planted on the _____ quarter section _____, Twp. 6 _____, Rge. 20

W. of the 4th Mer., in the district of _____ Raymond _____ Province of Alberta, for the season of 1949, in accordance with the rules and conditions printed on the back hereof and made a part of this Contract, and the Grower agrees to comply with and perform the obligations imposed on him by said rules and regulations.

2. The Contractor agrees to accept and the Grower agrees to pay, as full compensation for the said work the following prices, to wit:

THINNING 22 INCH ROWS	$13.00 PER MEASURED ACRE.
FOR HOEING 22 INCH ROWS	5.50 PER MEASURED ACRE
FOR WEEDING, OR WEEDINGS	3.50 PER MEASURED ACRE.

For pulling and topping and piling into piles from 300 to 600 lbs., or loading the beets as topped into low wagons or trucks not to exceed approximately 4 ft. in height, or placing in windrows suitable for mechanical loading, $19.00 per acre on a yield of 10 tons per acre, and over 10 tons a bonus at the rate of $1.90 for each additional ton, per acre, and under 10 tons per acre a deduction of $1.90 per ton shall be made for each ton, provided that there shall be no deduction on a yield below 8 tons per acre. In the event of an invasion of web-worm or other pest requiring the beets to be poisoned, the Labor agrees to assist the Grower to do the poisoning without extra pay, up to 50% of the total labor required.

(a) These conditions may be modified to cover mechanical operations _____

_____

_____

(b) Irrigation _____

(c) Fork Loading _____

3. It is mutually agreed between the parties hereto that $5.00 per acre shall be withheld from the payment due under this contract for thinning, and for hoeing $1.00 per acre, as a guarantee of the faithful performance of the contract by the contractor, provided, however, that if the contractor shall cease work before the completion of the contract under conditions which render the performance of the work possible, the contractor shall either accept from the Grower as full compensation, 60 per cent of the contract price per acre for the work done up to the time the contractor ceases to work, or in lieu thereof the contractor shall with the consent of the Grower, hire and pay other labor to complete the work and thus fulfil his contract with the Grower. The Grower shall furnish, if requested by the contractor, a holdback certificate showing that spring labor has been performed satisfactorily and the amount which shall be payable to the contractor on completion of the contract.

4. Payments for said work shall be made by the Grower to the contractor providing the respective classes of work have been done to the satisfaction of the Grower or have been approved by the Agricultural Superintendent or Fieldman of the Sugar Company, promptly as follows: Payment for thinning and for hoeing on the completion of each operation less guarantee agreed upon; payment for weedings on satisfactory completion of work; payment for pulling and topping when such work is finished.

5. The Grower reserves the right to cancel all or any part of the contract on such portions of the land as will not in his judgment pay to harvest, provided that full payment is made to the contractor for all the work theretofore done by him on such portions of the land.

6. It is mutually agreed between the parties hereto that the rules and conditions printed on the back of this contract governing the handwork to be performed by the contractor **form part of this contract** and are binding on the parties thereto.

7. It is mutually agreed that in the event of any misunderstanding or dispute between the parties hereto with respect to the interpretation of any of the provisions of this contract, including said rules and conditions, or as to the amount of work or character of the work performed hereunder, or the compensation due therefor, or respecting any claim by either party for failure of the other party to complete this contract, the aforesaid Agricultural Superintendent or Fieldman or the Sugar Company shall be arbitrator, and his decision shall be final and binding on both the Grower and the contractor.

IN WITNESS HEREOF, the parties hereto have hereunto subscribed their names the day and year first above written.

WITNESS _____
As to Grower

WITNESS _____
As to Contractor

GROWER _____ Julius Horvath

CONTRACTOR _____ Eugene Wagner

Wagner's agricultural worker contract with the Canadian government, 1949 (two pages).

Rules and Conditions Governing the Hand Work of the Within Contract

BLOCKING AND THINNING

This operation must be commenced by the contractor as soon as the beets show four leaves and the grower has them properly cultivated, and must be completed as rapidly as possible in the following manner, to wit: Beets to be spaced ten inches apart, or as ordered by the grower, leaving only one plant in each place; no double beets shall be left; in splitting doubles the stronger plant must be left; care must be used not to hoe dirt from the plants left. The grower must keep the crop cultivated so at least fourteen inches of the centre of the row remains clear of weeds and foul growth up to the time when the damage done to the leaves by cultivator prevents further use of that implement. The thinning must be done so that the remaining space will be entirely free from weeds.

HOEING

This operation must be commenced by the contractor just as soon as the grower orders and he has again properly cultivated the field, and must be completed as rapidly as possible in the following manner, to wit: By killing and removing all weeds in the land mentioned in the preceding paragraph, and reducing any double plants to singles, and hilling-up where plants are exposed.

WEEDING

This operation must be commenced by the contractor when the grower orders. It calls for the contractor's keeping the entire beet field free from weeds until the beet harvest is started, with the understanding that the grower is obliged to continue the prescribed cultivation until prevented by the damage done to the beet leaves. If it is necessary to go over the field more than once to keep the field clean, the contractor agrees to do so without extra pay. If the use of hoes at the time of weeding damages the beet leaves, the contractor must remove the weeds by hand.

Weedings shall not commence until August 5th unless the Grower orders otherwise. As soon as the field is cleaned and the work finished satisfactorily to the Grower, the contractor may be released by the Grower to go to other work until the beet harvest commences, provided he leaves his address or reports back to the Grower during his absence and not later than September 10th.

HOUSING

The Grower agrees to provide without charge for the contractor a habitable house, equipped with cooking stove, which may be occupied during the beet work and thirty days thereafter, or longer as per arrangements with Grower, and to arrange if necessary on account of distance, conveyance of food supplies and suitable water for culinary purposes, to transport laborers and baggage from station to farm. The contractor agrees to make good any losses or damages to the premises, household furniture and chattels occasioned during his occupancy.

PULLING AND TOPPING AND PILING OR LOADING

The harvesting of the beets shall commence at the time specified by the Sugar Company in their notice to the Grower to dig. The contractor shall report to the Grower by letter or in person not later than September 10th. If the contractor has not personally reported for work by September 20th, the contract may be cancelled and his holdback forfeited to the Grower who is free to hire other help. If the Grower has orders and has not commenced digging beets by September 25th, weather permitting, the contract may be declared cancelled and the Grower shall pay the holdback to the contractor who is free to seek other employment. The beets must be pulled by the contractor, and cleaned reasonably well of adhering dirt by knocking the beets together and throwing them into piles. If required by the Grower, the beets shall be topped and thrown into low wagons or trucks, or placed into windrows suitable for mechanical loading, at no extra expense. No beets shall be piled on top of beets that have not been pulled. The beets shall be topped by the contractor in the following manner, to wit: By properly topping average beets by completely cutting off all leaf structure at the base of the crown; extra large beets shall be trimmed of all leaf structure; they shall be free from leaves and excess dirt, stones, trash or foreign substance. The ground on which the beets are piled must be cleaned off by the contractor so that the loaders may fork the beets into the wagon free from clods, rocks, leaves, or other trash, or contractor shall operate V-out equipment to prepare the ground for the windrowed beets.

All beets left in the fields overnight must be properly protected by the contractor by covering the piles with beet tops to be removed by the loaders before the beets are loaded.

All tools for hand work except beet forks shall be furnished by the contractor.

In the event any hand work is not done with sufficient rapidity by the contractor, the grower may appeal to the aforesaid Agricultural Superintendent or Fieldman to either of whom authority is hereby delegated to decide whether the employment of additional help is necessary and to permit the engagement of additional help to do the work in question as cheap as existing conditions warrant. The grower is hereby authorized to deduct the amount paid such additional labor from the account of the contractor.

The Fieldman shall, on request, furnish the contractor or the grower a written statement showing the acreage of the respective classes of work when completed by the contractor if requested to do so to settle a dispute. The grower agrees to furnish the contractor a statement of the tonnage delivered to the Sugar Company from his contracted acreage.

The grower shall, on request, furnish the contractor a written statement of any charge made to the account of the contractor by the grower for monies advanced or for commodities sold or furnished by the grower to the contractor. Such statements will be furnished by the grower to the contractor at the time of the transaction and will set forth the amount of the charge and kind of commodity for which the charge is made.

The above conditions shall be binding upon both parties unless changed by mutual agreement and noted in writing on the contract.

Canada developed a humane, indentured-servitude system to address DP needs and meet local labor shortages. The government paid passage rather than the employer, reducing employer power. The time of indenture was shorter than the four to seven years common earlier and could not be extended. The agricultural workers could earn outside income when not busy in the field. And there were no negative consequences if they left their employer, although the Wagners were not aware of this. By the time the Zoltais came a year later, the program was even friendlier. The contract, as explained to them, was only for one year and the International Refugee Organization paid their ocean travel.

The Wagners viewed Canada's worker program as a godsend. Indentured servitude offered a way out of Europe and the imminent threat of war. Their days were filled with hard physical labor, but they were pleased with their new life and excited by the many opportunities in Canada. Like most of the over 50,000 DPs entering as domestic, factory, and farm workers, they made sure to fulfill their terms.

One of the challenges: they weren't paid for their work until after harvest. "How do we pay for clothes, food, and other things we need now?" Eugene Bácsi asked Jula the day they arrived. This question had been gnawing away at him, like shoes two sizes too small, ever since he signed on to come to Canada.

'Don't worry," Jula said. "I'll set up credit for you at the local store. You can buy what you need, then pay after harvest. You can also work in town when there isn't farm work. There's really only a couple months field work."

Before they began their field work, Olga worked three weeks at a Chinese restaurant in Raymond, returning whenever the beets didn't need attention. The restaurant was on the main street, sandwiched between stores and offices, its two large picture windows offering a ringside view of any action in the tiny town of a couple thousand. Smells of sizzling steaks and burgers, deep-frying potatoes, dominated the twenty-four table establishment. Only rarely did the predominantly Canadian clientele order the Chinese food on the menu.

Olga's job was to carry out empty pop bottles and wash dishes. With the place filling up most evenings after farm work was over, Olga kept fairly busy. The Chinese proprietor paid her forty-five cents an hour, close to double what the family estimated they would earn on the farm. And she was paid promptly, not months later!

When it became clear the parents couldn't handle the back-breaking farm work, Eugene Bácsi looked for full-time employment. By mid-summer, he was hired as a loom mechanic in a small textile factory in the town of Magrath, about twelve miles from the farm. His salary was excellent compared to farm wages. He was paid sixty-two cents per hour, the non-farm minimum wage for men. He rented a room in Magrath, since walking five hours to and from work every day wasn't feasible. The family only saw him on Sundays.

At the end of the harvest, the Wagners were paid for their farm work. The sugar factory handled measuring the fields and figuring out farm worker pay, making the process transparent.

"We got paid about $41 dollars per acre, like the contract promised," Eugene Bácsi said to the family seated around the wood table in their cabin.

"How much is that per hour?" Olga asked.

Eugene Bácsi added up their estimated hours on a piece of paper and divided it by the payment. "About twenty-five cents."

"After we pay the store, we'll have some left," Maria Néni said.

"If we add the money from the restaurant and factory," Eugene Bácsi said with head held high, "we can make our first payment to the government."

* * *

When the sugar beet season ended, the family dispersed: Eugene Bácsi remained in Magrath; Maria Néni, Olga, and Andy moved into Raymond; Gene headed to Toronto to scout opportunities for the family after their contracted term.

Uprooting the whole family and moving to the city was very risky, since there was no welfare safety net and no assurance of work or shelter. Finding work and a place to live, Gene eased their transition.

Olga thoroughly enjoyed the apartment she, Maria Néni, and Andy rented in Raymond, a few blocks from the restaurant. It was the second story of a single family dwelling. Officially it only had two bedrooms, but there was a large walk-in closet that Olga made into her own private room. Her brother teased, she could stand in her room and touch all the walls at once, but it didn't matter, it was hers.

She also marveled at the apartment's amazing appliances. A refrigerator, so food stayed fresh longer. A communal electric wash machine, so they didn't have to hand power the agitator. A gas stove and central heating, so they didn't need to chop wood or stoke a fire. Without the scent and smoke of burning wood, the apartment was different than anywhere she had ever lived.

Like a lot of farm towns in rural North America, the dozen streets of Raymond clustered around the main highway. Unlike neighboring towns, there were no bars, no liquor stores, no gambling, or houses of ill-repute—the Mormon town founders at the turn of the century had written the town charter to inhibit such establishments.

Olga and Andy attended school. Olga started in the tenth grade, and by February was able to pass an exam to advance to eleventh. She found school fascinating, a good place to learn English and study Canadian youth. High school, in Canada, was quite different than gymnasium in Hungary. Boys and girls were in the same school, even the same classes. Youth who wanted to go into a trade and those planning to study at a university were mixed together as well. Classes were more casual, no one wore a uniform. Back home, contact between boys and girls was very restricted, occurring only in dance class or other supervised places. Olga remembered teenage boys even being kicked out of their school if seen alone with a teenage girl. But here, the girls wore bright red lipstick and openly flirted with boys, often without an adult even around.

Olga kept her job at the restaurant, working after school. Soon, she was promoted to being a waitress part-time, and Maria Néni came in to help wash dishes. The Chinese proprietor liked Olga and Maria Néni, especially their work ethic. He offered to buy the family a farm if they would stay after their contract obligations. But a lifetime of the physically grueling farm work and the isolation of the Alberta prairie were not appealing to any of the Wagners.

While Olga didn't want to live in Raymond forever, she still found it exciting to meet all the different people who came to the restaurant: immigrants from Japan, China, Russia, Belgium, Germany, and many more countries. They followed religions she never knew existed, all believing theirs was the true faith. She listened to the Mormon customers enthusiastically explain their religion and customs. Hungarian Seventh-Day Adventists believed with absolute certainty the world would end in two months. Ethnic German Hutterites and Mennonites, who left Russia due to religious persecution when the country became Communist, were easy to identify, always dressed in black, the women with coarse ankle-length-woven dresses and knitted caps. The Hutterites lived together on a communal farm and sold the restaurant fresh, crisp produce. Olga felt their strict rules made Catholicism look flexible.

As the snow melted and buds appeared on the trees, the Zoltai family joined the Wagners in Canada. Olga had helped find a sponsoring farmer, asking Jula to query his contacts and directly asking farmers dining at the restaurant. Finally, Olga found them work on a German immigrant's farm.

Unlike the Wagners, who had to pay the government back for their cost of passage, the International Refugee Organization paid the Zoltais' ocean liner fare. They were only responsible to their farmer for the cost of train fare. And the Zoltais' labor contract was only for one sugar beet season, so both families would finish at the end of the 1950 harvest.

It was wonderful not to have thousands of miles of land and ocean between them, but fifteen miles of paved road still separated their homes and kept them from visiting as often as they wished. Once or twice a week, they were able to catch a ride or take a bus to see each other. At eighteen, Olga had matured, Tibor also, now twenty-four. Olga had cut her youthful braids, her figure had continued to blossom. She had become more confident, sure of herself. Tibor had put on much-needed weight, his hairline was receding, and his optimism was firmly back in place.

As they spent time together, their love bloomed. No one could be in the same room without sensing their attraction: their eyes tracking each other, their intimate smiles, their whispered words.

At first, Tibor was hesitant to ask Olga to marry him, since he didn't yet have a strong job prospect to support a wife. Both families convinced the young couple not to wait. They needed to follow their hearts.

Like Olga's parents, Lili Néni and Nicholas Bácsi had trouble with the back-breaking farm work. So the bulk of the hoeing fell to Tibor and Steve, physically challenging for Tibor with his bad knee. But his determination was strong. He and Steve quickly had a rhythmic chop and scrape in place, steadily working their way through the first hoeing.

Once their hands became dirt-stained and blistered, neither Tibor nor Olga had time to visit each other. But as soon as the young men finished their acres, they went to help the Wagner youth. With Gene in Toronto, hoeing their forty acres was a daunting challenge for Olga and Andy.

Whenever possible, the four youth hoed together. First they did the Wagners' acres and then the Zoltais'. Hoeing together gave Olga and Tibor the opportunity to spend more time with each other.

"Let's take turns telling stories. It'll make the work more fun," Tibor suggested. Seeing nods, he continued, "The story can be about a book you've read, a movie you've seen, or your own creation."

Turns lasted for the time it took to hoe a row, an hour or so. The youth worked adjacent rows and kept a similar up-and-down rhythm. No one wanted to fall behind and have the story stolen by the dust and wind. Each would strain toward the speaker not to miss a word.

Tibor has such delightful ideas, thought Olga. The stories made the long hours bent over a hoe fly by.

Steve was the best at recounting movies. He provided so much vivid detail that the characters and action came to life. It was almost as if you sat next to him in the theater.

Tibor was the best at imaginative fantasies. Olga's favorite was when man landed on the moon. It made a major impression because it had never occurred to her that man might travel there. In Tibor's story, humans traveled in an innovative metal spaceship, encountered special beings like dwarves who were green. The two species didn't have a common language, but with a lot of patience and sign language, they were able to communicate.

The hoeing progressed rapidly. So fast, they actually took on hoeing for another farmer, born in Canada to Hungarian parents. When he spoke Hungarian, he used English words with Hungarian suffixes and grammar. Olga enjoyed his speaking style.

"Watch-oj Tibor a ditch-en mert be-plug-ol az engine (Tibor, watch out in the ditch so the engine doesn't plug)," was a typical comment the farmer made. Learning English was not easy with all the rules and exceptions to rules, so Olga appreciated he made the effort to speak Hungarian.

Olga and Tibor continued to correspond when they weren't hoeing. Since neither family had a phone, this was their way to stay in touch. In July, Olga sent her first letter in English: "My Darling, I thought it is a good idea to write you an English letter. By examining you I found out how well you speak the language and after mine opinion it would be a great enjoyment to correspond with you in English. First of all we can practise correct spelling, vocabulary, the different part of the speech and not at least we might have some funn."

Olga had invested a lot of heart and effort in learning to read, speak, and even write in her new language. She glowed inside at her elevated status in the family as the main translator. The following poem captures the challenge all members of both families confronted in learning English.

> Let's face it - English is a crazy language.
> There is no egg in eggplant, nor ham in hamburger;
> neither apple nor pine in pineapple . . .
> And why is it that writers write but fingers don't fing,
> grocers don't groce and hammers don't ham?
> If the plural of tooth is teeth, why isn't the plural of
> booth, beeth?

One goose, two geese. So one moose, two meese? . . .
If teachers taught, why didn't preachers praught?
If a vegetarian eats vegetables, what does a
humanitarian eat?
Sometimes I think all the English speakers should be
committed to an asylum for the verbally insane.
In what language do people recite at a play and play
at a recital?
Ship by truck and send cargo by ship?
Have noses that run and feet that smell? . . .

Author Unknown

"I'm not finding work," Eugene Bácsi told his family releasing a sigh. It was summer and they were relaxing over dinner, savoring the daylight hours that lingered long into the evening. His plant had shut down and he was searching for another job in the area.

"My friend in Calgary wrote that her family easily found work." Olga was corresponding with a Hungarian woman she'd met on their train ride from Halifax to the prairie. Calgary, a 160 miles away, was the nearest big city, with a population of about 130,000.

Nicholas Bácsi joined Eugene Bácsi as he headed to Calgary to look for work. The fathers quickly found jobs at a landscaping service with help from local Hungarians. Eugene Bácsi also began teaching classes in Oriental rug weaving at the local arts council.

In early August after the third hoeing, Olga, Tibor, and Maria Néni joined the fathers. The young couple stayed in Calgary until October, when they returned to Raymond for harvest. Through the contacts of her Hungarian friend, Olga found work cleaning houses. She also helped translate for her father's rug weaving classes. Tibor found day-labor work.

Olga and
Eugene Bácsi
in Calgary
boarding
house,
fall 1950.

Intense pain had driven Maria Néni to a doctor in Raymond, who recommended she go to Calgary for an emergency hysterectomy. Accompanying the young couple to the city, soon she was scheduled for the operation.

Olga left their boarding house in the densely packed neighborhood and woodenly boarded a bus the morning of the surgery, her first day of work at her new cleaning job. She mindlessly followed the directions to get to the job provided by her Hungarian friend, her thoughts focused on her mother. If only she could have spent the day at her side.

Her mother had been in pain for so long from an ovarian cyst, almost twelve years. She had been putting off operating because she feared complications and infections from the knife more than the pain. But now the pain had worsened, and her mother had no choice.

Olga arrived at the plush neighborhood filled with gracious homes and rolling lawns. The woman of the house was cheerful and talkative. As the day progressed, she asked Olga about herself.

"Where are you from?" she probed. "When did you come to Calgary?"

As conversation continued, Olga explained her thoughts were with her mother who was having surgery.

"Which hospital?"

Olga told her.

"My husband works there!"

The woman called her husband to see if she could learn how Maria Néni was doing.

"My husband's your mother's surgeon. Your mother's case is quite serious, but the surgery's over. Your mother is recovering nicely."

Olga thanked her again and again, awed at the coincidence. The husband of this gracious woman was the surgeon! What a fortuitous start to their new life in Calgary.

Part II

Building a Future as Americans

8

Canada, We Want to Build Your Future (1950 - 1959)

Olga and Tibor Zoltai, 1950

Joyous bells ringing in the steeple announced Tibor and Olga's wedding day, November 18, 1950. The small brick Catholic Church in their densely packed neighborhood was mostly empty—only family and the president of the local Hungarian club and his wife had been invited—but incense lingered in the air and stained-glass windows added a glow to the off-white plaster walls.

Tibor, his light brown hair receding, stood proudly in a dark-blue double-breasted suit and dark red tie. Olga, in her gold wool wedding suit, brunette hair combed back in soft waves, reverently faced the vestibule as the elderly Canadian priest recited scripture and the traditional words that would join them as husband and wife.

When it came time for the vows, Tibor wasn't able to quite correctly repeat the English. "I, Tibor Zoltai," he said, "take you, Olga Vagner for my awfully vedded vife," starting a story that was retold for decades.

After the vows, Olga turned to look back at her parents. Her father's face was wet with tears. She rarely saw him cry, even during the hardship of the war and its aftermath. Her mother smiled at her, love in her eyes.

As the newly married couple strolled out of the church, the sidewalk was covered with a light layer of fresh snow. Tibor and Olga's side-by-side footprints were visible on the snowy sidewalk as they started their new life together. There hadn't been enough money for family, spread across two provinces, to congregate for the traditional Hungarian engagement party, nor could they afford the luxury of a white wedding dress for Olga to wear. But the love between them was strong. They had survived the war and emigration, and here they were, together.

Olga and Tibor had three marvelous honeymoon days in a Banff lodge, engulfed in the familiar scent of pine, the surrounding majestic mountains and alpine landscapes reminiscent of where they had met in the Austrian Alps. With no work, no obligations, nothing they had to do, they reveled in each other's company. When they returned, the couple moved into their own one-room apartment. At $50 a month, it was an exorbitant price for their income. Olga only earned $5 a day cleaning houses; this was half her month's salary. By the second month, they found a much more reasonably priced studio apartment at $20 a month. They shared a bathroom with other tenants and covered the grimy walls with fresh paint, but they were very pleased.

As soon as the grime was hidden under paint, they invited Tibor's parents over for dinner. Olga double-checked that everything was ready for their first guests, the secondhand Formica table properly set in the kitchen alcove, and the used sofa bed, two chairs, coffee table, and desk were neat. She uncovered the soup, the smell of cooking potatoes adding to the hearty smell of bacon and the lingering odor of paint cleaner already in the room.

She was planning to serve savory-sour potato soup seasoned with paprika, followed by Turós Tézta, Tibor's favorite dish. Olga had made the el dente pasta for the Turós Tézta by hand. Before serving she planned to add soft cottage cheese curds and thick-cut rendered bacon chunks. Rich homemade sour cream was set on the table for everyone to add themselves.

As the two generations of Zoltais sat down at the table, everyone chatted except Nicholas Bácsi. He immediately picked up his spoon and inhaled his soup.

"It smells of turpentine," Nicholas Bácsi said, setting down his spoon with a clink.

"We just finished painting," Tibor said. "The turpentine smell isn't quite gone." As Tibor explained, Olga began eating her soup.

"This soup tastes like turpentine!" Olga said, turning pink. Turpentine and vinegar were both stored in the apartment's one closet; both glass bottles looked identical and had transparent, free-flowing liquids. Had she accidentally put in a couple of tablespoons turpentine, instead of vinegar?

Thankfully the rest of the meal was delicious.

L to r. Lili Néni, Olga, and Nicholas Bácsi in Tibor and Olga's apartment in Calgary, 1950.

Like everyone in their extended families, Tibor and Olga took whatever work they could find, living frugally. Olga continued cleaning gracious homes with rolling lawns, working in a Chinese restaurant, and Tibor got a high-paying union job in a meat-packing plant, pulling the warm, bloody pig carcasses along on the assembly line and scrubbing the large slop trays.

To save money, they walked everywhere, rarely using the bus even when the wind whipped at their clothes on blustery winter days. They bought inexpensive food and made it stretch. They rolled Tibor's cigarettes, wrapping the moist, fragrant tobacco in white paper sheets, rather than buy them ready made.

In April 1951, Tibor was laid off. The couple moved to Toronto where both their families now lived. To accommodate the young couple, Eugene Bácsi and Maria Néni rented a larger place, one-half of a three-story brick duplex, putting Olga and Tibor on the second floor.

Olga found an office job at an insurance company that she enjoyed. Tibor looked for work in a dental lab as a technician specializing in gold. A Hungarian acquaintance in Calgary, a dental technician, had spent several evenings showing Tibor how to make gold crowns and bridges. With Tibor's science education in Graz, experience carving, and this instruction, he felt he could do the dental technician work.

But he was turned away by a number of labs.

Not ready to give up, his next visit was to a one-man operation. The meticulously groomed older proprietor wore a lab coat, vest, and tie. He looked Tibor over through his wire-rimmed frames. "I'll give you a chance to show what you can do," he said, leading Tibor to his lab. "Here's an order. If you do it well, I'll hire you."

It was a real order for a two-tooth gold bridge, complete with specifications. Tibor meticulously carved a model out of wax. He then used the model to make a plaster mold, and poured hot, molten gold into the mold. Once the metal hardened, he polished the bridge to a golden sheen.

"Good work," the older man said, painstakingly examining Tibor's finished product. "Can you start next week?"

Olga's father earned a decent salary, once again working in his field supervising weavers and maintaining looms in a textile mill. He also taught Oriental rug weaving classes through a technical school. A Toronto newspaper did a story on him in January 1952: "Mr. Wagner is about to set two precedents in his adopted land: He will introduce rug-weaving into the night school course at Central Technical School, for the first time in a technical school in this country; and as a teacher, he will be the first to require the services of an interpreter."

In February 1954, a picture of Eugene Bácsi and Olga appeared in the same newspaper with a caption about weaving being a family craft in Eugene Bácsi's home. "Since the family brought away from Hungary only what each could carry in a handbag," said the article, "family rugs were left behind but Mr. Wagner brought a few little tapestry-like pieces—400 knots to the square inch. After he came to Canada he copied a portrait of King George VI in this technique—it looks like a very fine petit point—finishing it just at the time of the king's death. He sent it as a gift to Queen Elizabeth who was so touched that she waived the usual Royal rule against accepting gifts from strangers." Pride in his eyes, Eugene Bácsi was always quick to point out that his son Gene actually translated the picture of King George VI into a knotting pattern.

Eugene Bácsi added the Queen's thank-you letter to his collection of family treasures, pleased the family was making a place for themselves in their new world.

L. to r. Olga, Tibor, Maria Néni, Eugene Bácsi, Andy, and Gene in Toronto, 1951.

After eighteen months in Toronto, the young couple had enough savings for Tibor's university tuition. Olga found a higher-paying job on a General Electric television assembly line to cover their living expenses so Tibor didn't have to work during the school year. She made $1.20 per hour, plus bonuses, but the work sucked the energy out of her.

GE's efficiency expert defined how many units it was possible to solder a minute. The fifteen-woman line had to work at this speed or faster, and the fastest woman, at the front, dictated the speed. Such pace required tremendous concentration, continuously using both hands, over and over, the hot tip of Olga's solder iron melted the solder. This released a small puff of noxious fumes and caused the shiny metal alloy to adhere the wire to the electronic part. Not one minute of stoppage was permitted. If a worker backed up two or more TV sets, she was fired.

By 5:00 p.m. each day Olga felt as limp as a wrung-out cloth. Just thinking about the job made her muscles ache, but she stayed at it two years. Once they could afford it, she went back to the insurance company.

Before registering for university, Tibor needed to define his major. In France he was driven by a yearning to write philosophy; now his career interests were more practical. He wanted a career where he could support his wife and future children.

"What fields will be in demand over the next few decades?" Tibor asked Steve and Gene. The three were ensconced on the secondhand sofa and chairs in the diminutive living room of the Wagner's duplex. All three, starting the university that fall in 1952, needed to pick an area to study.

"The country has a population of close to fourteen million," one of them said.

"Lots of opportunity to grow," another said.

"Land will need to be developed," the third added. "That will require engineers and scientists."

Steve decided to study forestry, Gene geophysics, and Tibor mining-engineering-geology.

Tibor and Gene were admitted as sophomores based on prior college transcripts. Steve started as a freshman, his university transcript from Graz successfully avoiding any question of high-school graduation.

Tibor studying in Toronto, 1953.

Tibor studied diligently during the school year and did field work for Anaconda Copper during the summer break. The first year he explored for copper in Quebec, the next two in New Brunswick. "For most of Canada," Tibor explained to Olga when she visited the first summer, "mineral rights are owned by the government, but anyone can lease the rights for specific tracts of land." A gesture reinforced the point. "Right now, there are a lot of companies competing to stake lucrative claims." Tibor's eyes lit up when he talked about his work. They were sitting on the bed of their pocket-sized motel room near Tibor's field-work site.

"Before we can explore an area," Tibor went on, "we have to get permission of the local priest—the most influential person in the community."

"Is it hard to get?"

"It's the toughest part of my job. So far, we've been lucky."

The couple had spent the better part of the week sightseeing in Montreal and Quebec City. Tomorrow Olga was accompanying Tibor to the field. "What time do we need to leave?"

"Seven should be fine," Tibor said. "You'll need to be careful, the bush can be dangerous. If you see a deer or moose, shimmy up a tree. But if you see a bear, don't climb, they can follow you up. Run. You can probably outrun it."

Tibor in the bush, 1950s.

The terrain they traversed was rocky. Spruce, fir, and poplar trees worked hard to grow in the thin soil. Rich earth smell filled the air.

There were many bare, scraggly outcrops of rock. Tibor thoroughly enjoyed his job; pride was in his voice as he explained his work to Olga: surveying an area, noting the kinds of rocks and formations present, learning geologic history, studying evidence of mineralization to identify possible copper deposits. In the process he would systematically break off rock samples with his pick to evaluate copper and other mineral content.

Although Olga didn't have to climb or run to avoid wildlife, later that fall during mating season, Tibor's pick hammering on rock attracted a moose. The massive animal was over 1,000 pounds and six feet tall with majestic antlers. He charged in, ready to defend his territory and mating rights. Apparently to the moose, the clunk of Tibor's pick sounded like the threatening thrashing of another moose's antlers in the brush.

Dr. Cheriton, Tibor's supervisor, was a lanky man with wavy black hair and an engaging smile. He had gotten his PhD. from Harvard a few years earlier. Tibor admired his abilities and knowledge, valued his mentoring. When Tibor completed his bachelor degree and there were no good job prospects, Dr. Cheriton encouraged him to pursue graduate studies at the Massachusetts Institute of Technology. Tibor was accepted to begin in the fall of 1955.

Before heading south to school, Tibor and Olga spent the summer in Bathurst, New Brunswick. They shared a small ocean cottage with the exploration team. Fine sand beach extended as far as they could see in either direction. The fresh smell of the salty sea breeze filled their cabin, and each morning they watched the fiery sun rise out of the cool Atlantic waters.

* * *

In surveying the rocky, forested terrain, Tibor found an anomaly in the geologic formation of the area. Pursuing a hypothesis, he discovered a major ore deposit so significant that later in the fall Anaconda awarded Tibor an annual scholarship for each of his four years at MIT, worth more than twenty-four months of his field work salary.

But with the aggressive competition to file claims, the rumor of Tibor's ore discovery charged the atmosphere like a lightning storm.

"A spy visited our field office today!" Tibor told Olga one day. They were sitting in their private room of the shared summer cottage. "He tried to steal our findings!"

"Oh, my God!" Olga said, her jaw dropping. "How?"

"He had a camera hidden in his cigarette lighter. He tried to sneak a picture of our survey maps."

"Did he get one?"

"No. We took away his camera."

The summer in New Brunswick was a magical time for Olga and Tibor. They spent many hours walking along the beach hand-in-hand listening to the waves, the smooth sand under their feet warm from the summer sun. They had time to admire the shifting sands, the changes brought by the tide, and the ocean life. During low tide, they could even walk a half-mile into the ocean and look at the many translucent jellyfish the tide left behind. Locals warned them to be cautious of these creatures, since they had a poisonous sting. Having never lived by an ocean before, Olga was mesmerized by all the sea life but especially the jellyfish.

When they were invited to the home of a local family for a cocktail party, shrimp was served in a cocktail glass with ambient sea water. Olga and Tibor exchanged glances, neither quite sure what to do. They carefully watched as the locals ate the shrimp then downed the sea water. They both ate the odd tasting dense seafood, but neither managed the warm salty water chaser.

Tibor and Olga's favorite experience was the Lobster Festival down the coast. They had never seen anything remotely like this. The festival was held on the beach. There were giant bonfires with large kettles of gurgling, boiling water. The unfamiliar pungent aroma of lobster mingled with the salty breeze and steam. The live drab colored lobsters with snapping claws were dropped into the boiling water and emerged motionless and glowing bright red! For $1 a piece, Tibor and Olga could eat all the lobster they wanted. The giant, vivid red mountains of discarded shells made a lasting memory.

As the birds prepared to migrate south, Dr. Cheriton gave Olga and Tibor a ride down the golden coastline to Massachusetts. Olga planned to find a job to support them, while Tibor worked on his PhD. in mineralogy.

At the U.S. border, a guard asked for their papers. Tibor and Olga had recently passed their Canadian citizenship exam and proudly presented their new passports and U.S. visas.

"Everything looks in order," the uniformed official said, returning their papers.

"May I please have an employment authorization?" Olga asked.

"You don't qualify, ma'am. In other respects you're a Canadian citizen. Regarding employment, the U.S. government considers you a citizen of your birth country."

Olga and Tibor exchanged worried looks. Back in Canada, they had been told that as a Canadian citizen Olga could work in the U.S. The advice obviously came from someone unfamiliar with the distinction the U.S. made between those born Canadian and those naturalized later in life. How were they going to be able to pay their living expenses? Olga stewed on the problem for days until she came up with a plan.

"I've an idea how we can make ends meet!" Olga said eyes alight. They were in their room at a boarding house in Boston. Tibor was sitting on the double bed looking over materials he had picked up at MIT.

"How?" Tibor said, looking up.

"I'll put an ad in the Boston paper: 'Willing to Baby Sit in Exchange for Room & Board for Student Couple.' I won't violate my visa, since I won't be paid money."

Olga got two responses to her ad. She selected a nice family in the suburb of West Newton. They had a beautiful house, garden, and rolling lawn not far from a bus line into Boston. The family had two adopted boys, ages eight and ten. Olga and Tibor got to use a large furnished bedroom and bathroom on the lower level of the split-entry house. Their food was provided by the family. In exchange, Olga cared for the boys, house sat when the family traveled, and shared in the cooking responsibilities.

It was easy work. While the kids were in school, Olga even had an opportunity to attend English classes for the first time.

The summer in New Brunswick, the school year in Boston were the couple's first deep immersion in North American culture. While they had submerged their toes in the cultural waters over the last few years, even took dips in the workplace, they always came home to Hungarian culture. In Calgary, they lived near Tibor's family and other Hungarians. In Toronto, they lived communally in Olga's parent's home for two years. Then they jointly bought a house with Tibor's parents, Steve and his Hungarian wife, Elizabeth. The three families shared communal meals and even had several Hungarian neighbors.

Now they were with Americans day and night. They talked English, ate American food, began to learn American culture. They learned that in America main meals don't always start with soup. Servings of meat are huge. Elders are addressed more casually. Less respect is shown for people in authority positions. Americans need more personal space, less touch. They bathe more frequently. They use deodorant, a product new to Tibor and Olga. Women shave their legs and underarms. The American life style is based on abundance. Americans regularly volunteer for worthy causes, a concept not practiced in Europe. The list went on. All the new rules made their stomach muscles tighten.

Along their journey to learn American ways, they sometimes misstepped. Like when Olga's employer had a coat delivered to the house in a completely sealed paper covering. Olga, trying to be helpful, accepted the delivery, carefully unwrapped the package, and hung it up in the closet. At the crestfallen look on her employer's face, she later discovered that her employer had specifically paid to have the coat wrapped in the protective covering for storage.

Many of the new cultural practices they took on as their own. Others they chose not to. They adapted personal space, greetings, and hygiene. They learned to like the abundant seafood eaten along the coast and wholeheartedly got into volunteerism. But they didn't change their frugal ways. Nor did they give up the European eating etiquette of constantly holding the fork in the left hand and knife in the right. They found the habit of frequently setting down their knife and moving the fork to the right hand cumbersome.

The young couple even entered the world of American consumerism. They bought their first car, a 1947 Studebaker for $100. The black convertible had red leather seats, a little stained and cracked, and the retracting roof hadn't worked in years, but that didn't matter. The manual transmission with its steady purr enabled them to drive the ten hours to Toronto to spend Christmas with family.

Sitting in the Studebaker's red leather driver's seat, Tibor glanced over at Olga. His wife shifted in her seat, folding her hands over her heavily rounded belly. Tibor smiled at her and Olga's eyes twinkled in return. The late spring sun shone brightly through their windows, reflecting their radiant mood.

After six years of marriage, they were expecting their first child. They had been wondering if the miracle was ever going to happen.

When the couple arrived at the Wagners' home in Toronto, they were smothered in hugs and kisses. After a few days of visiting, Tibor was up with the sun to continue his trek northeast alone. Olga was spending the summer with her parents in their newly purchased home, while Tibor worked again in the field.

On June 30, 1956, a week earlier than expected, Olga gave birth to a healthy baby boy. Peter Tibor Zoltai was called a "lightning baby," since labor was under two hours. Extended family came to visit Peter that first day, their excitement lighting up the sterile, bland hospital room.

Olga's parents came first, anxious to see their first grandchild. They exclaimed he looked just like 'this' Wagner family member and didn't he have 'that' family member's nose. Tibor's parents said he looked exactly like 'this' Zoltai family member and weren't his eyes the same color as 'that' family member. The process was repeated over and over as Olga's brothers, Steve and Elizabeth, and even Jenci Bácsi's wife came. Jenci Bácsi, his wife, and their children had joined the extended family in Canada four years earlier when Olga helped arrange for Nicholas Bácsi to be their sponsor.

Olga's smile reflected the joy of having her first child after years of waiting, being once again surrounded by family, and the irony of how everyone seemed to think Peter looked like a different member of their family.

Tibor wasn't able to be at the birth. But he, Olga, and Peter had precious time together in mid-July when Tibor visited Toronto. He was again working for Anaconda in New Brunswick, this time as a mining engineer, doing work on the copper deposit he had discovered.

Olga holding
Peter, 1956.

It was a lazy, warm August day. A light breeze blew in through the lace curtains of Olga and Peter's room on the second floor of Maria Néni and Eugene Bácsi's newly purchased three-story boarding house. Olga lifted Peter out of his basket on the table. He was wearing a white sweater outfit and booties she had crocheted with love. The innocent smell of new baby made her smile. As she gazed into his brown eyes and gently stroked his brown hair, she wondered, what kind of life will Peter have?

Would he want ties with Hungary? Or would he reject his parents' heritage and consider himself only Canadian? She pondered what kind of parent she would be. She wanted to be more flexible than her mother, but would Peter still be frustrated with her old world ways, like Andy was with Maria Néni?

Her parents were having trouble raising Andy in Toronto. Andy didn't have a Hungarian identity as a foundation to build on, like Gene and Olga did. Olga was proud of who she was and didn't feel a need to become Canadian at any cost. But Andy was only eight when they left Hungary, with the last five years under the upheaval of war. He spent four formative years in Austria where they moved four times and the locals resented them. At nineteen, Andy had been in Canada for seven years in three different locales. Until he was fifteen, he only had acquaintances outside the family, not even someone he could call a close friend. It wasn't surprising he was seeking an identity, a group where he belonged. He was so smart, Olga thought. He can speak three languages without an accent. He could be successful in whatever career he wanted, but he wasn't interested in education. All he really wanted was to be part of the Canadian world.

Contrasted with his enthusiasm, her parents only spoke a thousand words of English. They still went to a Hungarian church, a Hungarian doctor, a Hungarian grocery store. The big city outside of the Hungarian community was intimidating, not inviting like for the teenage Andy who spoke like a native.

Her parents were trying to raise him according to the Hungarian Catholic parenting style, with strict rules that worked when they lived in the small village of Raymond, but set off fireworks with Andy as soon as they moved to Toronto.

"Hey look, that car has keys in it," a somewhat intoxicated Andy said to friends the night before Peter was born. "Let's take it for a ride." The piercing sound of a police siren ended the adventure.

The boys were taken to the police station, fingerprinted, and booked. Andy spent the night behind bars for car theft. He was arraigned the morning of June 30. With solemn faces, Olga and her parents appeared in court on his behalf. He was released on probation.

Andy didn't like being arrested, Olga thought, as she reflected on the day. However Andy's independent spirit certainly bristled when Maria Néni laid on a guilt trip. Not just for stealing, but for Olga going into early labor after court. Even with his outward show of bravado, she thought the night behind bars made a lasting impression.

Olga would have been comforted if she could have seen the future. How Andy would never again be behind bars. How within a few years he would get into a good trade and successfully forge his own path.

In the fall, Tibor and Olga bundled up Peter, retraced their route to Boston, and continued to pursue their own path. The three of them moved into graduate-student housing near Massachusetts Avenue in the heart of the city, a block from MIT. The housing had been built for veterans returning from World War II, but the flow had evaporated so the housing was now open to graduate students. There was a sense of community amongst the young couples living in the two-bedroom apartments and cottages. The couples were all similar in age. The men attended MIT and the women had babies, regularly babysitting for each other's children. Olga furnished their unit buying items from departing graduate students that were functional but not pretty, the living room sofa was covered in enormous faded green and beige flowers that Olga found hideous.

Tibor's performance the prior year earned him a teaching assistantship with the world-renowned professor Dr. Buerger, who taught crystallography. This position meant no tuition and a stipend, which when combined with the Anaconda scholarship, covered expenses. Olga didn't need to work outside the home.

MIT Graduate Student housing, 1950s. Tibor and Olga's unit was on the second floor, far left.

But developments in the world did not stay outside their home.

"Revolution in Hungary! Revolution in Hungary!" yelled a newspaper boy, holding up the day's paper as he trotted along Massachusetts Ave. His high pitched voice was audible over the purring engines and other street noises. It was October 23, 1956.

Tibor and Olga rushed to buy a copy before the newspaper boy dove between cars. Hurriedly, they scanned the article. A revolution had erupted in Budapest against the one-party Communist regime.

Tibor and Olga followed the newspaper stories each day, hoping the freedom fighters would succeed. Hoping the U.S. would provide assistance. Hoping their homeland would once again be independent.

The first eight days were encouraging. It appeared the entire nation was taking up arms against the regime. The Russians were retreating. On October 31, Olga and Tibor were glued to President Eisenhower's television address when the president rejected any action, diplomatic or otherwise. The U.S. would not interfere in what was referred to as internal affairs of the Soviet Union.

On November 1, Hungary declared itself a neutral power. It withdrew from the Warsaw Treaty. Hungary's appeal to the United Nations for military help went unanswered. The Soviet troops and tanks returned. The Soviets crushed the revolution in a matter of days, as easily as red peppers are crushed into paprika.

"The U.S. handled things badly," Tibor and Olga explained to friends. "Radio Free Europe, which the CIA sponsors, encouraged Hungarians to fight, to believe Western support was coming. But when they fought, no help came. The Americans broke their promise!"

Over the next months, an estimated 200,000 freedom fighters and their families fled to the west, 80,000 coming to the U.S. Olga spent countless hours as a volunteer translator for local churches helping the refugees.

Olga particularly treasured the story of one 1956 refugee woman in her late fifties. It got to the core of what Olga thought was important in life. "When my husband and sons fled," the woman explained, "I stayed to tend my sick aunt. Once she was better, I set out for the border on foot. I was crossing at night and sunk deep into the mucky soil near the border." The muck adhered to her boots like honey. "I eventually had to yell for help. My plea was answered by a border guard. The guard was under orders to shoot all escapees and approached me with his gun raised. Seeing my age and situation, he didn't shoot but demanded: 'Why are you crossing alone? What do you have in your bag?' " The woman clutched her handbag as she continued telling her story. "I explained I had the three most important things in the world in my bag: my praying book, my family photo album, and my cookbook. He lowered his gun and helped me across."

Olga (*left*) and friend at international exhibit hosted by MIT student wives' group, late 1950s.

As 1956 melted into 1957, Tibor and Olga settled into a routine. Tibor took classes and worked on his PhD. research with Dr. Buerger while still finding time to spend with his wife and son. In the summer of 1957, Tibor worked again for Anaconda. The three of them spent magical summer months at the cottage on the coast of New Brunswick, reveling as Peter's first tentative steps evolved into sure-footed running.

While Tibor worked at school, Olga cared for Peter and joined the MIT student wives group. She enjoyed the group's activities, especially the international exhibit they hosted where she was responsible for the Hungarian booth. On several occasions, they were invited by the professors' wives for formal afternoon tea, a new and memorable experience for Olga. Everyone wore immaculate white gloves, stylish hats, beautiful fitted dresses, matching high-heeled shoes, and a touch of perfume. They stood around daintily holding delicate fine china tea cups with their white-gloved hands, and kept up light conversation.

"We interrupt this program for late-breaking news," reported the radio announcer the evening of October 4, 1957. "The Official Soviet News Agency Tass has announced that earlier today the Soviet Union created the world's first artificial satellite of the Earth."

They were driving to Washington D.C. to attend a scientific conference. Tibor cranked up the volume on the radio of their aging Studebaker.

"The Tass press release," the announcer continued, "states a rocket launcher carried the satellite to the necessary orbital speed. The world's first artificial moon, called Sputnik 1, is continuously sending out radio signals." The pinging beep of Sputnik's signal eerily projected out of the radio.

"How did the Soviets get ahead?" Tibor murmured. The purr of their engine and flash of headlights from oncoming traffic faded into nothingness. For hours they sat riveted to each word of the broadcast, wondering what did this mean to their new country.

Over the next several days, weeks and even months, Sputnik dominated all conversations. Among MIT staff and students was fear that the Soviets had ballistic missile capability. Tibor and Olga watched as Sputnik 1 had a 'Pearl Harbor' effect on American public opinion, providing impetus for increased spending on aerospace endeavors, and scientific education and research. In 1959, Congress increased the National Science Foundation appropriation four fold to $134 million. By 1968, the NSF budget grew another 370 percent.

It was an exciting time to be in science, Tibor thought. There was so much to learn, so much truth to uncover. The frontiers of science were expanding exponentially and he was part of it. He had an opportunity to further advance man's understanding of the laws of nature.

Tibor received his first NSF grant while still at MIT. Dr. Buerger, Tibor, and several other students were awarded funds to decipher how atoms were arranged in eight complex minerals. Tibor felt extremely honored to be Dr. Buerger's graduate student. Dr. Buerger was considered by many the father of modern X-ray crystallography. He looked the role: a tall, distinguished man with receding white hair and wire-rim glasses.

Tibor spent hours in Dr. Buerger's lab, shooting X-ray beams at silicate minerals—silicates comprise the vast majority of the earth's crust and mantle. Tibor's PhD. thesis focused on a particular silicate formed under high pressures deep inside the earth. He analyzed reams of data on how X-ray beams deflected using the revolutionary MIT Whirlwind Computer. The Whirlwind was considered the first real-time computer. It had the first graphic display and used advances in memory to double processing speed.

"In seconds," Tibor explained to Olga, his features rounded with awe, "the computer can complete calculations it would take me days to do with a slide rule."

"What's it like?" Olga asked.

"It fills a four story building: two stories for the processor, one for the power substation, and another for the cooling system. The processor has thousands of glass vacuum tubes! I write my code in sections. Then if the computer crashes when a tube burns out, I still have partial results."

"You're lucky to be able to use it."

"It's essential to my research!" Tibor spent many hours at their kitchen table meticulously writing code and organizing his stiff nine-by-four-inch punch cards for the priceless moments he had access to the computer.

On July 31, 1958, Tibor and Olga welcomed their second child into the world. That morning Olga had had an appointment with her doctor since the baby was a week overdue. Olga mentioned that it was her birthday.

"Would you like to have your baby today?" the doctor asked.

"Oh yes," Olga beamed, "that would be the best birthday present ever!"

"Then we'll induce," the doctor said.

Later in the day, Katharina Aniko Zoltai was born. She didn't acquire the nickname Kitty until a few years later. Like for Peter, Tibor and Olga gave her a first name that would help her blend into American culture. And a unique Hungarian middle name that would preserve her Hungarian roots.

A few days later, Olga opened the door to a big surprise: Maria Néni! Her mother had left her secure environment of Hungarians, got on a train where no one spoke Hungarian, crossed the border into a new country, and found her way to a place she'd never been.

Olga never would have thought she had the courage. Obviously her mother's desire to share this special time overcame her fears. She stayed for two precious weeks, helping care for the children and making sure Olga and Tibor got some rest.

Katharina (Kitty)
and Peter, 1958.

Like most of Dr. Buerger's students, Tibor planned to become a professor. He got his first opportunity for an extended teaching assignment when Dr. Buerger traveled for a semester. Tibor enjoyed teaching the class. But at the end was in a moral dilemma about grading himself, since he was both teaching and taking the class.

"Dr. Buerger, what grade should I give myself?" Tibor queried over the phone.

"I left you in charge. If you don't know the answer to that, what are you doing teaching?" Dr. Buerger replied. Tibor nodded to himself, he knew just what to do. He gave himself an A.

When Tibor graduated with his PhD., he hoped to work in a university where he could both pursue his love of teaching and independently conduct research. Unfortunately, the two Canadian universities that offered courses in crystallography had newly hired professors, so he and Olga realized returning to live in their adopted homeland wasn't in their future.

Tibor and Olga at
Tibor's MIT
graduation, 1959.

Steve, Gene, and Tibor's prediction back in 1952 that Canada would need scientists and engineers to build its future wasn't wrong, both Steve and Gene had successful careers in their fields, but the country's need for Tibor's specialized skills didn't coincide with his graduation. He accepted an offer in 1959 to become an assistant professor at the University of Minnesota.

9

Raising American Children, Well, Sort of . . . (1959 - 1969)

The Zoltai Family, 1968. *L. to r.* Peter, Kitty, Olga, and Tibor.

In 1959, Tibor and Olga sold the hideous flowered couch and packed up their limited belongings. They were headed west to Roseville, Minnesota. Roseville was a suburb of St. Paul. It had a high-quality school system and was conveniently located to Tibor's work at the U of M.

Minneapolis sat on one side of the Mississippi River, St. Paul on the other, similar to Budapest, where the cities of Buda and Pest straddled the Danube. But Olga and Tibor's new home was different from Hungary in every other way. Hungary boasted a thousand years of kingdom history. Minnesota had only become a state a scant 101 years earlier. Roseville, growing up out of farmland into a village, still held the smell of manure. The village was so small mail was delivered faster if it was addressed to St. Paul.

But here they were, excited about Tibor's new opportunities. Since he was a teenager, he had dreamed of becoming a teacher, a common thread across most of the careers he considered. Now he was starting a real teaching job: assistant professor at a renowned university.

"One objective of all scientific endeavors," Tibor explained to his Introduction to Mineralogy class in the large lecture hall, "is to state in the simplest terms possible those natural laws and concepts that explain natural phenomena." He taught students how crucial symmetry was to the world around them, how the symmetrical arrangement of atoms in a crystal defined many of its properties. An enthusiastic teacher, he paced back and forth, one hand in his pocket, deeply concentrating on his lecture. He encouraged questions and invented techniques and 3D models to help students visualize the complex spatial concepts.

His office was in Pillsbury Hall, the home of the U of M's geology department. The massive sandstone exterior wall angled in to frame an arched window next to his desk. In this fusty room, he met with graduate students wanting to interview professors to choose an advisor.

Tibor always looked the part of a professor, wearing wire rim glasses with a dark upper frame, the top of his head bald with short curly dark hair down the sides. "What areas of geology are you interested in?" he'd ask the students.

"I want to be a generalist," one said early that fall, "although the study of rocks and how they form is my greatest interest."

"You should consider doing your graduate work in crystallography," Tibor advised leaning forward, his voice vibrating with energy. "If you become a crystallographer and understand other fields in geology, you'll be able to bring a new level of atomic understanding to these areas and will be in high demand."

Tibor's enthusiasm was contagious. Soon Tibor had his first graduate student who helped him set up his research lab. His successful research began attracting other students, starting Tibor on a long and satisfying career where his groundbreaking work in developing a hierarchy and classification system for silicates earned him international recognition.

Tibor in X-ray Crystallography lab at University of Minnesota, 1960s.

*   *   *

The family lived in a small starter home their first few years in Roseville. In 1962, Olga and Tibor built a three-bedroom stucco house on Heinel Drive. Their new home was a lifetime away from their DP quarters, with ten times more space, central heating, running water, toilets, a television, and other features standard in Roseville but unimaginable luxuries just a few years before.

Under the lazy summer sun of 1963, their home radiated warmth and welcome like the other homes on their street. It had large windows, a two-car garage, a deck, and a gracious rolling lawn. The green smell of fresh grass, the croaking of frogs from the lake across the street, and the occasional car purring down the street provided the peaceful suburban setting Tibor and Olga sought for raising children.

While their home looked Minnesotan from the outside, inside it was uniquely Hungarian. Embroidered pillows, knotted oriental rugs, the smell of paprika, and Hungarian words echoing about made it different than any other house on the street. While Hungarian was the first language of its occupants, on occasion accented English also bandied about, since Olga insisted English was spoken when neighbors were around.

In many things Olga had adopted American and Minnesotan ways. She spoke English fluently, followed the American dream, and adjusted to the Minnesotan's vast need for personal space. But she worked hard to teach her children the old way too. She didn't allow Peter or Kitty to have the casual manners of their American friends. They answered the phone politely: "Hello, Zoltais' residence. This is Peter speaking." When they went over to a friend's house to play, they couldn't slink off without first greeting and shaking the parents' hands.

Sometimes Olga made learning the rules into a game: "Kitty, you need to eat with your arms down at your sides and elbows off the table. Here's a penny for under each arm, if they haven't fallen out by the end of dinner, they're yours to keep." She was creative but strict.

Being properly dressed was another part of manners she insisted on. But as with a number of customs from the old country, time and experience had a way of melting them away like snow in the spring.

"Mommy is it time?" six-year-old Peter asked, excited at his invitation to the birthday party of a classmate at school. "Can we go?"

"We can go now," Olga said smiling. She was wearing her dark hair pulled back and a dress complimentary to her hourglass figure. She'd dressed Peter in a gray herringbone wool jacket and shorts, a stiff collar shirt, and red tie. He would have readily fit in at a child's party in Hungary. Together they climbed into the Volkswagen bug that Olga regularly drove.

As Peter climbed out of the car, a group of boys was tearing out of the birthday boy's house to greet him. Peter went still. They were all dressed in casual, rumbled play clothes.

"Mommy, I want to go home," he said, climbing back into the car with his head down.

Olga removed his jacket and tie. She finally convinced him to stay. After that, to Peter's relief, the herringbone suit stayed in the closet for American children's parties, yet another area where Olga learned to adapt.

The trees dropped their leaves and the holidays approached. For Thanksgiving, Olga was preparing a traditional American feast: turkey, fixings, and all. This year she decided to add a cultural dimension to the family's American celebration, emulating the first Thanksgiving when Native Americans shared a feast with the new settlers. She invited a student from East Africa who attended nearby Bethel College.

"We're going to have a guest for Thanksgiving weekend," Olga explained to Peter and Kitty, sitting them down at the Formica kitchen table. It was early Thanksgiving Day. The hint of roasting turkey was beginning to scent the air.

"She's too far from her family to go home for Thanksgiving," Olga continued. "She's from Africa, thousands of miles away." Since Roseville was not racially diverse, Olga decided it was best to prepare the children. "Her skin is darker than yours. It's black."

"Will my hand get black when I shake her hand?" Peter asked looking at his hand.

Olga remembered her own similar questions as a young girl the one time she met a visiting black man in Hungary.

"No," she said, "her hand will not get white because you shake it either. She's just like you. It's just the color of her skin. In Africa the sun is very hot. People's skin got dark over thousands of years to protect them from the strong sunshine."

The family thoroughly enjoyed their guest. After that, they began regularly inviting foreign students and professors into their home.

Unlike Thanksgiving, which was a new holiday for Olga and Tibor, Christmas brought with it years of old-world traditions. Just as Maria Néni had done with her, Olga helped Peter and Kitty to memorize Christmas poems. They needed to have them ready for the Hungarian community celebration a week before Christmas. The Hungarian community served as Tibor and Olga's year-long extended family, helping fill their deep-seated need for extended family routinely in their lives. They relished spending time with their Hungarian friends and being surrounded by their native tongue and customs.

Almost a hundred immigrants sat with their families on folding chairs in the cavernous stone hall of the College of St. Thomas. The hall was comfortably warm and smelled of heated winter air. Listening to a Hungarian priest give the opening sermon, Tibor's mind drifted back to his youth when the Catholic Church had been his foundation and he had regularly attended mass. Olga was more distracted, monitoring her wiggling children.

After the sermon, several dozen children recited poetry. When it was Peter's turn, he stood in front of the microphone and looked out into the multitude of attentive faces. Olga caught his eye and gave a reassuring smile. The microphone magnified his small voice as he carefully recited his Hungarian poem. Kitty went next. At four, her wavy, light-brown bob stopped a foot shy of the shortest microphone height. An adult angled the stand to catch her whispered words.

Kitty and Peter in their costumes for the Hungarian Christmas Play, 1963.

After all the children finished, Olga helped her kids put on the costumes she and Tibor had made for the Christmas play. Peter wore his draping shepherd's headdress and cloak, and carried his stuffed lamb and staff. He proudly walked with the older boys to bring gifts to the new born king. Kitty, in a silky soft white dress, stiff tinfoil and cardboard wings, stood with the other angels by the manger rejoicing the birth of Jesus.

Afterwards Tibor and Olga chatted with old friends and enjoyed the Hungarian open-faced sandwiches and traditional desserts families brought to share. They smiled tolerantly at the echoing clatter of children's running feet as swarms tore around the hall, regularly circling the food table to sneak yet another rich dessert.

Christmas Eve Day finally arrived. Eugene Bácsi and Maria Néni had driven down from Toronto, and Olga dressed the family in special dresses, jackets, and ties.

Following the traditional Hungarian pattern, after a light breakfast, the family fasted until dinner. Olga and Maria Néni prepared a feast, starting with vegetable and dumpling soup, followed by Chicken Paprika. The aromatic smell of its spicy sauce mingled with the scent of fresh pine from Christmas decorations and the wood burning in the fireplace. The chicken was served over galuska, a dense free-form egg noodle similar to German spaetzle. Cucumber salad, its crisp texture softened by a tart sour cream sauce, balanced the main dish. Dessert was Beigli, a dense pastry filled with spiraling layers of moist, sweet poppy seed or walnut filling.

Dinner was barely over when the sweet ring of a bell announced the arrival of little Jesus and the angels with the Christmas tree and presents. As Olga and Tibor had planned, the children never even noticed Tibor was suspiciously missing from the table. They jumped up and ran into the living room. Next to the fireplace, a pine tree had appeared. It glistened with metallic ornaments, gold-painted walnuts, szalon cukor, silver tinsel, and colorful lights. On the oriental carpet underneath were unwrapped presents.

"Little Jesus and the angels have come!" Peter announced, bouncing about. "Hurry!"

"Patience dear," Olga said eyes laughing.

The adults ambled over to settle in the comfortable low-backed sofa and chairs. "Peter, why don't you recite your poem first." Peter and Kitty hurried through reciting their poetry yet again.

"Menyböl as Angal, le jöt hozátok (The angel from heaven came down to us) . . ." Olga began to sing and everyone joined in. While many notes of the Hungarian Christmas carols they sang were off-key and discordant, the songs were sung with enthusiasm. No one in the family had stellar voices. Peter often teased Kitty that hers was so bad, people were going to jump off the world. But on this special day, to Olga's relief, he kept his peace.

Finally Olga said it was time for presents. Peter checked out Olga's heart rate with his hard plastic stethoscope, then Eugene Bácsi's. Kitty carefully removed her new doll's cozy blanket so Doctor Peter could give the doll a check up as well.

Christmas scene in Zoltai home, early 1960s.

When Olga attended gymnasium in Hungary, Maria Néni dreamed Olga would have a chance to go to college. Olga lived the dream once both Peter and Kitty were in school. She began pursuing a biology degree at the U of M.

It had been fifteen long years since she had been in school. Going from a business school in German to college-level science classes in English was as hard as growing tropical ferns in the desert. When everyone left in the morning, Olga sat down at the Formica table with a steaming cup of coffee. The sun shining in through the large kitchen window glistened on the white pages of her textbooks as she slowly plowed through her assignments.

In addition to completing her own schoolwork, Olga helped Peter and Kitty study. Kitty was struggling with learning to read. She longed to be in a higher reading group, but she was in the lowest of three. Olga realized Kitty had trouble processing sounds and recognizing words—a learning impairment later christened dyslexia. Despite no education in teaching or guidance from school, Olga took on the problem, drawing on her memory of learning Hungarian. She began working with Kitty every night, cuddled on Kitty's double bed with backs resting against the headboard, feet tickled by the yarn on the bedspread, and Kitty's stuffed pink elephant at their side.

"What sound does this letter make?" Olga asked pointing to "é". She was teaching her daughter the Hungarian alphabet.

"ā," Kitty said.

"Good." She gently squeezed Kitty's arm.

Hungarian was a phonetic language, having a unique letter for each sound: a (aw), á (ah), b (bay), c (tzay), etc. rather than English with its forty-four sounds for twenty-six letters. Olga was using its phonetic nature to teach sounds. In a few weeks, she decided Kitty was ready to put sounds together into words.

At first she worked on Hungarian words, but soon they advanced to English.

"Sound this out," Olga said, pointing to cake.

"K-é-k," Kitty said with the smile-grimace she made when concentrating.

"Good," Olga graced her with a smile.

Once Kitty mastered words, Olga started helping her read a book. When they reached an interesting part, Olga said, "I need to do laundry." In a few minutes she checked to make sure Kitty was enthralled enough to keep reading. Within a year, she helped her make it up to the middle reading group.

Outside of serving as a phonetic tool and being the language spoken at home, Hungarian served as the family's secret code. This worked since there wasn't another Hungarian in the neighborhood or school.

"Can my friend stay for dinner?" Peter asked Olga in Hungarian. Olga was in the kitchen preparing dinner, and Peter knew Hungarian provided the means to share a thought just with family. Unlike in Austria where there were many Hungarians, their secret language was never decoded in Minnesota. The number of Hungarians in the Twin Cities was only a few hundred.

Olga remembered one time this hadn't worked so well. She and her brother Gene tried to get on an overcrowded street car during rush-hour in the late 1940s in Austria. "Push those two nuns over so we can get on," Gene had said in Hungarian.

"Don't push me," one of the nuns had replied in Hungarian glaring at him, "I'll push you back." Eyes wide, Gene apologized. He and Olga found another place to board the streetcar before it slowly crawled away.

Like traveling on the crawling streetcar during rush hour, Tibor's university education had been interrupted and protracted. In contrast, Tibor's career pushed forward like a supercharged express train.

Within five years at the U of M, Tibor already had attained the rank of full professor and became chairman of the department.

"What's new? Any developments?" Tibor asked, as he swept into the crystallography lab in the musty basement of Pillsbury Hall, cigarette in one hand and cold coffee in the other. He was always moving at a frenetic pace. In three to four minutes, he comprehended what was going on with his graduate student's research and rushed out again.

"Why are you carrying around cold coffee half the time?" Tibor was asked.

"I don't like to drink cold coffee," Tibor replied. "But I don't want to take the time to freshen it up." Tibor's philosophy about work was summed up in advice he gave to one of his graduate students: "Someone who's not as smart but works through the night, will come up with something sooner than someone who's smart but doesn't."

After years spent idling as a DP, Tibor was determined to push forward as hard as physically possible. Just managing the department took forty hours per week. With his teaching and research he was working eighty to one hundred hours. Olga didn't mind because he was regularly home for dinner and to participate in any evening activity. It usually wasn't until after family time that Tibor would pull out his research and work until the wee hours of the morning, surviving on five hours of sleep.

Peter and Kitty quickly figured out that while Tibor was working at his massive oak desk with a view of Heinel Drive, he was deep in concentration. It was an ideal time to ask for things.

"Daddy, can I've a cookie?" Peter asked, a mischievous smile on his face, knowing dinner would be in an hour and his mother would say no if asked.

"Yah, yah," he would reply, never really having heard the question.

Tibor served as department chair for eight hectic years from 1963 to 1971. Just like he adjusted to tremendous change in his personal life, he helped the department adapt coursework and faculty to reflect the phenomenal advances in the field of geology.

The number of faculty grew faster than ever before with the help of NSF funds, but Tibor's tenure was a time of tumultuous pressures inside and outside the department. "We need to improve our national ranking," a professor said at a department meeting in their sandstone building. "We're only fifteenth."

"The top schools don't have undergraduate programs. We need to drop ours and focus only on graduate students." This was the opinion of four vocal, powerful professors.

But Tibor and more than half the department didn't agree. "Eliminating undergraduate studies isn't consistent with the university's mission," Tibor said. "We need to focus on reflecting advances in geology and upgrading our facilities." These endeavors alone were a major challenge. The words of the Dean still rang in Tibor's head: "If I line up all the departments in the Institute of Technology, geology is the least important."

"If you could start your career all over again,' Tibor asked his graduate students at a social gathering, "what would you do?" Most said they would do something quite different.

"What would you do, Tibor?" a student asked.

"I'd do the same, except I wouldn't be department chair," he said. "That way I'd have more time for research." If he still had to serve as chair, he thought, he'd sit down more with colleagues and talk things out over beer. He'd adopt the casual Midwest leadership style rather than emulating the more formal style used in Europe and by Dr. Buerger.

No matter how much he adapted, he realized, there was always more to learn.

"You wrap the candy snugly in the middle of the tissue paper," Olga explained to Peter and Kitty. The family, clad in casual clothes, was seated around the coffee table in the living room. A fire crackled in the brick fireplace. The notes of an American Christmas carol encircled the room: "There's no place like home for the holidays, no matter how far away you go . . ."

The pine smell of the Christmas tree competed with the sweet smell of the szalon cukor Olga was demonstrating how to wrap.

Tibor ripped off another strip of tinfoil with a loud zip. He was making two-by-four-inch strips. He'd already finished cutting fringe on the six-inch white squares of tissue paper.

"Then put the foil around the candy and press it to hold the candy in place," Olga continued. A soft tinny crinkling followed as Peter and Kitty pressed the foil around the candies they were wrapping.

"Can I eat one?" Peter asked, seduced by the sugary sweet smell.

"Okay, just one," Olga said. He had a powerful sweet tooth and could consume the entire bag.

By the end of the evening, the tree was colorful and festive. The szalon cukor, along with the golden walnuts, ornaments, and lights lit up the house. Olga and Tibor no longer waited until Christmas Eve to decorate the tree in secret. It wasn't necessary. Neither Peter nor Kitty believed anymore, deep in their hearts, that little Jesus and the angels brought the tree and presents.

Over time even wrapping paper and the American Santa pushed their way into family traditions. However the main holiday and gift exchange remained on Christmas Eve, as it had been ever since Tibor and Olga were children.

"What country are you from?" a sales clerk asked Olga and Tibor when they were shopping in 1966. Even after more than seventeen years in North America, Olga and Tibor's noticeable accents caused strangers to ask where they were from.

"We're American!" Olga answered head high, looking the stranger in the eye.

"No, I mean what country are you from originally?"

"Hungary," Olga replied. "In central Europe," she added. Geography was not an American strong point in her experience.

Olga and Tibor had the opportunity for their first trip back to Hungarian soil after twenty-one years. They would be returning carrying U.S. passports. Maria Néni and Lili Néni had flown in to stay with the kids.

Olga packed a few last-minute items, the large, beige hard-sided suitcase still open on her and Tibor's bed. A warm summer breeze blew in the open window, letting in frogs croaking and the earthy smell of summer.

There have been so many changes since we left Hungary, Olga thought. The Communists have ruled for decades. Thankfully, the initial iron-fisted control relaxed after the 1956 revolution. Now Hungary had more liberal economic and political policies than its Soviet-bloc neighbors. But even so, would it be the homeland she remembered?

Olga's eyes became soft as her thoughts drifted to when Cousin Olga had visited the U.S. the previous summer. She knew Cousin

Olga's family was concerned about how badly harassed she would be upon her return, but thankfully that didn't happen. Cousin Olga shared how her family's lives had improved in the last few years. There were so many more goods and food products available. She mentioned crisp, juicy red apples that were now imported from the U.S., "Del-ē-check" apples; Cousin Olga pointed them out in the grocery store. Olga knew them as Delicious apples, and laughed that she hadn't recognized the Hungarian pronunciation.

When their cab arrived, Tibor carried the suitcases out. Having already said his good-byes, his mind was fully on their trip. He was looking forward to seeing family he hadn't seen in decades. To once again eat flavorful, succulent apricots right off the tree. He was glad he had been able to time their trip to present at an international geology conference in Moscow immediately afterwards.

Olga and Tibor
during first trip back
to Hungary, 1966.

Hungary officially still considered them citizens. Tibor had heard of ex-patriots being detained while visiting. He wasn't expecting anything like that, but he thought it was best to be cautious. He had a colleague in Russia who wouldn't let his absence at the conference go unnoticed.

They landed in Germany, drove though Austria, and entered Hungary near Györ. After extensive questions by Hungarian customs, they were allowed entry and instructed to go directly to the police station in Györ.

At the police station, they were escorted to a stale, drab-gray, sparsely furnished room and interrogated. The officer was predominately interested in Tibor and his family.

"Give me your passports," the officer said in a serious voice.

Tibor passed over both passports. "You'll notice a visa for Russia. We're expected at an international conference in Moscow when we leave Hungary."

"When did you last leave Hungary?" the officer said.

"1945," Tibor answered.

"Why did you leave?"

"To avoid fierce fighting."

"Where are your parents?"

"Toronto, Canada."

"What's your father doing?"

"He's retired," Tibor said. His fingers rolled and tapped a cigarette he had lit.

"What's your uncle doing?" The questions clearly indicated the officer was aware of the role his father and uncle had had in the military. "Are they planning to return?"

On and on it went, the officer recording the session. Finally, after thirty excruciating minutes, it was over. They were not going to be detained.

But each time they were to overnight in a new city, the scenario repeated: the stale gray room, the interrogation, the redundant answers. And thankfully, the redundant release.

It rained as they drove around in Győr, the dreary black weather and swoosh of the windshield wipers reflecting the sad, worn city. Many buildings still bore scars of war and fighting. Rubble had been cleared away, but gouges and holes remained in the buildings.

While there were a number of new factory apartment houses, these looked even more depressing. They were sheets of cement poured at a factory and erected to make four walls; beige plaster covering the cement was crumbling and chipping.

The dreariness evaporated when Tibor saw his cousin Charlie Kováts-Szabó. The exuberance of the hugs and kisses reflected the pent-up emotion of two decades. Oh to be back home, thought Tibor. When he left in 1945 he had wondered: how long would it be before he again saw the smoky towers of Győr? But not even in his wildest dreams did he think it would be so long. How he missed being with his cousins, his aunts, his uncles. How wonderful it was to meet Charlie's young daughters, to see the grown men his younger cousins had become, to have Olga meet and laugh with his family.

With each family member they met, they learned more about Communist Hungary.

"I'm headed to Sopron," a relative with young children said. "I've heard they have strollers."

"You mean they don't sell strollers here?" Olga asked.

"Sometimes they do, sometimes they don't. You have to go where an item's available." Seeing Olga and Tibor's perplexed looks, he continued. "Our way of manufacturing is different with the five-year plan. I just went to another city to get small pots the other day.

The factory's production quota is in liters of pots. Since it's easier to manufacture one fifty-liter pot than fifty one-liter pots, large sizes are easier to get."

Tibor's cousin Charlie Kováts-Szabó (*back left corner*), Olga (*ninth from left*), and several other of Tibor's relatives in Györ, Hungary, 1966. Damaged condition of building visible in background.

Their visit was a special occasion for all their hosts. Olga and Tibor were the first of the escaped relatives to return! It was wonderful to be back in Hungary. Olga had almost forgotten how deep her roots went, how part of her would never stop being Hungarian. She felt like a sun-loving plant moved from partial shade into direct light. To again be surrounded by Hungarian people, language, culture, and countryside. It felt so natural, so at home. But Tibor and Olga now spoke Hungarian with an accent, they were told. How disappointing to no longer speak any language without sounding foreign.

From Győr they went on to Budapest, then east to visit Cousin Olga. In Cousin Olga's backyard, Tibor got to fulfill his dream eating ripe apricots directly from the tree. The sweet aroma surrounded him as he picked the fruit, and the plump, ripe fruit of his homeland was as mouth-watering as he remembered.

Tibor and Olga knew Hungary would always own a portion of their heart. But as they returned home, they realized they were now more American than Hungarian.

Olga had lived in North America years longer than in Hungary. Even for Tibor the years were growing equal.

When the smell of new grass, buds, and flowers scented the Minnesota air, Olga again signed Peter up for the most popular American sport, baseball.

"Tibor, Peter's baseball team needs an assistant coach," Olga said. They were sitting down to enjoy a cup of espresso in the living room. "I think you should help." The American concept of volunteering had become as natural to Olga as her skin. She volunteered for the League of Woman Voters, the local schools, Campfire Girls, the International Institute, and many other groups. She also regularly helped Tibor find projects. Tibor already volunteered with Peter's Boy Scout Troop and at school science fairs.

Tibor took a sip of his coffee. "As long as I don't need to know the game." Tibor had never played, or even seen, a baseball game. Soccer was the sport of his youth.

The head coach welcomed him at an early practice on the local baseball field. "Tibor, you take the outfielders and have them practice catching flies." He handed Tibor a wooden bat and pointed him to the emerald green outfield.

Tibor took Peter aside. "Why are the boys supposed to catch mosquitoes?" he asked.

As Peter explained baseball to his father, another hole in his American cultural education was filled.

"My teacher says you're a famous geologist," Kitty said to her father once a thin coating of ice had formed on the lake. "He told me to ask if you'd come talk to my class."

"Okay," Tibor answered, "I'll come. What should I talk about?"

"Anything," Kitty said, shrugging her shoulders. Tibor came and gave a lecture on different kinds of symmetry.

"What was that about?" a friend asked Kitty afterwards with a bewildered look.

"Patterns in nature," Kitty said.

"What does that have to do with rocks?" her friend asked.

"My Dad studies minerals in rocks. It's important to the mineral's structure, I guess." Kitty was sorry she hadn't taken up Tibor on his offer to select what he covered. She thought he would somehow know what to teach kids—-wrong. Tibor always assumed everyone was highly intelligent and knowledgeable, which generally worked well at the university, however outside of academia he had to regularly be prompted to adjust his explanation to the knowledge of his audience. Peter and Kitty became experts at asking, "What does that mean?"

One of Olga and Tibor's major challenges raising children centered on religion: how to give them the formative moral teachings they had received through the church, without being practicing Catholics. Out of tradition, and because it was important to Maria Néni, they had baptized Peter and Kitty Roman Catholic, even allowed them to attend Sunday school with a neighbor to learn Christian traditions. But neither Olga nor Tibor wanted that to continue.

Through a close friend and neighbor, they found a religious organization where they felt at home. Olga and Tibor became active members, and the family began regularly attending Sunday services. In the Unitarian Society in Minneapolis, religion was not centered on specific religious beliefs. Members gathered around shared moral values that included the inherent worth and dignity of every person.

"I shared my idea for the commemorative coin," Tibor said to Olga in the main brick hallway of the church about a year after joining. His voice vibrated with enthusiasm. Tibor was helping with the 400th commemoration of the Unitarian religion. After twenty years of feeling spirituality homeless, now he found it energizing to be part of a spiritual community. The coin project made use of his spiritual beliefs, fascination with history, and even love of Hungary. As Tibor was delighted to point out, the Unitarian faith was born in Transylvania, an integral part of Hungary for a millennium.

But Tibor and Olga finding their spiritual home outside of Catholicism was a crushing blow to Maria Néni. Leaving the only true church was worse than death, Maria Néni believed. Their souls would rot in hell forever. She saw it as a personal affront against her and the religion that was interwoven with her very being. Olga didn't realize the depth of Maria Néni's anger until decades later, when Olga found a faded letter Maria Néni had written to a relative capturing the venom of her feelings. Being true to her own beliefs, she had alienated her mother.

For so long after loosing her faith in Catholic doctrine, Olga had maintained loose ties to the church to placate her mother, but what had that accomplished? It only delayed the anger and pain. She knew everything had a price; she was just disappointed at how high this cost was.

Unlike their evolution in spiritual beliefs, for Olga and Tibor being frugal was deeply imbedded and immutable. They had survived a time when a scrap of food was treasured, a second shirt a luxury. Like those who lived through the U.S. Depression in the 1930s, it was hard to throw anything away, even once their fortunes improved.

By 1968, Olga and Tibor moved the family into another new home on Heinel Drive, a block away from the first. While their new home had similar square footage and a stucco exterior, it was directly on the lake and was designed by an architect to have arresting views of Lake Owasso from almost every window. Yet even though they prospered, Tibor and Olga reused everything from broken furniture to plastic sandwich bags to spark plugs.

"Daddy, why are you saving ten broken hockey sticks?" Kitty asked when it was her turn to clean up the garage.

"You never know when the wood will come in handy," Tibor replied.

Perhaps the most surprising part: Tibor actually used a lot of the scraps he saved. He took great pride in always being able to fix any broken toy, machine, or furniture. The repair was functional, if not always attractive or long-lasting.

Tibor and Olga had no desire to part with their refugee mentality. It would have been easier for them to give up a lung. They still found it advantageous to help their pennies go farther. And their saved pennies helped to fund an extended visit to Europe in 1969.

Tibor arranged a half-year sabbatical to do crystallographic research with Professor Fischer in Saarbrücken, Germany. This time the kids were going along. Tibor and Olga thought they would easily fit into German life with all the exposure to European culture. But actually living in Europe made them realize how American the children were.

Olga had let Kitty buy a new outfit for the trip; the newest fad in Minnesota was brightly colored clothes. Kitty's Minnesota friends thought her new hot pink jeans were "soooooo co-ol", but when she walked down the street in Germany, where everyone wore dark, muted colors, passer bys stopped and stared.

"How was school today?" Olga asked a few weeks later.

"Okay," Peter answered. They were eating lunch in their furnished visiting professor flat. The contemporary dining room table was inviting with colorful placemats and the bread, cheese, and salami Olga set out.

"How's it different than back home?" Olga asked. She was never satisfied with a one-word answer. She wanted her children to consciously think about what was different.

"We have to memorize a lot more," Peter said, swallowing a bite.

"When the teacher comes in everyone rises and says together 'Guten morgen Frau Schmidt' or whatever the teacher's name is," Kitty piped in.

"The kids do e-v-e-r-y-t-h-i-n-g the teacher says in class," Peter said. "But when she leaves, they jump over desks and do crazy stuff."

School in America meant more student questions during lessons, less memorization, and more independent work. Olga liked the German second language training, the stronger emphasis on grammar, more respectful manners—lessons reminiscent of her upbringing. She watched her children adapt to the new environment, learning German, mimicking German manners, following school rules. At times they were still less disciplined, less meticulously tidy, less punctual; they climbed on monuments the family visited, not observing quietly from the sidewalk like the German children sitting with their parents. While her kids could be called unruly, at the same time she thought their experience with independence made them more responsible. The father of a German friend echoed her opinion: "I'd trust Peter with my car keys," he said. "But I wouldn't give them to my own children, not even my son who's two years older."

L. to r. Peter, friend, Olga, Kitty, and Tibor in Germany, 1969.

Olga wanted to further strengthen Peter's inter-cultural experience. She arranged for him to stay an extra three months with the Fischers. At thirteen, Peter adapted well to their routines. He even learned to play soccer, giving him a leg up on this sport just introduced in Minnesota.

Before Peter started his extended stay, Olga and Tibor took the family on a driving tour across Europe and into Hungary. They wanted Peter and Kitty to finally see their native country.

Crossing the border into Hungary was thankfully uneventful. The family traversed the country, seeing the traditional plaster and brick buildings, the rich green rural countryside, and the historic structures. They took a sailboat out on the glistening waters of Lake Balaton and visited relatives. They filled their bellies with scrumptious, ripe sour cherries picked directly off the tree.

Olga and Tibor became like supercharged batteries. Being continually on the go, visiting dozens of relatives and Hungarian sights didn't drain them—it energized them to new heights.

One warm day in July, the family was huddled around the TV with relatives and their friends, more than a dozen people crammed into the humid, sticky living room. There was no sound outside of the voices and crackling noises emanating from the TV. As they watched, they saw Apollo astronaut Neil Armstrong as he took man's first step on the moon.

"One small step for man, one giant leap for mankind," reverberated around the silence in the room.

"The Americans did it!" The Hungarians looked at Tibor and Olga and cheered, their faces alight. "They beat the Russians!" No love was ever lost on the Russians.

Watching the landing reminded Olga of Tibor's story about man traveling to the moon. The one he told in 1950, while they hoed sugar beets and lived in a wood shack without running water or electricity. She thought it was an outrageous idea. It had never occurred to her before then that man could ever make the trip.

Tibor's mind drifted to the rock samples the astronauts were collecting. The U of M was one of the institutions who would receive a sample. He wondered what the composition and structure of the moon rock would reveal about the moon and nature's laws? He marveled at how man's knowledge and his technology were rocketing forward.

So much change on so many fronts.

10

Olga Juggles Family and Counseling Immigrants (1970 - 1979)

Olga at International Institute, 1970s.

In 1970, a small package arrived that catalyzed in Olga and Tibor a dramatic adoption of American ways. Within a year the family's home language became English and Olga entered the workforce. Shifting from speaking Hungarian to English had a profound impact on the Zoltai family. Their lens on the world shifted.

On December 22, Olga gave birth to another daughter, Lilian Ildiko Zoltai. Olga was already thirty-nine, Tibor forty-five.

As soon as Lili was born, it was clear something wasn't quite right. She had a flat face with upward slanting eyes, small ears, and an enlarged tongue. The hospital doctors diagnosed she was Down syndrome, born with an extra chromosome, forty-seven instead of forty-six. The extra genetic material slowed her mental development.

"Lili belongs in an institution," a Pediatrician family friend advised Olga while she and Lili were still in their pallid, medicinal-smelling hospital room. "They're well prepared to take care of her there." This had been commonly done with Down syndrome children.

"I can't put her in an institution," Olga said, shaking her head. "She's my daughter." The idea of shutting her child away behind locked doors in an institution made her stomach turn. Lili was coming home.

Olga holding Lili, Dec. 1970.

* * *

222

Responding to Lili's weak cry in the middle of a chilly winter night, Olga went to her young daughter's crib. She lovingly cradled Lili, feeding her a bottle. Olga thought about how grateful she was that she no longer believed in the Catholic teachings from her childhood. They preached that an unhealthy child was punishment for the mother's sins. Intellectually she had rejected that long ago. But she realized somewhere deep in her subconscious the poisonous idea must still linger, since it had resurfaced several times since Lili's birth.

Understanding the genetic rationale helped her conquer the subconscious message. The genetics also helped her accept that Down syndrome was a permanent affliction. Maria Néni and Eugene Bácsi kept saying: "She'll outgrow it, just like you outgrew illnesses when you were two." But they didn't understand the genetic cause. Lili's condition would not change.

As with every life challenge they faced, Olga and Tibor discussed what they could do. While there was no 'solution', they thought about how they could make Lili's life easier. They decided it would be challenging enough for Lili to learn to speak, read, and write English. They discontinued speaking Hungarian at home. They also found an innovative pilot project at the U of M for Lili: Expanding Developmental Growth through Education. EDGE used early intervention to teach language development, enhancing Down syndrome children's success in learning to learn to read, write, and do math once school-aged.

When Lili was three months old, the family started taking turns giving her a thirty-minute lesson each day from the EDGE material, covering vocabulary and basic concepts. The lessons were repeated over and over again.

One lesson was about a ball. "Lili, this is a ball. It's round." Lili, in her infant seat, would track the ball with her hazel eyes. Olga put Lili's stubby hands around the ball to feel the round shape of the rubbery object. "See, it bounces." Demonstrated bouncing. "The color of the ball is red." And so it continued.

Olga gives Lili
an EDGE
lesson, 1971.

Olga decided it would be best for Lili to be surrounded with the stimulation of other children her age. An opportunity arose in 1971 to work as an immigration counselor at the International Institute. For years Olga had volunteered at the agency, helping new immigrant families, even serving on their Board of Directors. While she only had a few years of biology classes, not the social work degree the Institute sought for the position, she convinced the agency's director that she was the right person for the job.

Olga deeply valued being a wife and mother, but she thoroughly enjoyed her new job. In counseling refugees and immigrants, she took the lessons learned in her own assimilation and used them to benefit others.

Olga knew well the significant difference between refugees and immigrants. Refugees flee home to escape the danger of political upheaval and persecution based on race, religion, nationality, social group, or political opinion. They're unable to return. They often leave unexpectedly with just a suitcase, without important documents, like she and Tibor.

An immigrant comes to the U.S. for other reasons, such as economic opportunity, or to reunite with family. They plan their emigration and can choose to return.

Olga worked with both refugees and immigrants, helping them prepare visa applications, complete Immigration Naturalization Services (INS) paperwork, and representing them in their INS citizenship hearings. But if she could help them solve other problems in adapting to the U.S., she did that as well.

"I can't find job," a Russian client said, his heavily accented English filling Olga's office. A Russian refugee who had fled persecution because he was Jewish, he hoped Olga could help.

Olga sat at her smooth olive-green metal desk facing the doorway. In her forties, she was a compassionate-looking woman with a rounded figure, warm hazel eyes, dyed honey-brown hair, and smile wrinkles etched around her eyes and lips. Her compact office with off-white walls smelled faintly of paper and people. Behind her desk were a small row of windows near the ceiling and a large wall map of the world where clients could point out their homeland. On the wall shelves to her right were books, files, and folk art. On the wall opposite her, was a line drawing by a Ukrainian artist: a naked man inside a globe. To her, he represented humanity trying to break out of the world's constraints. Her dislike of writing and paperwork was evident in the backlog of files hidden in drawers.

Her client was seated in one of two chairs she had for visitors. "What was your job in Russia?" Olga asked, her head slightly tilted as she focused on his problem.

"I was professional wrestler."

"And you want to stay involved in wrestling?"

The strong muscles in his neck flexed as he nodded.

"Then I suggest you volunteer in a wrestling club."

His eyebrows rose. "I need job. Why would I volunteer?"

"I know volunteering isn't commonly done in Russia," Olga said, "but it is here. Volunteering in a wrestling club would give you a chance to see how a club works here, and give the wrestlers and managers a chance to get familiar with you. Once they get to know you, they might hire you."

When he followed her advice, he soon had paid employment at the wrestling club, and Olga smiled when he came to thank her.

Olga in her International Institute office, 1970s.

Taking on the added responsibility of Olga's new job was not easy on the family. Olga drastically cut back on volunteer work. She enlisted more help from Tibor, Peter, and Kitty with chores and started serving time-saving American meals like spaghetti, Sloppy Joes, grilled cheese sandwiches, and canned soups.

Only rarely did she still find time to make the more labor-intensive Hungarian recipes. Despite Peter and Lili's preference for American food, even they loved the familiar aroma of Chicken

Paprika and galuska, Hungarian crepes, or Olga's special chocolate crème tortes.

When Tibor's cousin came to visit from Toronto, Olga took the time to scout a source for cow kidneys and brains, a Hungarian specialty the cousin loved.

Peter was skeptical. He set the bag of groceries from Olga's car on the kitchen counter. "This is good?" he asked, eyebrows raised.

"It's a delicacy in Hungary," Olga said enthusiastically. When she brought the sautéed brown kidneys and wavy cords of translucent brains to the table, Tibor and his cousin dug in with gusto. But Peter, Kitty, and Lili gagged, staring at the slimy delicacy, pushing it around their plate.

Olga never served this meal a second time, no longer willing to invest the effort needed for traditional cooking if it wasn't going to be broadly appreciated.

Like all children, Olga and Tibor learned first from their families, then from society how to think about themselves and those different. They made a conscious decision to reject the prejudices taught to them. They knew what it felt like to be discriminated against, to be an outsider, a "damned refugee." They didn't wish that on anyone.

They worked hard to raise their children to respect and appreciate differences, to break the vicious cycle of prejudice. This concept, Olga thought, was so critical to making a democracy of people from diverse countries and cultures. But she still ran into prejudice based on religion, race, and ethnic differences. Even in her family.

One night, comfortably ensconced under her bed covers, Olga was enjoying a rare moment of peace, reading a political satire. Her night light was angled to illuminate the pages. The sliding glass door in the bedroom was open a foot, letting in a light summer breeze and the soothing smells of trees and lake. The high-pitched sounds of crickets echoed in the distance.

Suddenly Kitty rushed in. "Do you know what Ipapa said to me?" Kitty dramatically lifted outstretched arms before flopping down on Olga's bed. Tibor had just picked her up at the airport from a solo trip to Toronto to visit relatives, including Nicholas Bácsi, who was called Ipapa by the grandchildren. It was 1974.

"What?" Olga put down her book, knowing her moment of escape was over.

"That the Jews are responsible for Watergate! They caused all the problems in the Nixon administration! Can you believe it? He didn't even hear my arguments why that can't be true. His mind was already made up. Forget the facts."

Ipapa's anti-Semitic views were reflective of the Hungarian society of Olga's youth. She decided it was time for a history lesson. "Like here in the 1930s and 1940s, Hungary discriminated against people who were different." She looked into her daughter's turbulent eyes, the same hazel color as her own. "They considered true Hungarians white, Christian, and strongly committed to Hungary as a nation. They resented racial and religious differences. Hungary wasn't immune to the wide spread anti-Semitism in Europe. You remember learning about anti-Semitism in school, right?"

"Yeah, and the Holocaust."

"A very sad chapter in history."

"Why were Jews hated?"

"Jews weren't allowed to own property, so many went into banking and business. They were very successful and powerful." She paused. "This caused resentment and distrust. They also valued education, so their children went on to be even more successful."

"You, Dad, and your parents aren't anti-Semitic." Kitty was still angry at her grandfather.

"You have to want to reject what you're taught. Ipapa believed in it. He was always a very rigid person. Not open to a different way of looking at things."

After Kitty left, Olga turned out her light, but her mind still churned. She was glad Kitty was comfortable enough to talk about things bothering her. Talking about unpleasant things was one area of parenting Olga was determined to be different than her mother.

To think Olga grew up not even knowing her grandfather was an alcoholic. She had to hear about it from a cousin, when she was an adult. She asked her mother why she didn't tell her. All her mother said was, "You didn't need to know."

Olga's heart hammered at the memory. Things needed to be aired, whether others wanted to talk about them or not. She had made sure her children understood the changes life would bring.

"Did you vote?" Olga asked Tibor as he walked into the kitchen. The smell of frying breaded pork cutlet permeated the room.

He nodded. "Did you?"

"Yeah, I canceled out your vote." They smiled. It was a family joke; Olga voted Democrat, Tibor Republican, but they always made sure to vote. It wasn't a right to be squandered.

"Hi, Peter," Olga said when he walked in. "Did you vote?"

"Yeah, what's for dinner?" Peter said sniffing the tantalizing aroma. His brief answer held a wealth of meaning. Because Peter was born in Canada, he held dual citizenship until he turned eighteen and voted.

It would have been so easy to escape the draft for the Vietnam War by choosing to be a Canadian citizen. Many young men were going through a lot more effort to dodge the draft by faking maladies or fleeing to Canada. But Peter consciously chose to be an U.S. citizen with all the privileges and duties it entailed. His notice to register for the draft had come earlier in the year. He promptly turned it in despite not wanting to be a soldier. Thankfully the war ended before his number was called.

"... He (a relative in Hungary) was jailed for making anti-Communist remarks," Tibor said later, setting down his fork and knife.

"What'd he say?" Peter asked.

"Oh," Tibor said, lighting-up a cigarette, "things like: 'Even the clouds are freer over Austria.'"

"We don't always like what the U.S. government does," Olga added, her head tilted, "but at least we can openly express our opinions."

Zoltai Family. *L. to r.* Lili, Olga, Peter, Kitty, and Tibor, 1974.

* * *

With each client success, Olga gained confidence in ideas to help the foreign-born. This gave her strength to pursue her newest idea with powerful conviction. It would have been easier to stop the flow of a mighty river than stop her crusade. Calling half way across the world, to a man on his honeymoon in Thailand, was merely a pebble in the flow.

"Just a moment please," the hotel clerk said in the polite voice of a well-trained customer service worker.

"Hello?" the Institute director said.

"Hello, this is Olga. I—"

"What's up?" he asked in a strained voice.

"I'm sorry to bother you," Olga said, her voice fast paced, "but a fantastic opportunity for the Institute has come up and there isn't much time to act." A few months earlier the fall of Saigon had ended the Vietnam War. About 125,000 Vietnamese, who feared reprisals by the Communist party for their work with Americans, were seeking asylum in the U.S. Olga's own refugee experience helped her understand what horrible times these people were going through. She yearned to help.

"The government announced an Indochinese Refugee Assistance Program," Olga continued. "They're actually offering money to help resettle refugees!" Funds for resettlement were unprecedented. "I know the Institute hasn't done this kind of work, but it fits with our mission. And we can make it work financially! I've had people already call to volunteer to be sponsors. We could place refugees with these sponsors and use the money to hire a Vietnamese caseworker to coordinate the effort."

"I see," he said, digesting the news.

"If we don't act quickly," Olga said, "I think those interested in being sponsors will go to other agencies."

"Okay," the director said, pausing briefly. "It's consistent with our national goals, but we need to get board support. Set up a board meeting for shortly after I return. I'll review your proposal when I'm back, then discuss it with the board."

Olga and the director's enthusiasm were able to overcome reticence on the board. Their application moved forward to the Federal Government, soon funding and refugees began to arrive.

While resettling refugees was a first for the Institute, they were not Olga's first. She always liked to joke that Tibor was the first refugee she resettled; she had arranged his family's immigration to Canada. Since then, there had been others as well, but nothing like the scale she was embarking on.

Olga took on developing and supervising the resettlement program. She hired a Vietnamese caseworker. In addition to finding families and churches to sponsor refugees, the two were a resource for both sponsors and refugees to help resolve issues in communicating, adjusting to their new culture, finding work, or other challenges.

Being the first in the Twin Cities to have an ethnic Vietnamese caseworker was a phenomenal asset. Within two years, the International Institute of Minnesota would successfully resettle eighty-four Vietnamese refugees.

Olga's expanding success fortified her rock-solid self-esteem. Heaven help the individual who did not treat her as her own person, equal to any man or women.

"Mrs. Tibor Zoltai, would you come with me?" A nurse made the mistake of saying to Olga at the doctor's office one day.

"I'm a unique individual," Olga instructed with a direct piercing look, "separate from my husband. I've my own unique name, Olga Zoltai. Please use it!"

Feminism, a young seed deep within her in 1948, had grown into a massive tree.

She made sure to raise her children the same regardless of gender. Olga split traditional household and yard chores equally between Peter and Kitty. She equally celebrated successes, rewarded good grades, and encouraged career dreams.

"I got my report card today," Kitty said to Olga, taking off her mittens to set the half sheet with mainframe boxy print on the kitchen counter.

"Nice job!" Olga said her eyes sparkling. The sparkle was replaced with a scowl as she remembered Tibor's comment when Kitty was seven and really struggling to memorize her Hungarian Christmas poem. "That's OK," Tibor had said. "She's cute. Someone will marry her." Kitty's high school report cards certainly proved him wrong, Olga thought. Olga later handed the half sheet to Tibor with his coffee.

"An A-," he teased Kitty, rolling his lit cigarette between two fingers. "What happened?"

While he was proud of both Kitty and Peter's good grades, Tibor's core belief in gender roles hadn't migrated from what he wrote to Olga in 1948. He believed the man supported the family and his intelligence and career were more important. The wife's primary role was caregiver, so her heart and caring nature were more important. But his respect for Olga, combined with both Olga's pit-bull tenacity pursuing her ideas and the growing pressure from the American women's movement, shifted his day-to-day behavior toward treating the genders equally. Tibor and Olga shared all major decisions, equal partners in life. He thoughtfully listened to her ideas and fell in with her organization of his life outside of work. Tibor even fell in with her plans when Olga told him she wanted to get a college education, and later when she decided to work full-time. He knew these were important to her. So while his belief stayed firm, his practices bent like a fir tree whose upward growth was stunted by a massive rock.

On a cold morning in mid-February 1976, Olga was at the airport to welcome new clients, a Laotian refugee family arriving on the 6:00 a.m. flight from Thailand. Olga's breath condensed and froze as she briskly walked from the parking lot into the terminal. When she first came to the North American prairie, she had a tough time adjusting to the long frigid winters. She had acclimatized long ago, although she still resented the bitter cold.

She had greeted many other Southeast Asian families and knew the critical things to bring. Most important were plenty of blankets and jackets. The new arrivals were prepared for tropics, not the below-zero weather that awaited them.

She met two women from the partnering sponsor churches in the terminal entrance. They had followed her advice and were well prepared, loaded down with warm items.

The corridor where the refugees waited was empty. But even if it had been full, it would have been easy to pick out the family. Their small stature, almond-colored skin, dark hair, and Asian eye fold were distinctive. The ten of them huddled close together, as if to ward off the unfamiliar surroundings. There were two adult males, two adult females, four older youth, and two toddlers. The head of the extended family, a young male, was dressed in summer weight pants, jacket, shirt, and tie. The women wore thin shirts, skirts, and sandals; the toddlers only T-shirts.

"Welcome to Minnesota." The three women greeted the new arrivals, smiling.

"It's nice to meet you," the head of the family replied, smiling and nodding. Having worked with the American forces, he spoke fluent soldier English. The others looked shyly and somewhat bewildered at their hosts.

"How are you?" the sponsors asked.

"Fine," the head of the household said.

"Would you like a jacket?" the sponsors offered.

"No, thank you," he said.

"The paperwork we received said you were Meo," Olga said. "What's Meo?" This was the Institute's first Laotian family and she had no idea who the Meo were. Up until now, all their refugees had been Vietnamese.

The head of the household recoiled, grimacing. "We're not Meo! We're Hmong." Meo was a very derogatory Laotian slur for the Hmong, Olga later learned. The Hmong had been important allies in the Vietnam War, rescuing downed American pilots in the mountainous jungle and serving as foot soldiers.

"We're Laotian citizens," he continued. "Our tribe lives above 3,000 feet in the mountains."

Before going outside, the women gently persuaded the family to put on jackets or blankets. Even with the added protection, the cold air was far outside the realm of anything they had ever experienced. They tried to breathe, but inhaling the cold air froze their windpipes. The severe pain was frightening. They wished they were anywhere warm.

Sights, smells, clothes, weather, language, nothing was familiar.

"Is this the ancient part of the city?" the head of the household asked on the car ride to the apartment the sponsor had prepared for them.

"Yes," answered the sponsor, unsure if their reaction was positive or negative.

"Where are the leaves on the trees?" he said.

"The trees don't have leaves in winter," she said. "In winter the sun only shines on us at an angle, so it's colder. Soon it'll be spring and the sun will shine on us more directly. It'll be warmer and the leaves will return."

An explanation so bizarre to the new arrivals, they thought she must be lying. Maybe she didn't want to admit Agent Orange, a defoliant used during the Vietnam War, had destroyed their foliage.

The apartment was ready with food, pots and pans, beds, pillows, blankets—everything. But the insulated building with electric heat, indoor bathrooms, and an electric kitchen was new and confusing. Even with the generous material support and ongoing help, Olga knew the family's adjustment was going to be extremely difficult. She remembered how hard hers had been, and she hadn't come from a lush tropical jungle, arriving in deep winter, in a big city with no residents of her ethnic group, and only a handful of people from her side of the world.

They did have one thing in their favor that she didn't have, Olga thought. There was now a government support network and a resettlement program to help them.

On that winter day, Olga didn't realize the significance of the occasion. This family is reported to be the first Hmong family to be formally resettled in Minnesota.

"Happy birthday, dear Lili, happy birthday to you." Family and friends sang loudly and gaily, the winter chill and the dreary browns of December 1976 in direct contrast to the warmth and good cheer in the playroom.

With a big smile, Lili blew out the six candles on her cake. Olga knew Lili loved all birthdays, but her own in particular. Her delightful, happy giggles filled the room.

Lili was developing nicely, Olga thought as she watched her play with her friends. She was friendly, spoke in sentences, knew her letters, and could even dress herself in simple clothes. The EDGE preschool she attended since she was two-and-a-half had made a big difference, preparing her for school.

Lili at her birthday party, Dec. 1977.

With a backbone of steel and Tibor at her side, Olga had fought the local school placing Lili with children unable to learn to read and write. Appealing to the school board, Olga won the right for her daughter to be mainstreamed with a Special Education plan. Olga, always a zealot for a good cause, was proud of Lili's accomplishments. And Olga's vast experience in arguing cases with the INS and starting the Refugee Resettlement program gave her experience on how to successfully take on the government.

As zealous as Olga was about Lili's education, she was equally zealous about Peter and Kitty learning another language, understanding other cultures. She had believed in this for decades, her experiences at the Institute reinforcing her thinking. Peter had the chance at thirteen in Germany, Kitty went abroad the year after high school and lived with a Dutch family in the Netherlands.

"Are you glad you went?" Olga asked, a few days after Kitty returned. They sat in the living room, a breeze blowing in the familiar smells of Lake Owasso summer through the open sliding glass door. "What'd you learn?"

"The biggest thing was about me!" her daughter said. "I thought I knew all about Europe. I'd fit in, no problem. And I did fit in. But I changed so much; I began to feel like a stranger to myself. I guess I had to learn what I can change, and what I can't."

"I wish I could've been there to help you," Olga said, with a sad smile. She had been through it herself. You have to decide, she thought, what you're willing to change and what's innate to you.

Of all the opportunities Olga and Tibor had to be immersed in other cultures, the one that made them fully realize the limits of their ability to adapt was their trip to Venezuela in the fall of 1978. Exactly forty years after Olga's family awaited their ship's departure for their new life in South America, Tibor, Olga, and Lili got the chance to go to South America for a nine-month sabbatical.

Besides frustration with the inefficiency and corruption of the Venezuelan government, one of Tibor and Olga's main impressions was the large gap between the 'haves' and the 'have-nots'. The 'haves' had nice homes and were well educated. In the cities, the 'have-nots' lived in shanty villages, although with TV antennas.

Despite the dire predictions of danger from Tibor and Olga's 'have' friends, the family departed on a visit to see the Warao Indians, the second-largest indigenous tribe. They drove twelve hours to the end of the paved road, then hours more to the end of a pot-hole-ridden dirt track. They boarded a thirty-foot dug-out canoe made from a single log.

Shoving off before sunrise, they traveled until past sunset in heavy mist and rain. The boat, powered by two outboard motors, was guided by two Warao scouts who spoke Spanish. The boat meandered down small, earthy-smelling, yellow waterways that wove through marshes and green tropical islands of dense vegetation. The hum of the outboard and light rain was interrupted by the guttural call of howler monkeys and the croaking of great white egrets.

For many hours the Zoltais saw no other humans. Near dusk they saw Warao huts clustered in villages along the shore overhanging the water. The rough wood floors of the huts attached to stilts several feet above water level.

The structures only had floors and thatched palm frond roofs, no walls. Hammocks were slung between the stilt poles. Adults dressed in western garb with bare feet and naked young children gathered around a central clay fire pit.

"Amazing," Olga said eyes like saucers, "this is like traveling into the pages of the National Geographic." She knew some of her clients came from worlds nearly as far from Minnesota as this. It gave her further appreciation for their life's journey.

"In many respects," Tibor said, "the Warao still live in early stages of the stone age. They're hunters and gatherers."

The natives they met the next day had short, wide stature with bronze skin, high cheekbones, and dark hair and eyes. Many, especially the children, had somewhat distended stomachs typical of malnourishment. "The people suffer from diarrhea," one of the guides explained when asked about the residents' health. "Half of the children don't reach five-years-old." They later were told by a nutritionist that the Warao used to be nomadic. To make them accessible, Europeans convinced them to no longer wander, which destroyed their fragile sanitation balance. They still pulled drinking water from one side of their hut and poured refuge off the other.

Without the migration, their drinking water became contaminated with parasites and infections.

Warao Indians in Oronoco River Delta, Venezuela, 1979.

Communication with the residents was limited. Warao had to first be translated into Spanish by the guides, then into Hungarian by the family friend who traveled with Tibor and Olga. Tibor did, however, get a chance to converse with a Warao chieftain.

"I'm chief of this area," the guides translated, as the chieftain spoke. "Each village has a chief and he is the chief of these chiefs," the guides added.

"I'm also the tribe's doctor," the Chieftain said. "I've never lost a patient."

"How do you heal them?" Tibor asked.

"I heal with song and prayer."

In Warao culture the natural doctor, or shaman, communicated through song with the supernatural to maintain order in the world.

The trip was the most fascinating Tibor and Olga had ever been on in their lives. The Warao culture was incredibly interesting, a world unfathomably different from their own. It was also distressing to see how Western culture had disrupted the very fabric of the Warao world.

While in Venezuela, Olga and Tibor experienced a wide spectrum of social classes. Hungarian and other European immigrants were more educated. They hadn't blended with the native residents. The Hungarian immigrants, and even their children, spoke beautiful Hungarian and surrounded themselves with Hungarian culture. Olga remembered how close her family had come to immigrating to Chile. If they had, she wondered, would her life have been closer to this?

One night, Olga and Tibor had an opportunity to attend an event held at the Hungarian House. Hungarian Scouts were meeting in an adjacent room. Having been involved in Scouts across five countries, their curiosity led them to stop in.

Their jaws dropped as they realized the prize being given out in the Scout Ceremony was Tibor's novel! The one he'd written about Boy Scouts in the DP camp then donated to the Hungarian Scouts when he and Olga lived in Toronto. Tibor learned his book was being used in several countries, there had been several printings.

Nine months in Venezuela felt incredibly long. When they returned to the U. S., Olga was a nervous wreck and literally got down on her hands and knees, to kiss the rich Minnesota soil. "I never thought I'd return alive!" Olga said. "The traffic was out-of-control!"

It wasn't just the traffic that made it difficult for Olga and Tibor to adapt to life in Venezuela. Their lack of Spanish, the slow-moving bureaucracy and corruption, Olga's isolation, and the extreme wealth and poverty all added to their discomfort. Older, more rigid in their ways than when they immigrated to North America, they didn't bend as easily now.

From their trip, Olga felt newly grateful to the twist of fate that resulted in her family immigrating to North, not South America. Both she and Tibor valued the equality, integration, and freedom of being U.S. citizens. They had raised North American children and lived truly American lives, albeit seasoned with Hungarian paprika.

11

The Harvest of Their Careers
(1978 - 1993)

Tibor in his office at the
University of Minnesota, 1980s.

Olga Presenting at the
International Institute, 1990s.

After close to twenty years at the U of M, Tibor still looked the part of a professor, albeit a more experienced one. His hair salt and pepper, he sported a thick mustache along with wire-rimmed bifocals. Concentration and drive still shone in his eyes, but major health problems since the late 1960s, especially the loss of feeling in his fingers, had stopped his work in the lab. Poor health also contributed to him stepping down as department chair.

Students no longer viewed Tibor as frenetic, now he was rather laid back.

Frontiers of science had blasted forward. The breakthrough work of Tibor's early career was now foundational knowledge. His current efforts focused on theoretical concepts, literature reviews, and guiding graduate students' research on how structure and shape drove fiber properties.

One morning in 1978, Tibor, armed with espresso made on a Bunsen burner in his lab, sat at his desk immersed in journals on asbestos and other fiber research spanning 400 years and six languages. Spring sun shone in through his basement-office window, illuminating the words on the often fragile, yellowing pages. Atomic models and carefully organized mountains of journals surrounded him on his desk and every cabinet. Tibor, still aware of how deprived of reading he'd been as a POW, cherished every book, every page. He was impervious to the smell of the cigarette smoke and dust that pervaded his office.

As he lit a cigarette, Tibor was pondering asbestos fiber. What made it so strong and indestructible? The health hazard from breathing asbestos was now broadly understood. But there was scientific confusion about what was and wasn't asbestos.

Tibor had personal experience with the deadly impact of asbestos exposure. It provided him extra impetus to unlock the science behind it. He wanted to make sure asbestos was correctly identified, the critical properties of it as a biological hazard understood and guarded against.

In the 1960s, Tibor's father had developed lung cancer. His employment at the Austrian tile and pipe factory mixing asbestos, crushed rock, and water in the late 1940s was thought to be a factor. He survived with aggressive treatment. Then in 1975, his uncle Jenci Bácsi died from Mesothelioma, a rare, incurable cancer of the protective sac of the lung, which almost exclusively came from asbestos exposure. The asbestos fibers became airborne during the manufacturing process and took up residence in his lungs, beginning a long, slow disease that took twenty to fifty years to kill. Tibor feared his devastating losses to slow-killing asbestos disease were not yet over. Unfortunately his premonition proved true.

His father would die of Mesothelioma in 1980, his brother Steve in 1998.

Mesothelioma took every family member who directly worked with those blasted tiles and pipes. If only they had understood the risk!

But it took a few more months for Tibor's work on asbestos to take a public turn.

One of many gatherings Olga and Tibor hosted in their backyard.

Hot summer sun and fully leafed-out trees reflected in the water behind the Zoltai's Heinel Drive home. Home was only a fifteen-minute drive from Tibor's office, yet it always gave Tibor the feeling of being away from it all.

On this glorious Sunday, Tibor and Olga were hosting the Hungarian Literary Club. Tibor was sitting by the edge of the lake in a lawn chair, enjoying the earthy smells of summer, chatting with a long-term member's son, Richard Mandics.

"How do you like it in Duluth?" Tibor asked Richard. "What're you working on?"

Richard, a stocky young man with wavy brown hair and intelligent eyes, always enjoyed talking with Tibor. Even when he was a child, Tibor talked to him with respect. Richard answered with excitement, telling Tibor about his new job as an intern reporter with WDIO-TV in Duluth.

"I hear a lot about Reserve Mining dumping asbestos in Lake Superior," Tibor said, pausing for a puff on his cigarette.

Richard didn't know anything about it and leaned in slightly.

"As a scientist I've a strong opinion about it," Tibor said. "The material they're calling asbestos isn't really asbestos. I don't have a reason to side with one group or the other. Of course, I care about the environment. But I think the issue needs to be dealt with on a scientific basis."

Richard returned to Duluth, did some homework on the case, and with Tibor's technical help put together a proposal for a story. He got to be the on-camera reporter for the thirty-minute exposé that aired in August 1978.

"To understand the Reserve case at all," Richard reported, standing in front of the camera with Lake Superior and the Reserve Mining operation in the background, "it must be kept in mind that the material in the tailing, which is thought by some to be hazardous, is not true asbestos; although, it has been incorrectly called that over the years."

"In the early seventies people started to think quite a bit about the dangers of true asbestos. Several studies done on asbestos workers showed a dramatic increase in lung disorders. With that as a backdrop in 1973, both the U.S. Environmental Protection Agency and the Minnesota Pollution Control Agency released preliminary reports, which said that particles in the Reserve Mining tailings were virtually identical to the killer amosite asbestos. By the spring of 1974, Judge Miles Lord became so convinced that the public was being endangered by Reserve, he ordered the company shut down."

"But there are those that say they can tell the two substances apart," Richard reported over the image of Tibor working at the university. "And they say the differences between them are quite considerable. Notable among these scientists is Dr. Tibor Zoltai, a mineralogist at the University of Minnesota who is an internationally recognized pioneer in the field of asbestos study. His interests began with a study he was commissioned to do by the PCA in 1975. That study was mainly intended to help clear up the confusion in definitions that existed at that time. But Dr. Zoltai ended up learning a lot more. He became convinced that the substance in the tailing and true asbestos are not identical and that they behave quite differently."

The camera zoomed in on Tibor. "Mineralogically speaking, are there reasons to assume that the two would behave in the same way in the various circumstances that they might encounter?" Richard asked.

"Oh no, no," Tibor said. "Because one of them is stronger, is more durable, it's flexible, and it's more inert in chemical environments." Tibor's hand emphasized the point. "That one, the asbestiform variety, will survive mechanical treatments, processing and will survive in different environments such as biological systems much more than the weak, decomposable, and brittle, form in the tailings."

Tibor strongly advocated the fibrous substance in the tailings should be studied for health risk. He was concerned the fibers could be dangerous, but not because they were asbestos. That was an unjustified scientific leap.

As the story was picked up by the Twin Cities and national media, Tibor's opinion was very unpopular. The Reserve Mining case was the first major battle where the government forced a company to change its operation because of a negative impact on the environment. Tibor was life-long member of the Sierra Club, yet he was in the awkward position of the scientific facts not agreeing with his politics.

His convictions were challenged just like when he was a DP and had a very unpopular opinion on Catholic Doctrine. This time it was not a personal matter. It was a professional challenge in the public eye. With the reinforcement of years of experience and maturity, he had the strength to weather the storm without harming his self-worth.

"Did you hear what happened in Iran—?!" Olga, wide eyed, opened the front door for Kitty, not even bothering with hello. It was April 1980.

While they walked into the living room, Olga and Kitty exhausted what they knew about the failed attempt to rescue the American hostages in their sixth month of captivity. They were being held by Iranian students demanding extradition of the deposed Shah of Iran.

"Since last summer," Olga said, settled on the low-backed settee, "I've had a number of political asylum cases from Iran." The Institute had never had asylum seekers before, but these individuals sought refuge from persecution like refugees.

Unlike refugees, they didn't have a visa permitting them to settle in the U.S. Most were here with a temporary visa, or some had even been smuggled in. Either way, they had no legal right to stay.

"They described a lot of torture by the new regime." Olga's brows furrowed. What she visualized was in sharp contrast to the greening grass, the buds sprouting on the trees, the lapping lake outside the living room's picture window. "The worst case was a student whose sixteen-year-old sister was caught in a student demonstration against the government. They put her in jail and were going to execute her, but believed Muslim law forbad executing a virgin. So they raped her. Then executed her the next day."

"No," Kitty gasped.

"My client also demonstrated. He fears for his life if he returns."

"Will he be able to stay?"

"I think so," Olga said. "His asylum was approved, but he still has to apply for permanent residence and a work permit." While Olga didn't yet know it, many more waves of asylum seekers would flow in from conflicts erupting around the world: Ethiopia, Congo/Zaire, Liberia, and others.

Olga began to focus her client time on these cases, while her staff of five caseworkers ran the Institute's blossoming refugee resettlement program. She loved the technical, ethical, and moral challenges of developing a persuasive INS case for asylum seekers who wanted to stay in the U.S.

The stakes were high. Often imprisonment or death awaited them if they were deported. These new cases stretched Olga to come up with yet more creative approaches.

With only one child still at home, Tibor and Olga found the space and time to take on more volunteer projects and invite even more guests into their home. In May 1981, they welcomed three Laotian refugee sisters.

The sisters had escaped the repressive Communist government in Laos by crossing the fiercely guarded, snake-infested Mekong River in the dead of night. After eighteen months in a crowded refugee camp in Thailand, they arrived in Minnesota.

"What was your first impression?" Olga asked the middle sister, Bounnhong. Olga and Bounnhong were sitting on cushioned wood chairs at a Formica topped table, the air redolent with the sweet smell of freshly steeped green tea.

"Just still freezing." Bounnhong hugged her warm cup of tea, shivering as she remembered. "I have no clue that America look huge. Everything so big. We see big buildings in Thailand but not as big as here." She paused, looking into her tea. "Felt kind of afraid. So new to us. Didn't want to say wrong thing."

For both Olga and Tibor the experience of sponsoring the sisters and seeing them blossom into Americans was powerfully rewarding. So much so, that in years to come they would sponsor an Ethiopian boy, a Hungarian family, two Transylvanian families, and more, but their closest relationship would always remain with the Laotian sisters. They were like daughters.

Laotian sisters. *L. to r.* Bounnhong, Buma, and Vansy at Buma's wedding held in Olga and Tibor's home, 1982.

A month after the sisters arrived, Tibor and Olga hosted one of their regular get-togethers for Tibor's graduate students. The graduate students, Peter, and the Laotian sisters sat on the patio, chatting. Tantalizing smells of grilling meat rose out of the barbeque.

The sky began to turn from pleasant blue to dark iridescent green without much notice by those in the gathering. All of a sudden a forceful gust of wind demanded their attention.

Then the electricity went out.

As Tibor headed into the house for candles, the air pressure crashed. His ears filled with pounding.

"A tornado!" Tibor yelled. The china cabinet started shaking. He grabbed it.

"Everyone to the garage!" Olga screamed over the hammering, reckless wind. "Get under the pool table!"

A tower of water rose out of the middle of the lake. It climbed and climbed, swirling water reaching twenty feet toward the sky. Lawn chairs appeared above the neighbor's house, somersaulting crazily on their roller coaster ride toward the lake.

The guests dashed through the house to the garage. Sirens began to blare over the loud, rumbling wind.

Olga headed back to the patio, thinking the embers might fly out of the wildly gyrating barbeque kettle and start a fire. She tried to wrestle open the glass door. The force of the wind was stronger. It held in place.

Then abruptly there was silence. A strange, inscrutable lack of sound.

The wind had stopped. An uncomfortable, unnatural calm descended. The tornado was gone, its visit was no more than a minute.

Everyone slowly walked back to the patio, gazing at the fallen trees that littered the lawn.

"We should eat," Olga said after a silence, "there may be another wave coming."

Another wave coming? she thought. Why would she say that? Tornadoes don't come in waves. But the fear and the siren had triggered a memory from the days when Sopron was bombed. After a bombing raid, her family always ate immediately since any moment the siren might blare again.

"Sure, let's eat," the others said.

In the yard, their canoe was wrapped around a tree, eight mature trees were down, and their neighbor's porch had taken up residence. One of the downed trees had snapped in half forming an upside-down V over the Dodge pick-up Peter had driven over—the first vehicle he had ever purchased new.

Amazingly there was no structural damage to their home or even a scratch on Peter's truck!

In a neighbor's yard, a three-foot-thick oak had been rotated, splintered, and knocked over, the tornado twisting it as easily as a dishcloth. Many other mature trees were down. Those still standing had trash high in their branches. One home had a canoe firmly planted in the center of their picture window. Another was bare of windows.

Damage from tornado, 1981. Picture taken one block southeast of Tibor and Olga's home.

Like Tibor and Olga's place, the rest of their street had escaped the full brunt of the storm, but up hill, one block southeast, the situation was different. Sixty homes were missing all or part of their roofs. Six houses were demolished. Incredibly, no one was killed!

Tibor's arm traced the direction the storm traveled. "The tornado must have touched down on the hill, bounced up, passed over our street, and landed in the lake." They later learned the tornado cut a fifteen-mile swath of destruction through the Twin Cities with winds of more than 200 mph.

"Today was really something," a graduate student commented as he was leaving. "Your gatherings are always so interesting, Tibor. What are you going to do next time? How will you top today's entertainment?"

While it certainly wasn't as dramatic as a tornado, a powerful force drove Tibor. Since his DP days, he wanted to both understand and help others understand nature's laws. He also clung to his youthful dream of publishing a book.

"I've been thinking about publishing a textbook on mineralogy," Tibor said one day, entering Dr. James Stout's musty-smelling office. Tibor and Jim had offices across the cabinet-lined hallway that ran down the middle of the Pillsbury Hall basement. Since Jim joined the faculty in 1972, they co-taught Introduction to Mineralogy. Because they didn't find a text including all they felt a student needed to learn, they primarily used a plastic binder of their own material.

Jim looked up from his work.

"I've always wanted to write a book," Tibor said. "Current textbooks have such a gap in material. Would you be interested in co-authoring it?"

"I don't think I've got time," Jim said, although he was honored to be asked by a man he viewed as one of the world's experts in symmetry and crystal structure. But Tibor didn't let the idea drop.

While it wasn't a novel like the ones Tibor wrote in DP camp, nor a philosophy book like he dreamed of writing while is Paris, the mineralogy textbook was published in 1984. He wrote a Hungarian colleague, "I worked on the book for ten years. If I had known how long it would take, I probably wouldn't have embarked on writing it. But now, I'm glad I did."

Alongside working on the textbook, Tibor continued to pursue nature's laws regarding fibers. While he and his students conducted research, served as scientific experts on state and national committees, and published a dozen papers on the impact of surface structure and shape on asbestos properties, Tibor wanted to do more. He wanted to correlate asbestiform properties to their health effects. Tibor applied jointly with a group of health professionals to NSF for funding this critical work, but the grant was turned down.

Unfortunately, asbestos wasn't a topic of interest to the scientific community. Important to industry, but not sexy scientific research, and NSF dollars were no longer as readily available. Regardless, Tibor continued to advocate for the critical need to define the link between fiber properties and health.

The shrill ring of the telephone sliced into the dark silence. Olga awoke, heart pounding, and looked at the clock. It was 2:00 a.m. She shivered when her feet touched the wintery cold wood floorboards of their Summit Avenue home—they had moved into their brownstone mansion a couple of years earlier—and reached for the phone.

"Hello," Gene said in Hungarian, his speech slurred. "She left me."

"I know, Gene," Olga said gripping the phone. "You need to stop the drugs and the drinking. You get violent when you drink."

"My life is ruined. Why should I care?"

"You need help," Olga said. "You can still get your life—"

"My life is so hard . . ." He rambled on about his failed marriages, never listening to what Olga had to say.

Sometimes a consequence of giving unwelcome advice was to drive those away she loved. Her brother Gene would no longer talk to her if he was sober. He didn't want her advice. He knew if he called, he would get an earful, so he only called when he drank.

Olga despaired over this. How to use her well-developed problem-solving skills to help people she loved? Unlike clients who came to her office looking for advice, family and friends didn't necessarily agree there was a problem. Even if they did, they often weren't receptive to Olga's solutions. Gene wasn't the only one driven away by her pit-bull conviction to an idea. Dozens of times Olga heard variations of, "I know you want me to do that. You've told me many times, but I'm dealing with it my own way!"

By the summer of 1985, Gene's chemical use put his job in jeopardy. He chose to address the problem in his own way, a dismal solution: He committed suicide.

When she heard the news, Olga became extremely angry. He was so talented, a real artist, very intelligent. Why did he throw it all away?

She knew Gene's life wasn't easy. He had to finish four years of military school even though he hated it within months, lost his homeland, started a new life in Austria, then Canada.

But he had so much raw talent. What a waste. She was able to help strangers solve their problems.

Why wouldn't Gene listen to her? Why wouldn't he get help?

Olga hated when she wasn't able to solve people's problems, even if they weren't family.

"The Hmong are having so much trouble finding work," Olga said to her coworker. The two were seated at a long smooth plastic topped table in the Institute's linoleum floored basement break room. It was

1989. The tools the Institute had to help their Hmong clients just weren't enough.

"Yeah, they're struggling more than others," her coworker answered, sipping his steaming coffee.

"I've an idea how to help," Olga looked straight at her coworker. "A class combining both nursing assistant and English language instruction. Nursing assistant pay is better than an entry-level job. With added language help, more of our clients should be able to pass the licensure test."

The coworker admired how Olga could generalize observations from working with specific clients to come up with ideas for new programs. He nodded, adding, "That's shift work, which would really help with childcare." The Hmong tended to have large families, so childcare was a huge barrier to employment.

"Exactly!" Olga said, eyes aglow. "It also fits with their respect for elders. I talked to Lyngblomsten nursing home and they've a shortage of nursing assistants. They're willing to work with us."

Olga and her coworker submitted a grant request, and the state of Minnesota approved funding a pilot. The first group had high passage of the licensure test but was not very successful in the workplace. The program staff addressed the problem by adjusting client screening criteria and adding a workplace component to cover proper dress, chit chat with coworkers, body language, and workplace rules, to teach cultural harmony.

Olga was delighted with the way the program blossomed from her seed. While it never became as broadly popular among the Hmong as she had hoped, it helped many foreign-born clients move ahead.

* * *

Tibor and Olga chatted with other Minnesota Hungarians, while they waited in the air-conditioned airport luggage area in the summer heat of 1991. Loud speaker announcements, luggage dropping down metal slides, and people shuffling echoed about the cement room. Tibor and Olga had greeted many visitors from around the world in this room, but today's guests were exceptional. Tibor, serving as President of the Minnesota Hungarians, had arranged a welcome delegation to show support for the new visitors, the Hungarian Special Olympics Team.

Ever since Lili had entered their lives, Tibor and Olga had an appreciation for how precious people with disabilities were. They now advocated on their behalf.

Being able to support these young adults, repressed in their native land, was particularly meaningful.

As the athletes entered, Olga noticed Peter Baga, a twenty-two-year-old tennis player. Peter was trying to hide behind the other athletes. He was five-foot-ten-inch with a sinewy build. Olga's eyes were drawn to his grossly deformed face. His eyes were several inches too far apart. He had a huge, crooked nose with a deep pit on one side.

Peter Baga before surgery, 1991.

How difficult it must be for him, Olga thought. There have been so many advances in the U.S. in plastic surgery. Could something be done for him?

Being a case worker was so interwoven into her nature, it didn't shut down just because she was off Institute time. Since the athletes were only in town for a short stay, she knew she needed to work fast.

"Peter has a paramidline cranial facial cleft," Dr. Shilling, a plastic and facial reconstructive surgeon explained to Olga in his modern office. "This is a rare birth defect that occurred when he was developing in his mother's womb. In the U.S. you don't see grownups with this deformity. It's surgically corrected in infancy." Dr. Shilling's voice began to sparkle. "I think I can help him!"

Dr. Shilling only had an hour free to make arrangements due to his surgery schedule. In that narrow window, amazingly, he reached all six heavily booked specialists and the hospital administrator he needed to donate services and facilities. They all said, "Count me in."

Olga crossed the last remaining hurdle the day before Peter was scheduled to depart. She got the Hungarian Embassy to extend his stay by committing that he was welcome in her and Tibor's home during recovery. The Minnesota Hungarians would fund his return flight.

The more Olga interacted with Peter, the more she began to wonder if he even had a mental disability, or was he just slow from growing up in the isolation of an institution. Olga shuddered as she thought about how several close friends had recommended she institutionalize Lili when she was born.

"I love my new face," Peter said to Olga before he left. His grin was infectious, Olga thought. She had never seen him smile before the surgery. "My mother left me in the hospital when I was born," Peter told Olga. "When I was growing up in the institution, everybody teased me. With my new face, maybe my family will accept me."

Over time his face healed nicely. While his dream of reuniting with his family didn't come true, he walked with head up and eyes looking about, no longer fearing being ostracized.

Dr. Shilling went on to embark on a multi-year partnership with a Hungarian medical center. He trained two Hungarian surgeons on the procedure, conducting fifty-one facial reconstructive surgeries, mostly on young children. Olga and Tibor were proud to help initiate this project that gave Hungarian children an equal chance in life.

Since his stroke in 1990 while attending a conference in China, Tibor had aged a lot. His hair was more white than brown, his glasses trifocals with an additional pane to compensate for strained muscles from decades of viewing 3D drawings. His physical frame was a shadow of his former strength. One day he made an important decision. It was time to retire.

In his long career, he'd taught the natural laws of mineralogy to more than a thousand students and nudged forward man's understanding of nature. Man knew exponentially more about nature's laws now, than when Tibor first became involved fifty years earlier. Today even retail stores sold programmable calculators more powerful than the four-story computer he'd used at MIT.

What natural laws will scientists uncover in the next fifty years? Tibor thought. How will technology change lives?

Not long before Tibor retired, an issue of *Acta Crystallograhia*, a crystallography journal, was dedicated to him in honor of the existence for thirty years of his sharing coefficient used in classifying silicate structures. Tibor was surprised, but pleased, when he received another accolade a few years later. A former undergraduate student named a new mineral after him, in recognition of his contributions to mineralogy, both as a researcher and as an educator.

The newly identified mineral bore the name Zoltaiite.

Two years later, Olga retired too. "Area Immigrants Are Soon to Lose Their Patron Saint," read the front-page headline of the *Minneapolis Star-Tribune* on July 26, 1993. "They are known as 'Olga cases'," the article read, "immigrants and refugees whose situations are heartbreaking, and among the toughest to sort out and resolve. Over the years, Minneapolis immigration lawyer (and International Institute board member) Sam Myers has often told Olga that there didn't seem to be any legal way to help her clients, however compelling their situations. 'She would say, 'There's got to be a way, Sam,' Myers recalled. 'And, there typically was a way.' Once convinced that her case was right, Zoltai would take it upon herself to prove it to everyone, from attorneys like Myers to immigration officials. She would look for the loopholes and discretion in the law. She would argue, always politely, for her clients. More often that not, they would win.

"To hear people talk about Zoltai is to hear them describe the former Hungarian refugee in saintly terms. 'Who would not talk to Olga Zoltai?' Myers said. 'It's like not talking to Jesus! It's like not talking to Mahatma Gandhi!' Zoltai, 62, has been a caseworker, a counselor, an advocate and a surrogate mother for thousands of foreigners who have come to her at the International Institute . . . colleagues say her creative approach to solving problems will be missed."

Olga, with her gray hair, large wire-rimmed glasses, and rounded face etched deeply with smile wrinkles was a lifelong friendly advocate and confidante. She felt extremely lucky to have had such an interesting career. "I love to give back to this country that has given me so much!" Olga often said.

The programs she started continued long beyond her retirement. By 2001, the Nursing Assistant program graduated over 700. The Institute resettled close to 15,000 refugees, laying claim to being the largest sponsor of Hmong and Somali in Minnesota, and most likely in the entire U.S.

12

A Legacy of Cultural Mosaic
(1982 - 2001)

Tibor and Olga holding grandchild Alex, 1985.

For a number of years, Olga made monthly trips to Toronto to help her parents and Tibor's mother. It shattered her heart to see how sad Eugene Bácsi was in his nursing home room. As always, her mind was seeking a solution.

That's when Tibor and Olga decided to move from their lake home to an old mansion on Summit Avenue in St. Paul.

"The grandparents are getting older," Olga explained to Peter and Kitty, who were surprised at the idea. "They could have their own apartment, yet we could take care of them."

"Lili will never be able to drive," Tibor said. "On Summit she could catch a bus. We know the house's in bad shape," he added. "But we couldn't afford it otherwise."

Rain came in, half the rooms had falling ceilings, the porch was about to collapse, the wood floors were uneven and gummy. The list of problems in this house went on and on.

But Tibor's architectural and engineering background allowed him to see beyond obvious drawbacks. He knew the house was structurally sound: a solid foundation, the plumbing and electricity in reasonable shape, and a relatively new roof. Tibor and Olga had so many ideas on how they wanted to restore the house. It was in St. Paul's historic Ramsey Hill district. With hard work, they thought it could return to its former glory.

The massive Romanesque brownstone building with towers, turrets, and large arched windows was built in 1883 by fuel and transportation baron Chauncey Wright Griggs. Its flamboyant history intrigued them. It had been a social club, a stockbroker's residence, an art school and gallery, and the home and business location for a self-proclaimed warlock.

"The self-proclaimed warlock painted the front hall blood red," Tibor said. "While the family we bought it from painted over with white, you can still see the red underneath." The white paint was the last dwellers' only improvement.

In the children's room, walls and woodwork were bright orange. The walls sported thousands of pin holes from being used as a dartboard.

In the master bedroom, the warlock had gone for effect, silver metallic wall paper covered with intertwined naked bodies printed in black.

"With the yellow from the swaying light," Tibor said swirling his hand, "I could see how from the sidewalk you could think you saw moving bodies. The warlock certainly worked to promote the house as haunted. It was good for business,"—the warlock published occult books, his printing press in the original kitchen. The adjacent master bath had similar orgy wallpaper with a cherry-red ceiling light and tiles.

Tibor went on to show other occult oddities, like the cement cat caskets and pentagram painted on the basement floor.

The whole building had a musty smell and a cold, damp feel. But with Tibor and Olga's imagination, the old grandeur was visible under the dirt, wear, and occult decorating. They admired the grand central staircase of oak rising twenty-six feet, the original wood-and-marble fireplace mantles, the hardwood floors, panels and trim, the distinctive stone arches, the leafy capitals.

On October 30, 1982, Olga, Tibor, and Lili moved in.

First, Olga took down the filthy ten-foot high drapes, ripe from decades of use. Removing the drapes for cleaning proved to be a mistake. The next morning, the front page of the *St. Paul Pioneer Press* Halloween edition had their new home with the headline: "Haunted Houses: Several homes in Twin Cities tell their own ghost stories." The caption under the picture read: "The house at . . . Summit Ave. may be the most notoriously haunted house in St. Paul." But Tibor and Olga had no drapes to shut out the numerous gawking sightseers that night.

Now they owned the most famous haunted house in the Twin Cities. It didn't bother them. They joked that their homeland,

Hungary, was for a millennium the home of Transylvania, the setting for the famous book on Dracula.

A refugee family sponsored from Transylvania a decade later lived in the house for close to a year. The family was related to Béla Lugosi, who played Count Dracula in the original 1931 movie. A funny twist of fate.

Tibor and Olga's home on Summit Avenue.

Regrettably Tibor and Olga's parents never came to live in the house. Lili Néni soon died. Maria Néni cherished the Hungarian Catholic Church too much to leave Toronto, and Eugene Bácsi didn't want to leave Maria Néni.

But Olga did get her dream of sharing the house with extended family. In June 1985, Peter, his pregnant wife Margie, and four-year-old son Barrett returned to the Twin Cities so Peter could accept a new job. The younger Zoltai family had their own apartment on the second floor. This was one of the six apartments Tibor and Olga rented, but they were delighted to have family there instead.

In Hungary, extended family often lived together. Olga and Tibor loved this closeness over the distances separating family in America.

A month after moving in, Alex, Peter's second son, was born. When Eugene Bácsi came to visit that winter, he affectionately called roly-poly Alex, little chicken catcher, a name he used for Peter decades earlier.

Tibor bought a camcorder to record the grandchildrens' antics. "Make him crawl, Barrett," Olga said, as Tibor filmed. Alex was sitting on his knees between Olga's legs on the cream-colored linoleum floor of the enclosed porch of Peter's apartment. Lighting there was best for filming, and the smell of flowers rose from Olga's garden below.

"Okay," Barrett said moving away, "come here." Alex's eyes followed Barrett and smiled, but his rounded body stayed put.

"Come here, Alex," Olga said, moving next to Barrett. Alex gave Barrett and Olga a great big toothy grin and bounced up and down, but he didn't move forward. Only later while trying to film Barrett, did Tibor capture clips of Alex speedily crawling to interfere with Barrett's play.

Watching the video was a novel treat. It was sharper, less bouncy, not silent like the movies Tibor had taken of his children. He didn't have to pull out the reel-to-reel projector and screen. The video played right on the TV.

"You're movie stars," Tibor said, as the kids giggled at themselves on TV.

* * *

266

Forty years had passed since they left Hungary. Both Olga and Tibor still treasured links to their homeland. Olga collected and celebrated everything Hungarian: folk art, old Hungarian household tools, and Hungarians themselves. She loved to talk about everything Hungarians accomplished, pointing out that a Hungarian was the first to isolate Vitamin C—from paprika, of course. She bragged about the twelve Nobel Laureates of Hungarian origin, pretty impressive for a small country.

Tibor was happy to contribute details. A Hungarian laid the foundation for the theory of symmetries in quantum physics, discovered the properties of cathode ray tubes, developed the use of radioactive tracers to study chemical processes, and defined the physiology/pathology of balance in the inner ear.

"Kitty, did you know that Hungary had an important role in Minneapolis becoming the milling center of the world?" Olga asked raising an eyebrow. The family sat at the round kitchen table, the sunlight lazily lighting up the room. While no room in their house was small, the kitchen was the coziest, full of lingering aromas from Hungarian cooking.

"Really?" Kitty asked. Kitty was a scientist for the Pillsbury Company.

"In the late 1800s, the milling baron Pillsbury bought equipment and hired experts from Hungary to be able to duplicate their process for making much finer flour out of hard wheat. Because of this superior process, Minneapolis became a milling center and grew into a big city." Olga beamed at having recently discovered this.

"Is there any industry where you can't point out a successful Hungarian?"

Olga could happily point out Hungarians in any industry, even entertainment. Tony Curtis, Jerry Seinfeld, Mariska Hargitay, Paul

Newman, Harry Houdini, Paul Simon, and Steve Spielberg all had Hungarian ancestry, she told Kitty.

Tibor's link to all things Hungarian tended to be tied to history, another one of his passions. He believed that to understand history was to gain insight into people. Through understanding both, man had an opportunity to influence the future. He collected old coins and maps, researched family genealogy, studied historic linguistic interrelationships, and investigated historic places and events. His linguistic interests grew as he started looking at the link between Hungarian and Finnish, two Finno Ugric languages.

While he enjoyed all his projects, his favorite was the family tree. "I've traced several branches of my family back seven or eight generations," Tibor explained to a visiting Hungarian professor in the mid-1980s. "It looks like one branch may even go back 400 years."

"On our way here," the guest said, "we stopped in New York and visited a friend who's into genealogy. She was excited about a new lead she just uncovered for the Hungarian branch of her family. She traced the Beéry Balogh family back 600 years."

"The Beéry Balogh family?" Tibor said straightening up. "That's one of the branches of my family tree. Perhaps we're related!"

"Why don't you give her a call?" the guest suggested. Tibor called. The woman was in fact a relative!

Tibor loved uncovering new relatives, stories, and family documents, like finding treasure. Wonderful nuggets of gold, like unearthing a story that his ancestors were involved in receiving Napoleon in Győr after the French Army defeated the Hungarian nobles, like discovering the letter that a noble ancestor, who had visionary ideas on class structure, wrote in the mid-1800s abdicating his nobility and declaring nobility an unnatural state.

"She's a distant cousin!" Tibor exclaimed to his guest, sounding like a child who just won a prize. "We're going to exchange material on our common branch."

Tibor went on to tell the story of Nicholas Bácsi's father. "My grandfather was christened Steven Beéry, legitimate son of Joseph Beéry. Until he was eighteen he had bright prospects and lived the privileged life of a son in the prestigious Beéry family. But, when he was eighteen, Joseph and Joseph's brother, had an argument. It came out my grandfather was really the son of the brother, a Roman Catholic priest, and the priest's housekeeper." Tibor stroked his chin. "My grandfather was forced to take the housekeeper's last name. To hide his shame, he left town and changed his first name as well, starting a new life as Eugene Mersich."

"How difficult that must have been!"

"I remember grandfather as a bitter man that never smiled." Unlike some relatives, Tibor didn't hide the circumstances of his grandfather's birth. To the contrary, he thought it made an interesting story. And facts were facts.

For their first six years on Summit Avenue, Tibor and Olga spent the majority of evenings and weekends restoring their historic home. They got help from students and immigrants looking for part-time work. Most work they did themselves, since professional fees were beyond their budget. They both enjoyed this project that combined their love of history, their desire to preserve old things, and their refugee mentality. It recycled a beautiful, historic old building and provided bountiful space for housing extended family and their numerous visitors from around the world.

By 1988, the house was restored. It was on the National Historic Registry, and their work was featured in an article in the *Historic*

Preservation Magazine: "Tibor—living up to his wife's admiring description as a 'Renaissance man'—launched into historic research on the home at the same time that they began actual labor. Tibor handled major structural repairs, including modernizing the kitchen while maintaining its antique face. 'It would have been much easier to add new cabinetry, but that would not have been right for the house.' Olga painted, wallpapered, experimented with methods to clean original brass hardware and scoured estate sales for suitably large-scale furnishings."

The article continued: "With the help of the Minnesota Historical Society archives, the Ramsey County Abstract Office and the St. Paul Public Library, Tibor collected old photos and newspaper clippings. Admirers cite this research as an example of the thoroughness that distinguishes the Zoltai's restoration. 'I ran into a large number of problems,' admits Tibor. 'One solution I'm very proud of involved the porte cochere (a covered loading area for carriages),' which had been dismantled in 1939. Its foundation had been left in place, and Zoltai found the original stones buried in the back yard. 'I had an 1886 photograph, and using that I rebuilt it, including the proper wood trim and carved column heads.' "

The most unusual renovation project spawned out of an art show they hosted. Tibor and Olga invited the current director of the art gallery-school, which had been housed in their mansion from 1939 to 1964, for the show and a tour of the house.

"Did you know," the director said gazing at Tibor's restorative handiwork, "the art school removed the woodwork from your front room when they left?"

"We heard that," Tibor said.

"It was used for a number of years at our new site. But we no longer have a place for it. We've been wondering what to do with it."

"I'd be interested in buying and reinstalling it." Tibor knew about the woodwork and was hoping the gallery-school might see fit to sell it.

"It really belongs with this house," the director said. "I'll give it to you."

After almost a year of hard work, Tibor was ready to show the refurbished room.

"Two truckloads of broken-up wood pieces arrived," Tibor explained when unveiling the renovated room to one of his long-time Hungarian friends. "It was like a puzzle. I had no idea how the pieces went together. I measured the dimensions of each pieces, as well as the dimensions of the room, and wrote a computer program to determine how they best fit together. There was three feet of straight crown molding missing, so I shortened the room a foot-and-a-half by adding a false front around the fireplace."

Walnut window trim, wood panels, wood crown molding, wainscoting, and bookshelves snugly framed the cream-color wallpaper. Even the half-circle of windows in the front didn't show any sign of looking forced. Everything fit together beautifully.

"You haven't seen the best part." With a smile, Tibor pushed a button hidden on the east side of the fireplace about five feet from the floor.

With a buzz and a pop, a panel, perfectly aligned with the other wood surrounding the fireplace, shot open a half inch on the west side. Tibor pulled it wide open revealing an eight-rung stepladder.

"I built this secret room for the grandchildren." Tibor reached in, flicking on the light switch.

The guest maneuvered up the child-sized opening, fitting his head and shoulders into the room. The hidden space was four-feet-cubed. It had a warm, cozy feel, the walls painted off-white, inviting recycled multi-colored squares of shag carpet remnants on the floor.

"I think the grandchildren will forever remember my secret room," Tibor said.

His prediction proved true. Tibor and Olga continued to add grandchildren and each adored the secret room. Early in 1987 a healthy baby girl, Corrie, joined Peter's family. Six months later Kitty gave birth to her first child, Dan.

As soon as they were old enough to climb, there was one more child who eagerly buzzed and popped open the door to ascend into the magical room.

Lili points out hidden ladder to secret children-sized room in Summit Ave. home front room, 2000s.

For decades, Tibor dreamed of a sabbatical in Hungary. He had been actively trying to arrange it for ten years. On several occasions, he had been a guest speaker, but all his attempts to arrange a longer stay were denied by the government due to fear that a Hungarian-American professor would be a corrupting influence, interfering with university students' Communist indoctrination.

But in 1989, the University of Veszprem invited Tibor as a guest lecturer with government approval.

"That's great," Olga said. "When?"

"Fall term. The honorary doctorate from Miskolc helped smooth the way."

Tibor and Olga had already been planning to go Miskolc, Hungary, for the honorary doctorate award ceremony in early September. Olga would need to return to Minnesota after a few weeks, but Tibor was able to extend his stay.

If one of Tibor's American students watched him lecture in Veszprem without sound, they would not have seen anything different than at the U of M. The familiar pacing with his left hand in his pocket, the overhead slides of crystal structures and data charts, the stroking of his chin as he pondered a point were all in evidence. The experience was all Tibor hoped for. He enjoyed having the intellectual interchange with colleagues in his native tongue and sharing his knowledge with his homeland.

During his stay, Hungary celebrated the thirty-third anniversary of the failed 1956 Hungarian revolution. Tibor and his colleagues were glued to the TV, watching developments. The speaker of the Hungarian parliament and acting head of state addressed a crowd of some 100,000 people assembled in Kossuth Square, the location where the first mass rally occurred in the 1956 uprising.

"As provisional president of our Republic," the speaker declared, waving the constitutional amendments from a balcony of the parliament building. "I greet . . . the citizens of our country, our friends abroad. I ceremonially announce that, with the declaration of the Constitution amended by the National Assembly, as from today,

October 23, 1989, our country's state form and name is the Republic of Hungary."

Incredible, Tibor thought. Hungary was independent. It was a democracy! And he was here to witness it! Even if he tried, he could never have planned to be here during such a historic change.

He joined the exuberant celebrations throughout the country, tears in his eyes as his voice melded with others, singing the Hungarian anthem, "God bless Hungarians."

While Olga wasn't in Hungary to directly experience this historic event, she wasn't left out of the celebration.

"Olga, there's a call for you." A coworker came down to the break room in the International Institute. "They say it's urgent."

Olga picked up the call in her office. "Olga Zoltai speaking."

"I'm calling from the White House," said an unfamiliar voice. "We'd like to invite you to join President Bush in the Rose Garden tomorrow, to attend a special Hungarian reception."

"Oh?" Olga said raising a brow. "Give me your name and telephone number so I can call you back." She called immediately, to her surprise the White House answered. The invitation was authentic. Olga was one of a hundred Hungarian-Americans asked to be at the White House for a historic ceremony on October 26. The president would announce Hungary's Most Favored Nation Status, granted for becoming an independent state.

"It was lunch time when I got the call," Olga later explained to the Institute's newsletter writer. "I was on the plane for Washington eight hours later. My husband was in Hungary on a teaching assignment and missed being included. But my oldest son and daughter were delighted to go. I couldn't reach my daughter until 5:00

p.m., but she was all set to go within two hours. It meant so much to have both of them with me for this once-in-a-lifetime occasion."

"Boy, security is tight," Peter said the next morning when they entered the White House grounds. A full background check had been run on each family member in addition to the on-site questions, the physical screening, and the metal detector they passed through.

"I'm glad we left plenty of time," Olga said.

In the Rose Garden, the family took seats, dressed in their best wool suits and fancy shoes. Olga, who loved gardening, noticed the crabapple and lindens bordered by low pruned hedges. Roses and seasonal flowers were interspersed to add color.

Over a hundred folding chairs sat in rows, with the center aisle leading to the stairs and glass doors of the oval office. The two central pillars of the imposing west-wing colonnade were flanked by the U.S. flag and a flag with the President's seal. A lectern adorned with the President's seal and an elegant wood signing table and chair were positioned in front of the entrance.

A row of TV cameras focused on the lectern and table.

"It's hard to believe we're only feet from the office of the president!" Olga whispered eyes wide.

"Did you notice all the Secret Service?" Peter said.

"They're all over," Kitty answered. With dark suits, ear pieces, concealing glasses, and tensed like animals ready to pounce.

"I bet they had to add extra when they heard Mom was a Democrat," Peter said.

"It looks like they're ready to start," Olga said, shushing the banter.

The doors opened. President George H. W. Bush, the first Bush president, took his position at the lectern. Four officials spread out behind him. The President announced the U.S. was extending

Unqualified Most Favored Nation Status to Hungary. He signed the document at the table and was off in minutes.

Bush's action made Hungary the first nation to be freed from trade restrictions that had been the centerpiece of U.S. trade policy toward the Communist world.

Rose Garden ceremony awarding Hungary Most Favored Nation Status, Oct. 1989. Kitty, Olga, and Peter (*photographer*) attended.

While Olga and Tibor eagerly watched changes on the world stage, they also thoroughly enjoyed their growing clan at home. Emily, Peter's second daughter, joined the family in 1989.

With their extended family adding new members regularly, they developed the tradition of having infant carriers as the centerpiece at family dinners. Most dining room tables could not accommodate such a delightful and lively centerpiece. The six-by-four-and-a-half-feet pseudo-marble table in Tibor and Olga's dining room had space.

The family's dining room table from their Heinel Drive home looked like a toy in the eighteen-by-twenty-three-feet dining room. Olga found the massive replacement, like most of the furnishings in the house, at estate sales in this historic part of town. She had a great eye for a deal.

Early in 1990, Olga got an unexpected opportunity to double the size of her table when a prospective renter visited.

"I was looking for a larger place," said the woman with disappointment. Olga was showing her the second floor apartment, vacant since Peter and his family had moved into their own home. "I guess it won't work."

"I've got such fond memories of this house," the woman continued as she glanced around the room, her eyes lingering on the features. "I took art classes here as a child." After they chatted a while, the woman asked. "Is there any chance you could give me a tour?"

They stopped in each room, on the grand stairs, and then in the front entry way. Olga gave her standard explanations.

"We're Hungarians," Olga said, eyes smiling, "and we always try to be hospitable. You may have heard the house is haunted. But don't worry, we have an emergency kit." Tibor had it mounted at the front entrance, a display box with a wooden stake and mallet, a clove of garlic, a silver cross, and a glass vial with holy water from Rome.

The tour proceeded as hundreds of others, until they came to the dining room. The massive room was lined with mottled gold-and-brown wallpaper and white woodwork. An ornate white marble fireplace sat along one wall. Light from three sets of large windows reflected off the wallpaper, giving it a golden glow that off-set the damp chill of the brownstone. The woman's eyes were immediately drawn to the white pseudo-marble table.

"That's the table from my parents' house!" the woman said. "You must've bought it when they moved out." The woman's parents had owned two matching tables. Olga had bought the one for sale.

"My sister has the other half. She's getting married and no longer wants it, or the matching buffet."

"I'd like to buy them," Olga said, her eyes alight.

The very next day, the dining room table expanded to twelve-by-nine-feet and the matching buffet graced the room.

That fall, when Kitty's daughter Karen joined the family, there was plenty of space at the table for her infant seat.

Dining room of Summit Avenue home with expanded table.

Tibor and Olga sat encircled by grandchildren. It was 1994, and everyone gathered in the basement of the International Institute for the Hungarian Christmas party. More English than Hungarian was spoken now, but Olga and Tibor beamed when each grandchild played their instrument or sang an American Christmas carol.

"Santa and St. Nick are about to come," Olga said to the grandchildren seated around her. And soon St. Nick in his draping red cape trimmed in gold, with flowing white undergarments and the traditional gold bishop's headdress, strolled in.

"I'm St. Nicholas," he said in a gravelly high voice. His face was barely visible under the beard and shoulder-length white hair. "Children in Hungary celebrate my special day on December 6. The night before my visit, the children clean their boots and shoes and put them outside their door. Before they awake, I stop by on my white horse and put sweets and fruit in their shoes if they've been good. But if they've been bad, what do I put in their shoes?"

"Coal," a grandchild yelled, being very familiar with the Hungarian tradition.

"Sticks," another child called out.

There was a burst of noise. "Ho, ho, ho! Merry Christmas, boys and girls!" yelled the American Santa. His boots clicked on the linoleum floor. "Sorry I'm late. I had trouble finding a parking spot for my reindeer. He held his jiggling belly, laughing. "Have you children been good?"

"Yeah, yeah, yeah," was the reply.

Hungarian St. Nick and American Santa bantered back and forth, teasing each other, asking the children how they were similar and different. The children hollered out what were the same and different about their clothes, their celebration day, how they traveled. Afterwards each grandchild, and all the other children present, got a turn to sit on Santa or St. Nick's lap and receive a bag filled with candy, fruit, and a toy.

Before exiting, Santa sat down on Tibor's lap. "Have you been good?" he asked to the laughter of the crowd.

Throughout the skit, the magic of the season shielded the younger grandchildren from the knowledge that Kitty was dressed in the St. Nick costume, Peter in the Santa. Olga and Tibor loved being co-conspirators in the secret, happy their offspring were carrying on the magical Hungarian traditions.

Hungarian Christmas party, mid-1990s. Grandchildren Dan and Karen dressed in Hungarian costumes sang a duet. Peter and Kitty put on Santa-St. Nick skit.

"How was your luncheon?" Olga looked up from watering her profusion of lush vines, shrubs, and flowering plants. They added a rich, earthy scent to the solarium in the back of the house. Tibor, president of the Minnesota Hungarians, had been invited along with other ethnic community leaders to a political event in Minneapolis. Tibor was on his eighth year as president, and Olga had served a two-year term in the 1970s.

"Interesting." Tibor sat down in a chair at the solarium table. "There were a lot of elected officials. I sat next to Mayor Sharon Sayles Belton. She talked to me like I was some important dignitary. I don't think she'd any idea who I was!"

"And the president?" Olga joined him at the table.

"President Clinton stopped by and spoke. I got to shake his hand." Tibor smiled. "Twice, actually. They even took my picture with him." President Clinton, in town for a fundraiser, had specifically requested this function to meet ethnic community leaders.

"So you, the life-long Republican, shook the hand of a Democratic president. And I, the life-long Democrat, attended a ceremony in the Rose Garden with a Republican president." Olga chuckled.

"Neither of us ever met a president we voted for." Tibor added, laughing.

Tibor shaking President Clinton's hand, 1996.

Once Olga and Tibor were both retired, they increased the frequency of their visits to Hungary, going almost every year. Even though Tibor's health was dramatically deteriorating, the trips continued. Their itinerary slowed down. They spent a couple of weeks at a mineral spring spa near the sandy shore of Lake Balaton. Tibor found bathing in the soft, warm water soothing and invigorating. Olga enjoyed massages and the relaxing feel of the heated mud-pack therapy.

They loved spending time with family and seeing the changes in Hungary. They marveled at how much more vibrant the cities were becoming.

Győr was no longer a dreary, war damaged city. Reconstruction of the city center had begun in the 1970s. By the late 1980s it was revitalized. In 1989, Győr even won the European award for monument protection. Red, white, violet, and yellow flowers in window boxes and gardens made it particularly attractive.

Hungary was also becoming a market economy, and experiencing a lot of growing pains. A whole generation who had grown up with guaranteed jobs now found unemployment a very real challenge. The older folks on pensions especially suffered, their incomes not keeping up with the cost of living as prices sky rocketed when controls were lifted.

"If the situation in Hungary had changed within ten to twenty years of our departure in 1945," Tibor told a visiting Hungarian ethnographer, chronicling their and other Hungarians journeys to the U.S., "we probably would have gone back. Then our life changed so much with children, even grandchildren, we didn't consider it."

Tibor and Olga loved interacting with people from around the world, not just Hungary. Peter and Kitty teased their parents that the real reason they got a bigger house was so they could run a free international hotel. At every visit, there was bound to be guests— professors, contacts through the Unitarian church, relatives, friends, previous clients. Karen became convinced Olga could go to any country in the world and she would know someone.

The *U of M Relations* publication in fall 2000 reported: "Professor Emeritus Tibor Zoltai and his wife, Olga, believe that a global perspective is essential for students. Therefore, they created the Zoltai International Scholarship for students who demonstrate an interest and willingness to broaden their education through an academically related experience in Hungary... they also created the Zoltai Graduate Fellowship for students (from Hungary) who have been admitted for graduate study at the University of Minnesota.

" 'We feel very strongly that we've been given a chance in the United States. We were born in Hungary and feel very strong ties there, too. This is our way to say thank you to both countries,' says Olga Zoltai.

" 'We've lived in Austria, France, and many places. But we like it here in Minnesota. We like the atmosphere and attitude of the people,' says Tibor Zoltai. 'We believe that to appreciate all the benefits of Minnesota, students need to explore other places to understand what they have at home.' "

Olga and Tibor tried to instill cultural appreciation in their grandchildren, playing a major role in each youth's life. When Alex was in high school, he interviewed Olga for a paper on someone he respected. Dan had a similar assignment a few years later and chose Tibor.

Peter's blended family. *L. to r.* Corrie, Alex, Emily, Peter, Ryan, Deb, Jason, and Barrett, 1996. Pictured in Summit Ave. solarium.

*   *   *

At Olga and Tibor's fiftieth wedding anniversary celebration in November 2000, the grandchildren shared a special memory they had of their grandparents. Lili, Peter's family, and Kitty's family were invited.

Seated around a table in an alcove at a local Italian restaurant, the children were dressed in casual American clothes, a mix of t-shirts and nice jeans, as well as dressier shirts and pants. No one wore the trendy jeans with holes that Olga dreaded. In contrast, Tibor and Olga looked like they could have walked in off a street in Europe. Olga was dressed in a dark brown pants suit with a white turtleneck, a patterned tan scarf, and decorative broach. Tibor wore a jacket, sweater vest, white shirt, and tie. His wire rimmed glasses, mustache, and goatee added a European flair. It wasn't just their clothes preferences that told of their foreign roots They both still had Hungarian accents, although Tibor's was much heavier than Olga's.

Alex was the first grandchild to speak after the dinner.

"We went to Mexico last November," Alex, age fifteen, said. "We'd go out shopping. I'd just watch you barter, Nagymama (Hungarian for grandmother). You'd get stuff for about 200 pesos down to about ten pesos."

"I don't know if the rest of you ever heard this story," Olga said, "I went with Barrett, Alex, Nagypapa, and Lili to Mexico. Nagypapa got sick with gout, and he couldn't walk. I thought what am I going to do with those two kids? You know, how can I keep them busy? So I figured out that if they're going to swim a hundred laps each day they're going to get a certain amount of money, right?" She smiled at Alex. "Then we went shopping with all that money."

Alex folded his tall lanky frame to give Olga a hug, and then reached over her to hug Tibor.

"One of my favorite memories is when we go on trips," Emily, age eleven, said. Her quiet voice was hard to hear over the restaurant din. "Like when we went to Cancun and when I came with you to Edmonton. It was really fun. When we stay at your house and you always make it a good time, get us movies or take us shopping."

Olga got up and hugged Emily. "Thank you." Emily, not yet a head taller than Tibor seated, squeezed behind Olga's chair to give Tibor a hug.

Tibor and Olga at fiftieth wedding anniversary party when Emily shared her favorite memory, 2000.

"You taught me Lorem (a Hungarian card game with eight parts)," Dan, age thirteen, said. He stood by his place at the far side of the table, trapped by chairs and people from going over to Olga and Tibor. "We couldn't remember the seventh game. And when we made galuska."

"We have to make some more, right?" Olga smiled.

Ryan, age nineteen, Peter's step-son from his second marriage said, "I liked the wedding, the Hungarian theme and dancing." Tibor and Olga treasured that Peter and Deb included Peter's heritage in their celebration.

"My best memory is about the garage sale and helping Altrusa," Karen, age ten, said hesitantly, boxed-in near her chair. "And it was kind of fun to be in charge of the toys." Altrusa, a woman's service club that Olga was active in, held a garage-sale fundraiser for the homeless at the Summit house.

"How about the Ping Pong playing?" Olga asked. Olga still loved Ping Pong as much as she did on the ocean crossing as a refugee.

"My favorite memory is the wheelchair races," thirteen-year-old Corrie said, with a wide toothy grin. Olga and Tibor chuckled.

Tibor laughed at all the memories, although he didn't say much. Battling many medical conditions—diabetes, kidney failure, congestive heart failure, gout, a Staph bone infection—his energy was sapped.

At age six, doctors predicted he would never see forty. At age seventy-five, Tibor still surprised medical staff with his tolerance for pain, his ability to recover from death's door.

Olga cared for him at home, keeping him alive until he was able to fulfill his last wish: to die at home.

Olga's busy, filling a pitcher with filtered water in the kitchen—she not only has a faucet for cold and hot water, but one for filtered water as well. The afternoon sun shining in the window above the sink glistens on the water surface. The large pseudo-marble table in the dining room and the smaller table in the adjacent solarium are set with burnt orange placemats for twenty. It's November 2001, and soon the family will arrive for Thanksgiving dinner.

The smell of chicken with paprika fills the room. Olga smiles, remembering when her grandchildren were young and she served American food for holidays. But when the children were in elementary school, she had asked them, "What should I make for Christmas dinner?" "Chicken Paprika and galuska," they said, and soon they wanted it for every holiday, even Thanksgiving.

Strains of "My Country 'Tis of Thee" interrupt her reverie. She heads for the side door, knowing which doorbell plays that song.

The whir of Tibor's automatic wheelchair gets louder. He meets Olga at the door.

A chorus of "Hello Olga and Tibor," and "Hello Nagymama and Nagypapa," comes from the arriving crowd.

After the delicious feast, Olga asks her traditional Thanksgiving question.

"What are you thankful for?"

"Friends and family," several say.

"Our trip to Hungary," Karen said. Mark, Karen, and Dan got their first chance to step on true Hungarian soil this summer.

Kitty's family in Hungary, 2001. *L. to r.*, Mark, Kitty, Dan, and Karen.

"The good food," Dan said.

"That I only have to answer this question once a year," chuckled a grandchild.

"That more people were not killed in the September 11 terrorist attack." A pause follows this sobering comment. The comment triggers in Olga childhood memories of World War II and the multitudes that died in bombing raids.

America is lucky, Olga thought, that bombing is a highly unusual occurrence.

"That I've gotten so many opportunities in my life and am surrounded by family," Tibor says, his voice hoarse with emotion.

There have been so many changes in my life, Tibor thought. He always tried to look for the possibilities, the silver lining. How could he make something good happen?

"That this country has given us so much and allowed us the freedom to be ourselves," Olga says. While born under the Hungarian flag with only stripes, the land of Stars and Stripes had become their home.

There's a chorus of agreement, then everyone goes back to eating. It's time for dessert.

.

Bibliography

General

Zoltai, Olga in discussion with the author, Jan. 2007 through Apr. 2009.

Zoltai, Tibor and Olga Zoltai in videotaped discussion with author, Jun. 1997.

Europe

American Hungarian Federation. "The Treaty of Trianon: A Hungarian Tragedy - June 4, 1920." Copyright 2003 – 2007, American Hungarian Federation. http://www. americanhungarianfederation. org/news_trianon.htm.

Anonymous. "1921 The Treaty of Trianon & the Dismemberment of the Kingdom of Hungary." *Family Research Austria-Hungary Maps & Atlases*. Copyright the DVHH, Inc. http://www.dvhh .org/research/austria-hungary/au_hu_maps.htm.

Canadian Institute of Ukrainian Studies. "Displaced Persons." *Encyclopedia of the Ukraine*. Copyright 2001, Canadian Institute of Ukrainian Studies. http://www.encyclopediaofukraine.com/ display.asp?linkPath=pages\D\I\Displacedpersons.htm1.

CIA. *The World Factbook*. "Europe: Hungary." https://www.cia.gov/ library/publications/the-world-factbook/geos/hu.html.

Columbia Electronic Encyclopedia. "Hungary: History." Copyright 1994, 2000-2006, on Infoplease. Copyright 2000–2007 Pearson Education, publishing as Infoplease. http://www.infoplease .com/ce6/world/A0858706.html.

Columbia Encyclopedia. "Trianon, Treaty of." New York: Columbia University Press, 2001–07, 6th ed.

D'Olier, Franklin (Chairman), Henry C. Alexander (Vice-Chairman), et al. *The United States Strategic Bombing Survey: Summary Report (European War)*. Sept. 30, 1945. Copyright 1997, Chuck Anesi. http://www.anesi.com/ussbs02.htm#pagei.

Donauschwaben Villages Helping Hands "The Treaty of Trianon & the Dismemberment of the Kingdom of Hungary." 1921. *Family Research Austria-Hungary Maps & Atlases*. Copyright the DVHH, Inc. http://www.dvhh.org/research/austria-hungary/au_hu_maps_.htm.

Eli Lilly and Company. "Sepsis Overview." Copyright 2008, Eli Lilly and Company. http://www.sepsis.com.

Elwood, David. "The Marshall Plan: A Strategy That Worked." Bureau of International Information Programs, U.S. Department of State. *America.gov: Engaging the World*, Apr. 3, 2008. http://www.america.gov/st/educ-english/2008/April/0080423213601eaifas0.2363535.html.

Feltus, Pamela (Accreditation Coordinator at American Association of Museums). "The Berlin Airlift." *U.S. Centennial of Flight Commission*. NASA. http://www.centennialofflight.gov/essay/Air_Power/berlin_airlift/AP35.htm.

Gati, Charles. *Failed Illusions: Moscow, Washington, Budapest and the 1956 Hungarian Revolt*. Palo Alto: Stanford University Press, 2006.

Gracza, Ralph (engineer at Györ airplane factory, 1944) interviewed by author, Aug. 26, 2007.

Graztourismus. "Places of Interest." *Welcome to Graz*. http://cms.graztourismus.at/cms/ziel/1390812/EN/.

Gregor, Neil. *Haunted City: Nuremberg and the Nazi Past*. New Haven: Yale University Press, 2008.

Harry S. Truman Library and Museum. "Student Activity: Harry Truman and the Truman Doctrine." http://www.trumanlibrary.org/ teacher/ doctrine.htm.

Hutchinson, Edward P., ed. *Legislative History of American Immigration Policy, 1798-1965.* Philadelphia: University of Pennsylvania Press, 1981.

Lam, Michael. "317th Bomb Squadron Roster: Squadron Statistics," and "316th Bomb Squadron Roster: Squadron Statistics," April 13, 1945. *88ᵗʰ Bomber Group.* Copyright 2004-2009, Michael 'Mike' Lam. http://www.b17pbemgame.com/317th bomb squadron roster.htm.

Library of Congress. "A Country Study: Hungary." *Country Studies.* http://lcweb2. loc.gov/frd/cs/hutoc.html.

Lőrinczy, György. *Sopron.* Budapest, Hungary: Corvina Kiadó, 1971.

Kaczmar, Olga, ed. (contributors: former DPs and their descendents). "Welcome to Displaced Persons' Camp: Table of Contents." *Michigan Family History Network.* http://www.dpcamps.org/.

Milac, Metod M. *Resistance, Imprisonment and Forced Labor: A Slovene Student in World War II.* New York: Peter Lang Publishers, 2002.

Naturpark: Thüringer Schifegebirger, Overe Salle. "Our Nature Park: General Description of the Nature Park." http://www.thueringer-schiefergebirge-oberesaale.de/www/tsos/welcome/informations/.

Noyes, Arthur A. "Cut is Likely for Food Ration in Austria." *Stars and Stripes*, Southern Germany Edition, Feb. 11, 1946. USFA Veterans Association. http://www.usarmygermany.com/Sont USFA.htm.

PBS. "The Berlin Airlift." *American Experience.* Copyright 1997-2007, PBS Online. http://www.pbs.org/wgbh/amex/airlift/timeline/ timeline2.html.

Pipes, Jason. "World War II Axis Military History Day-by-Day." Copyright 1996-2008, Jason Pipes. http://www.feldgrau.com/ (listed in top 100 WWII web-sites by D. Smith and R. Jensen).

Skelly, Patrick G. "Combat Chronology: U.S. Army Air Forces; Mediterranean - 1944, Part 2," Dec. 6, 18 and 19, 1944. *Military History Network*. http://www.milhist.net/usaaf/mto44b.html.

Soros, Tivador. *Masquerade: Dancing Around Death in Nazi Occupied Hungary*. Translated by Humphrey Tonkin. New York: Arcade Publishing, 2001.

Strachen, John. "Report on Undernourishment in Feffernitz DP Camp," unpublished report to B.R.C. Supervisor, Feffernitz DP Camp, May 16, 1946. (Luke Kelly's personal collection from grandfather stationed at Feffernitz).

Szulc, Tad. *The Secret Alliance: The Extraordinary Story of the Rescue of the Jews since World War II*. New York: Farrar, Straus and Giroux, 1991.

Thompson, Boyd. "301st Bomb Group Mission Summary of the: 32nd, 352nd, 353rd and 419th Bomb Squadrons, April 1944." *Boyd Thompson's 32nd Bomb Squadron, 1942 -1945*. http://32ndbombsquadron.com/32ndmissns.html.

UK Government. *The National Archives*. Foreign Office Records, FO 1020/2424. "Repatriation of Hungarians." vol. I, 1946. Kew, England.

United States Army. "Headquarters 450th Bombardment Group (H) AAF, APO-520, U.S. Army, S-2 Narrative Report," Dec. 6, 1944. *Official Home of the 450th Association*. Mark Worthington, Craig Linn & the 450th Association. http://www.450thbg.com/ real/s2/1944/december/6december.shtml.

United States Holocaust Memorial Museum. "Introduction." http://www.ushmm .org/museum/exhibit/online/dp/history.htm.

Vernant, Jacques. *The Refugees in the Post-War World*. New Haven: Yale University Press, 1953.

Wagner, Andy (brother of Olga Zoltai) discussions with author throughout 2007 and 2008.

Wagner, Olga and Tibor Zoltai, over 100 unpublished personal letters exchanged between Apr. 1948 and Jul. 1950, translated by Olga Zoltai and Kitty Gogins.

Wagner unpublished DP Documents including: "Military Government, Austria, Permit (for travel); Military Government of Austria, Temporary Registration;" permission to be convent boarder; documentation of Eugene Wagner employment in Stainz and Graz; "Polizeiliches Sittenzeugnis;" invitation to IRO interview for Canadian emigration; "Preparatory Commission International Refugee Organization, Certificate for the Purpose of Emigration to Canada; 'Scythia' Platzkarte für Bett; Canadian Immigration Identification Card," 1945-1949.

WorldStatesmen.org. "Hungary." Online encyclopedia. Copyright 2000-2009, Ben M. Cahoon. http://www.worldstatesmen.org/Hungary.htm.

Wyant, Sophia (resident in Feffernitz DP camp 1945-1946) interviewed by author Jan. 14, 2009.

Wyman, Mark. *DPs: Europe's Displaced Persons, 1945-1951.* Ithaca, NY: Cornell University Press, 1989.

Zoltai, Tibor. *Pali Fel a Fejje* [Pali Hold Your Head Up], 3rd ed. Garfield, NJ: Hungarian Boy Scout Association, 1978.

Zoltai, Tibor interviewed about his youth by Dan Gogins for school project, 2001.

Zoltai, Tibor, "Diary in a DP Camp, Oct. 31, 1945 through Aug. 1948," unpublished, translated by Olga Zoltai and Kitty Gogins.

Zoltai, Tibor, "Diary of a Györ Youth, Jan. 1945 through Oct. 1945," unpublished, translated by Olga Zoltai and Kitty Gogins.

Zoltai, Tibor and Olga Zoltai audio taped interview by author, 1975.

Zoltai, Tibor and Olga Zoltai interviewed by Jenö Hetthésy (Hungarian Ethnographer). Video record translated by Kitty Gogins, 1993.

Zoltai unpublished DP Documents including: "Certificate of Residence; Office National D'Immigration, Centre de Fribourg (Bade), Attestation; Ausweiskarte; DP Index Card, Vorläufige Aufenthaltserlaubnis; Certificate of Discharge; International Refugee Organization Certificate;" and other official documents, 1945-1950.

Canada

Alberta Cash Labor Contract – Sugar Beets: Contract for Hand Labor for the Season 1949, signed by Eugene Wagner and Jula Horvath, June 20, 1949.

Alberta Cash Labor Contract – Sugar Beets: Contract for Hand Labor for the Season 1950, signed by Nicholas Zoltai and A.C. Winkler, June 12, 1950.

Anonymous. "Why English is so Hard, the English Lesson." *An Educational Emporium's: English and Grammar Links*. http://www .aneducationalemporium.info/t~eng.htm

Applied History and Research Group, University of Canada. "The Peopling of Canada: 1946-1976." Copyright 1997, Applied History Research Group. http://www.ucalgary.ca/applied_history/tutor/ canada1946/.

Applied History Research Group, University of Calgary. "Frontier Town to Modern City: Calgary 1895-1946." *Calgary and Southern Alberta*. Copyright 1997. http://www.ucalgary.ca/applied_history/ tutor/ Calgary /FRAME1895.html.

Belland, M. *The Birth of Bathurst Mining Camp: A Development History of the Austin Brook Iron Mine and No. 6 Base-Metal Deposit*. Province of New Brunswick ,Department of Natural Resources and Energy, Mineral Resources, Popular Geology Paper 92-1, 1992.

Canada's Immigration Museum: Pier 21. "The Netherlands' Trunk." Copyright 2009 Pier 21. From the Timmerman Family Collection of the Pier 21 Society. http://pier21.ca/culturetrunk/ netherlands/ photos/.

Cragg, Margaret. "Traditional Rug Weaving Can Be Practical Hobby." *Toronto Globe and Mail,* Feb. 12, 1954.

Employment Standards Contact Centre, AB, Canada, email to author, Jun. 20, 2007 "Employment Standards (Request #128780)." (Outlines 1949 minimum wage data for Alberta.)

Ford, Edward, unpublished letter to Wagner Maria. Written in London, Buckingham Palace, May 2, 1952.

Kanadai Magyarsag [Canadian Hungarians]. "Egyetemi tanar let a D. P. cserkészfiú!" [The DP Boy Scout Becomes University Professor!], 1959.

Library and Archives Canada. "Irrigating Sugar Beet Field," 1904. Notman/Library and Archives Canada/C-020310. http:// www.collectionscanada.gc.ca/index-e.html.

Martin, Gwen L. *Gesner's Dream: The Trials and Tribulations of Early Mining in New Brunswick.* Fredericton, NB, Canada: Gwen Martin and Canadian Institute of Mining, Metallurgy and Petroleum, New Brunswick Branch, 2003.

New Brunswick Natural Resources. "PARIS Assessment Report Details, Assessment # 471706." *Geological Survey.* Submitted 1956. Copyright 2007, Natural Resources.

Toronto Globe and Mail. "Hungarian Rug Maker to Give Night Classes with Interpreter's Aid," Jan. 16, 1952.

Town of Raymond. "History of the Town." *Welcome to Raymond: Home of the First Stampede.* http://www.raymond.ca/2ndlevel.php?pg=a06.

Van Ballenberghe, Victor. "Rutting Behavior of Moose at Denali National Park." *Biological Science.* http://www.nps.gov/akso/AKParkScience/ Denali/Rutting%20Behavior%20of%20Moose.pdf.

Wagner, Eugene and Central Technical School. *Oriental Rug School of Instruction.* Toronto, Canada: Central Technical School, 1952.

Massachusetts

Computer History Museum. "Exhibits: Timeline of Computer History, 1951 and 1953." Copyright 2008, Computer History Museum. http://www.computerhistory.org.

Hungarian Online Resources. "1956 Revolution." Copyright 1993, Hungarian Online Resources. http://hungaria.org/1956/ index .php?projectid=2&menuid=14#23.

Launius, Roger. "Sputnik and the Origins of the Space Age." *NASA History Homepage.* http://www.hq.nasa.gov/office/pao/History/ sputnik/ sputorig.html.

National Science Foundation, Division of Science Resources Statistics. "National Patterns of R&D Resources: 2002; Data Update (current to October 2002)." *NSF*, Arlington, VA (NSF 03-313). http://www.nsf.gov/statistics/nsf03313/.

National Science Foundation. "The National Science Foundation: An Overview of the First 50 Years." *National Science Foundation History.* http://www.nsf.gov/od/lpa/nsf50/nsfoutreach/m/hist_z2/ hist_stc.htm.

New York Times on America Online. "Sputnik: The Times Looks Back." Copyright 1997, The New York Times Company. http://www. nytimes.com/partners/aol/special/sputnik.

Old Computers.com, "MIT Whirlwind." An Online Museum since 1995. http://www.oldcomputers.com/museum/computer.asp?c=1047&st=1.

Tech: Newspaper of the Undergraduates of Massachusetts Institute of Technology. "MIT Receives Grant; Team of Four Starts Crystal Research," Mar. 3, 1959. Copyright 2009, The Tech. http://tech.mit .edu/V79/PDF/N5.pdf.

Technology Review. "The Atomic Pattern of Crystals," May 1959. Boston, MA, MIT publication (NSF Grant announcement).

Minnesota

General

Burant, Stephen R. "Hungary – A Country Study: Introduction." *Encyclopedia of the Nations,* May 25, 1990. Based on the Country Studies Series by Federal Research Division of the Library of Congress. http://www .country-data .com/cgi-bin/query/r-5747.html.

Byrne, Malcolm, ed. "The 1956 Hungarian Revolution: A History of Documents: A National Security Archive Electronic Briefing Book." *The National Security Archive,* Nov. 4, 2002. http://www.gwu.edu/~nsarchiv/NSAEBB/NSAEBB76/.

Darling, Edward. *400 Years.* Minneapolis: First Unitarian Society of Minneapolis, 1968. (Design and production of booklet and the medal by Tibor Zoltai).

Encyclopedia of World Biography. "Encyclopedia of World Biography on Charles Alfred Pillsbury." Copyright 2005-2006, Thomson Gale. http://www.bookrags.com/biography/charles-alfred-pillsbury/.

Fulop, Agnes. "Olga Zoltai Outstanding Achievements." *Minnesota Hungarians,* 2009. http://minnesotahungarians.com/?q=node/78.

Gamm, Ruth. "Local Woman Recalls Hungarian Christmas: 'The Baby Jesus Brought our Gifts.' " *Suburban Life (MN),* Dec. 20, 1967.

Gati, Sally. "1956 Hungarian Revolution." *Starting Over in America: The Story of Hungarian 56ers.* http://fog.ccsf.cc.ca.us/~sgati/gatiproductions/starting_over/revolution.htm.

Hungarian Ministry of Foreign Affairs Budapest. "Honored Creativity, Nobel Laureates of Hungarian Origin." *Fact Sheets on Hungary.* 2000. http://www.kulugyminiszterium.hu/NR/rdonlyres/5A0C3086-3A74-44AA-B283-535261661B09/0/nobang.pdf.

International Dyslexia Association. "Definition of Dyslexia." *Just the Facts . . . Information Provided by The International DYSLE IA Association®*. 2008. http://www.interdys.org/ewebeditpro5/upload/Definition_Fact_Sheet_3-10-08.pdf.

KMCSSZ (Külföldi Magyar Cserkészszövetség). "Hungarian Scouts in Exile." http://www.kmcssz.org/indexe.html.

Kraft, Christine. " 'Fun' Fund-raiser: Research project Will Benefit from Bazaar for Downs Syndrome Babies." *Roseville Sun-White Bear Lake Sun- Shoreview-Arden Hills Sun,* Sept. 14, 1971.

Lerner, Maura. "A Gift Beyond Measure." *Minneapolis Star Tribune,* Jan. 25, 1999.

Lerner, Maura. "Dr. Shilling's Legacy: A Minnesota Surgeon Changed Hungarian Medicine, One Face at a Time." *Minneapolis Star Tribune,* Jan. 24, 1999.

Majeski, Tom. "Twin Citians Give Hungarian New Face." *St. Paul Pioneer Press,* Sept. 15, 1991.

Minneapolis Unitarian Society. "A Cake with 400 Candles." *Minneapolis Unitarian.,* May 21, 1968.

Minnesota Climatology Working Group. "25th Anniversary of the Har Mar Tornado Sunday June 14, 1981." State Climatology Office, DNR Waters, University of Minnesota. *Climate Journal.* http://climate.umn.edu/doc/journal/tornado19810614.htm.

Minnesota Governor's Council on Developmental Disabilities. "With an Eye to the Past," (Project EDGE featured). http://www.mncdd.org/past/1960/1960s-30.html.

Myslajek, Bounnhong (Laotian refugee sponsored by Olga and Tibor Zoltai, May 1981) interviewed by author, Jan. 25, 2008.

National Cancer Institute. "Mesothelioma: Questions and Answers." *National Cancer Institute Fact Sheet.* http://www.cancer.gov/cancertopics/factsheet/Sites-Types/mesothelioma.

Old Farmers Almanac. "Weather History." Copyright 2009, Yankee Publishing Inc. http://www.almanac.com/weatherhistory/index.php.

PBS. "Jimmy Carter: People and Events; The Iranian Hostage Crisis, Nov. 1979 – Jan. 1981." *American Experience.* Copyright new content 1999-2001 http://www.pbs.org/wgbh/amex/carter/peopleevents/e_hostage.html.

Shilling, Bruce. "A Message from Bruce Shilling." *A New Week: Wayzata (MN) Community Church,* Feb. 28, 1995.

Schilling, Bruce (arranged facial surgery for Peter Baga in Aug. 1991) interviewed by author Mar. 27, 2008.

St. Paul Pioneer Press. "Little Bit of Hungary," Nov. 4, 1964.

University of Minnesota. "Zoltais Help Students Travel." *University Relations,* Fall, 2000.

University of Minnesota. "The Down's Syndrome Child: Fighting Low Expectations." *Update: A University of Minnesota New Publication,* Fall 1973.

Valentine, Dotty. "Women from East and West Will Note United Nations Day." *Suburban Life (MN),* Oct. 23, 1963.

Wurzer, Cathy. "Remembering the 1981 Tornado." *Minnesota Public Radio,* June 14, 2006. Copyright 2009, Minnesota Public Radio. http://minnesota.publicradio.org/display/web/2006/06/14/tornado/.

Zoltai, Olga, Tibor Zoltai, et al, unpublished video of "Tibor and Olga's Fiftieth Wedding Anniversary," November 18, 2000.

Zoltai, Tibor. "Comments on the Origin of Hungarian and Other Finn-Ugorian Languages." *The Eighth Tribe,* November, 1979.

Zoltai, Tibor, "Györ Branch of the Family Szentgyörgyvölgyi, Veöreös," unpublished, 1996.

Zoltai, Tibor, unpublished diary while on sabbatical in Caracas, Venezuela, Fall 1978 through Spring 1979.

Zoltai, Tibor and Paul Rupprecht. "History and Background of Minnesota Hungarians." *Minnesota Hungarians.* http://minnesotahungarians.onza .net/history.htm (Feb. 7, 2007).

House on Summit Avenue

Anderson, Marvel. "Old World Ingenuity in St. Paul." Open House. *Historic Preservation Magazine,* Jan. - Feb. 1988, 14-20.

Driscoll, Andy. "If the Walls Could Speak." *St. Paul Grand Gazette,* Oct. 1984.

Giese, Don and Bill Farmer. "Newsmen Spend Sleepless Night." *St. Paul Pioneer Press,* Feb. 27, 1969.

Greising, Chris. "Spooky Sights." *St. Thomas University Aquin, St.* Paul, MN, Oct. 19, 2007.

Grossman, Mary Ann. "Halloween Haunts." *St. Paul Pioneer Press and Dispatch,* Oct. 28, 1985.

Miller, Kay. "Words from Other Worlds: If it's Occult, Carl Weschecke Probably has Published a Book About it." *Minneapolis Star and Tribune Sunday Magazine,* May 11, 1986.

Peddie, Sandra. "Haunted Houses: Several Homes in Twin Cities Tell Their Own Ghost Stories." *St. Paul Pioneer Press,* Oct. 31, 1982.

St. Paul Grand Gazette. "Encore Summit Avenue," June 1985.

Zahn, Laura. "Homey Haunts." *Minneapolis.St.Paul Homes,* Oct. 1987.

Zoltai, Tibor, "The Chauncey W. Griggs Mansion," unpublished history.

Olga Zoltai's Career

Asian American Press. "Dayton Presbyterian and Macalester-Plymouth United Congregations Celebrate 30th Anniversary of the First Hmong Family Sponsored by their Church Communities," Nov. 19, 2006.

Baker, Ann. "Value of Ethnic Identity Defended." *St. Paul Pioneer Press/Dispatch*, April 15, 1978.

Borden, John (caseworker at International Institute, 1975-2005, then director, 2005-current) interviewed by author Jun. 20, 2007.

Borden, John. International Institute refugee records, unpublished, June 20, 2007.

Davies, Phil. "Faces of Change." Minneapolis Federal Reserve, *Fedgazette*, Sept. 2008.

Graupman, Jane (ELL teacher involved in starting Nursing Assistant Program at International Institute) interviewed by author Feb. 1, 2008.

Graupman, Jane. "New Americans in Minnesota," unpublished presentation, International Institute of Minnesota, 2007.

Hoyle, Bob (Director of International Institute, 1970-2005) interviewed by author Apr. 3, 2008.

International Institute of Minnesota. "Meet Olga Zoltai: Olga, Meet President Bush." *International Institute of Minnesota's Interpreter: For the Friends of the Institute,* Win. 1989.

International Institute. "A New Chapter for IIM's Casework Supervisor." *International Institute of Minnesota's Interpreter: For the Friends of the Institute,* Sum. 1993.

Myers, Sam (immigration lawyer, long-term International Institute board member, and case work committee chair) interviewed by author, Aug. 24, 2007.

Owens, Christine Wilson. "Hmong Cultural Profiles." Copyright 1995-2009; University of Washington. Harborview Medical Center. *Ethnomed.org,* Aug. 2007. http://ethnomed. org/ethnomed/cultures/hmong/hmong_cp.htm#language.

Pfeifer, Mark and Serge Lee. "Hmong Population, Demographic, Socioeconomic, and Education Trends in the 2000 Census." Chapter 1 in *Hmong 2000 Census Publication: Data and Analysis*. Washington DC: Hmong National Development, Inc and Hmong Cultural and Resource Center, 2004.

Povell, Marc. "The History of Vietnamese Immigration." *The American Immigration Law Foundation*, Jun. 2, 2005. http://www.ailf.org/awards/benefit2005/vietnamese_essay.shtml.

Rhodes, Jack. "Minnesota is Still 'New Land' to Many." *St. Paul Sunday Pioneer Press*, July 25, 1976.

Saint Paul Dispatch. "International Institute Helping the Foreign-Born to Adjust," Oct. 25, 1973.

Shefchik, Rick. "Faces of the New St. Paul." *St. Paul Pioneer Press*, May 3, 1992.

Tai, Wendy S. "Area Immigrants Are Soon to Lose Their Patron Saint," *Minneapolis Star Tribune*, July 26, 1993.

Vang, Chia Youyee. *Hmong: in Minnesota*. The People of Minnesota. St. Paul, MN Minnesota: Minnesota Historical Society, 2008.

Vellenga, Kathleen (chair of sponsorship committee for Hmong family arriving Feb. 16, 1976) interviewed Jan. 31, 2008.

White House Museum. "The Rose Garden." http://www.whitehousemuseum.org/grounds/rose-garden.htm.

Tibor Zoltai's Career

Brataas, Anne. "Health Experts Tangle with Asbestos Puzzle." *St. Paul Pioneer Press*, Dec. 11, 1983.

Bartholomew, Paul R., Franco Mancini, Christopher Cahill, George E. Harlow and Heinz-Juergen Bernhardt. "Zoltaiite, a New Barium-Vanadium Nesosubsilicate Mineral from British

Columbia: Description and Crystal Structure." *American Mineralogist*, 2005.

Committee on Nonoccupational Health Risks of Asbestiform Fibers (member: Zoltai, Tibor). *Asbestiform Fibers: Nonoccupational Health Risks*. Board on Toxicology and Environmental Health Hazards, Commission on Life Sciences, National Research Council. Washington D.C.: National Academy Press, 1982.

Edwards, Harold (earned PhD under T. Zoltai, 1988) interviewed by author, Aug. 31, 2007.

Engels, Nora. "A General Sharing Coefficient for the Classification of Structures with Defined Polyhedron Complexes." *Acta Crystallographia*, Oct. 3, 1990.

Finger, Larry (earned PhD. under T. Zoltai, 1967) interviewed by author, Jul. 27, 2007.

Institute of Technology. "Tibor Z. Zoltai: Institute of Technology Retirement Dinner," U of M unpublished announcement, 1991.

Jahanbagloo, Cyrus (earned PhD. under T. Zoltai, 1966) interviewed by author, Aug. 1, 2007.

Mandics, Richard. "An Investigation of the Reserve Health Issue." *WD10 TV Station*, Duluth, MN, August 18, 1978.

Mandics, Richard (WDIO Duluth reporter from 1976-1979) interview by author on Jun. 25, and Nov. 3, 2007.

Morrison, Blake. "Geologist Says Mineral Might Be the Culprit in Rare Cancers." *St. Paul Pioneer Press*, Dec. 21, 1997.

O'Hanley, David (earned PhD. under T. Zoltai, 1986) interviewed by author, Jul. 25, 2007.

Papike, Jim (earned PhD. under T. Zoltai, 1964) interviewed by author Aug. 30, 2007.

Rapp, George (Rip) (U of M geology professor Minneapolis Campus, 1965 -1976) interviewed by author Sept. 6, 2007.

Reserve Mining v. United States Environmental Protection Agency. 514 F.2d 492 (8th Cir. 1975).

Schwartz, George, editor. *A Century of Geology, 1872-1972, at the University of Minnesota.* Minneapolis, MN: Dept. of Geology, University of Minnesota, 1972.

Stephan, Katy. "Two New Department Heads Plan Improvement, Expansion." *U of M Minnesota Daily*, August 2, 1963.

Stout, Jim (U of M geology professor, 1972-current) interviewed by author Aug. 9, 2007.

Time. "Crisis in Silver Bay," Oct. 22, 1973. http://www.time.com/time/magazine/article/0,9171,908077,00.html.

Time. "The Classic Case," May 6, 1974. http://www.time.com/time/printout/0,8816,943689,00.html.

Walker, Jim (earned Masters under T. Zoltai, 1981) and Randy Walker (Dept. of Health, interacted with T. Zoltai on asbestos) interviewed by author Jul. 29, 2007.

Weiblan, Paul (U of M geology graduate student, then professor, 1965- 1997) interviewed by author Aug. 27, 2009.

Zoltai, Tibor. "Asbestos and Health Hazards." In *Society of Mining Engineers Annual Meeting*, Los Vegas, NV, Feb. 27-Mar. 2, 1989.

Zoltai, Tibor and James H. Stout. *Mineralogy: Concepts and Principles.* Minneapolis, MN: Burgess Publishing, 1984.

Zoltai, Tibor and James H. Stout. *Mineralogy: Problems and Solutions.* Minneapolis, MN: Burgess Publishing, 1985.

Made in the USA
Lexington, KY
22 November 2010